'The anecdotes, [...]
sounding recipes make you not only want to get in the kitchen but to find a way to be friends with Angela just so you can hear more!'

Ravneet Gill, author of *Sugar, I Love You*

'This book deeply touched my heart as well as my taste buds! A visceral memoir like no other! So grateful for its existence!'   Naomi Shimada, author of *Mixed Feelings*

'Angela's writing is so relatable. Chinese takeaway can't taste the same again when you know how much love, sacrifice, and soul families have put into each dish. Finally takeaway food is represented wholeheartedly by someone who really gets it'

Elaine Chong, BBC Journalist

'[*Takeaway*] points to something very universal: about food, about labour, about survival in a new place, about shame, and about the inheritance of generational trauma. It also happens to be exceptionally funny'

Jonathan Nunn, editor of Vittles

'*Takeaway* is a brilliant book that offers a unique perspective on something familiar to so many – the Chinese takeaway'

Melissa Thompson, BBC Good Food columnist

'*Takeaway* feels like coming home. It is a testament to the resilience of Chinese families and a tender reminder to cherish the many ways love is shown'

Tori West, author of *It's Not Just You*

ANGELA HUI

TAKE AWAY

Stories from a childhood behind the counter

First published in Great Britain in 2022 by Trapeze Books
This paperback edition published in 2023 by Trapeze Books,
an imprint of The Orion Publishing Group Ltd
Carmelite House, 50 Victoria Embankment
London EC4Y 0DZ

An Hachette UK Company

3 5 7 9 10 8 6 4 2

Copyright © Angela Hui 2022
Illustrations by Georgina Leung

A CIP catalogue record for this book is
available from the British Library.

ISBN (Mass Market Paperback) 978 1 3987 0556 2
ISBN (eBook) 978 1 3987 0557 9

Typeset by Input Data Services Ltd, Somerset

Printed in Great Britain by Clays Ltd, Elcograf S.p.A.

www.orionbooks.co.uk

For 爸爸, 媽媽, 子健 and 子康

Shine bright, Lucky Star takeaway, you may be no more, but your memories live on

Contents

A note from the author: Appetisers

The East and Southeast Asian (ESEA) community in the UK and across the world has been uniquely scrutinised. In March 2020 (when the first UK lockdown began), the Metropolitan Police reported a sharp spike in anti-Asian hate crimes, coinciding with the Covid-19 pandemic. Reported incidents increased by 179% and were 2.79 times greater than the number reported in the previous year. The misplaced fear and ignorance have prompted a rise in racism and attacks across the world. Viral videos of elderly Asian-American people being pushed to the floor, beaten and slashed across the face, and the mass shootings in Atlanta in March 2021, leaving eight people dead – six of them Asian women – have brought the issue into the wider public eye. Hardworking family-run Chinese takeaways and restaurants have been hit hard, targeted and vandalised. For a lot of people, East and Southeast Asians were seen as the embodiment of the disease and that stigma definitely kept people away. Ethnicity is not a marker for disease and that's why it's more important than ever to shine a light on these small, independent businesses during a period when they're struggling to survive.

This is a book I've been working on my entire life. It's also a book I feared to write, dredging up all the pain, the racial abuse, the alienation and the loneliness – things I have spent most of my life burying. But before I sat down at my desk to take on the mammoth task of writing this book, I truly didn't grasp the magnitude of how alive racism against the ESEA community is. Of course, I knew bigotry has always been here in the UK, animosity soaked in deep, but hidden from view. The attacks that are happening now validate my long-held suspicions of racism towards ESEA people, backing up the tales of my family fending off drunk, racist customers and vandalism attacks on our shop. Coronavirus has only sharpened this inchoate prejudice and renamed it 'kung flu'.

Chinese takeaways in the UK are often seen through the lens of exoticism and fetishisation. The East and Southeast Asian people who own these establishments are framed as unskilled workers, unhygienic and lesser beings. The Chinese takeaway in the UK deserves respect, not just for functioning in hostile environments, but because it's a unique thing in itself. A spice bag in Ireland, Liverpool's salt and pepper chips, and an old east London Chinese takeaway dish 'Jar Jow' are all expressions of what it means to be Chinese in the West. Food is adapted to regional preference and local palates in order to survive, but it's something that should be considered as innovative rather than looked down upon. They're willing to bend the food and bend the culture for what their clients need, serving anybody who would pay them. The dishes we sold at our shop were far removed from what my family and I typically ate for our family meal before service – whole steamed sea bass, tong (Cantonese soup), steamed egg, kai lan choi (Chinese broccoli) with oyster sauce, lap cheong (Chinese sausage) and steamed spare ribs with fermented black beans and boiled white rice. You'll find recipes for these, and more of my childhood favourites, in the pages of this book. Anglo-Cantonese food is loosely based on traditional Cantonese cooking and this simplified, watered-down Western version is what Brits have come to know and love.

Chinese takeaways were born in the post-war years at the start of the 1950s. They were few and far between back then but, with the introduction of new fast-food chains, competition grew and so did Chinese takeaways. Before long, they were springing up all over the country and almost every village in the UK had their favourite local takeaway. At the height of its popularity in the 1970s, shops were opening at a rate of three a week, and towards the late 1990s there were more than 5,000* takeaways nationally; by 2002, the number of takeaways had almost doubled, reaching 9,500.

---

* Statistics from G. Benton and E.T. Gomez, *The Chinese in Britain, 1800-Present*, Palgrave MacMillan, 2008, p. 130.

Despite its 'inauthenticity', the Chinese takeaway has proved to be a huge success for over 50 years and has become an institution across the UK. These Chinese outposts settled in largely white communities, offering mildly exotic Chinese food to Brits who had never even heard of soy sauce and were more accustomed to eating beans on toast. Takeaways tended to avoid direct competition, so you'll rarely see more than one Chinese takeaway in the same village; this is why the ESEA community here in the UK feels so dispersed and isolated compared to big cities and communities like New York, San Francisco and Los Angeles. In the early days, Chinese ingredients weren't as available as they are now, so immigrant owners couldn't display the full extent of their gastronomy skills and had to use what was available. However, food is always more than the sum of its ingredients.

All my life I've hated being East Asian, especially a Chinese takeaway kid, but how does a person learn to hate something that they were born into? We cannot choose the situation or backgrounds that we are born into, but we can choose what to do with the privilege we are given and make positive change for the next generation. I struggled to share my story or speak up about it for years. I lacked confidence, I shrank myself and obscured my identity to take up less space because I thought I wasn't important and that my story didn't matter. I created this feeling of never being good enough and it made me very self-critical; it's something I am still trying to navigate through and grow out of now. This understanding of resilience through adversity is what will allow me to become a stronger person. Growing up as one of the few Chinese families in my village in the South Wales Valleys, I never felt normal or like I fit into any boxes. I had been indoctrinated since birth to assimilate, suppress my East Asian identity, and reach for white adjacency, not only for survival but as a goal and a way of life to get on in Britain. Being Chinese, I'm technically a minority that's privileged, but excluded. East and Southeast Asians are considered so white-adjacent that they are no longer identified as a person of colour, but still experience systemic racism.

For years, many have suffered due to a culture of quietly ignoring inappropriate comments and staying silent, the abuse slipping under the radar, hidden behind an Asian stoicism. It's a deeply rooted cultural thing where there is a sense of shame in speaking up or discussing it. It's also rooted in the fact that there is a facade of being this 'model minority', of excelling, not complaining and keeping going. It took me too long to find my voice and I've silenced myself for so long (it is in our Asian nature to stay quiet), but I don't want this to be the case for the next generation. My parents risked everything to migrate to a Western country to create a better life and now it's our turn to tell the story of our immigrant parents, to embrace our culture and to speak up in order to fight racism.

It's important that we take up space, grow our

awareness of the hierarchy of systems of injustice. While I'm new to it, I am trying to be aware of privilege and acknowledge it. I hope this might encourage others to try it too. It's a feeling that invokes acceptance and self-love, and inspires many to shout, so as to avoid being misunderstood when given the chance to speak aloud. Our voice is our most powerful tool and, right now, people are quite literally dying to be heard. Every person must take action in their own communities to learn from their ESEA neighbours, friends and peers so we can fight racism together. May the next generation have more luck finding their voices to speak up for one another – something that I seriously lacked when I was a child.

In these fear-filled times, I hope this book will serve as a refuge of nourishment, a fortune cookie of joy and an education to what goes on behind closed doors in the nation's favourite takeaway.

Prologue: On the Menu

When we think of takeaway food, we usually think of convenience. No time to shop, no time to cook and no energy left after an exhausting day at work. Fancy a Chinese? A succulent Chinese meal? Yeah, go on then. But what about the people who cook for you and serve you?

I was that kid you saw running around behind the counter with toys spread out and cartoon drawings plastered on the red-brick walls next to handwritten signs while you waited for your food. I had access to some cool things – lai see (red pockets) and red eggs for my birthdays, all the chips and spring rolls I could eat, the pleasure of celebrating two different New Year's Days every year, with treats like lobster egg noodles and whole roasted duck during the Year of the Dragon. And, when I was old enough, I was tall enough to serve and plunge chicken balls into the deep fryer. As a child, I didn't see the complexity of the British Chinese take-away story hidden among the aromatic dishes being served. To me, the takeaway was just home, the place where I grew up.

Like many Chinese immigrants who came to the UK believing that the British streets were paved with gold, my parents left post-war Hong Kong in 1985 to search for a better quality of life. Mum never got a shot at a proper education, she was five years old when the Cultural Revolution happened – a socio-political movement that was one of the bloodiest eras in Chinese history – and she fled chaos from her famine-stricken ancestral village in Shenzhen, illegally swimming across borders to be with family in Hong Kong. Dad dropped out of high school and started working as a street hawker flogging cart noodles at the age of 13. They were essentially uneducated and this severely limited their job prospects. With little money, no knowledge of English and only low-paying manual labour jobs on offer, they went wherever there was work and live-in accommodation, moving from Bournemouth to Reading, then London, and finally settling in Wales. In the end, my parents saved up and opened their own Chinese takeaway called Lucky Star on the luckiest day of the century: 8 August 1988. It's an auspicious date because the number eight is lucky in Chinese culture, signifying good wealth, fortune and prosperity – three key factors needed for a young, growing immigrant family.

My parents, brothers and I lived above the takeaway and we barely left the building. My home town of Beddau, which means 'graves' in Welsh, is a former mining village in the South Wales Valleys. Our shop backed out onto the old, derelict colliery and coke works, a vision of poverty and profundity. Most Welsh coal mines were closed by the end of the 1980s when my family arrived and their ends were hastened by the Thatcherite decree. It's a sad story of deprivation, hardship and decline, and what's left are grim scars of despair, worklessness and industrial gravestones.

Beddau was gloomy, rainy and had an insular community, with a population of just over 4,000 people, so everyone knew each other and knew each other's business, which was both a blessing and a curse. Home to walls daubed with crude graffiti, stocky rugby lads drinking flagons of White Lightning in fields and youths who would set fire to our wheelie bins, it was a sleepy nowheresville where there was not much to do and, as the name suggests, a place where all good things went to die. We were also far from the hustle and bustle of the nearest Chinatown or any Asian supermarket, so I was surrounded by white neighbours, white teachers and mostly white friends. Diversity was therefore pretty much non-existent around these parts. It felt secluded from the rest of the world.

Despite dying of boredom and being apart from anyone who looked like me, being in Beddau did mean being in the beautiful countryside, surrounded by lush, rolling green hills and flowing rivers – wherever you stood there was a high chance of spotting fluffy white sheep in the distance. There's a stark contrast between the rich joyous beauty of the landscape and the high un-employment rates and limited prospects, but it's the melancholy of the people who try to scratch out a living in these parts that make this place what it is. It's the tangible optimism, the wicked humour and the mischief from these tight-knit communities. It's the neighbour who stops you in the street to ask, 'How's it going? s'appenin', butt?' Or the local hairdresser asking about your loved ones: 'Dawn! Alright, love? How's yer mam doing? Tell her I said hiya.' It's the welcoming, friendly natter of people going about their day-to-day, and that is the essence of the Valleys. This was, for better or worse, the green, green grass of my home, and I wouldn't have traded it for the world.

The complexity of the British Chinese takeaway story, and my story growing up in Beddau, cannot be unrav-elled through an inked menu alone or categorised neatly into rice, chow mein, curry and chop suey dishes. But the shop can tell us a little bit about ourselves – how we Brits treat one another and how we accept the new and the different. Our takeaway was the place to go for the neighbourhood pub afterparty. A place for some food and chat where women gossiped and beaming elderly men came to stave off loneliness. The telephone rang constantly and a stream of people would pop in to pick up orders in hot foil containers stacked in white plastic bags. It was a juxtaposition of us being treated like immigrants, but also being keepers of something instinctively British.

These little windows into history can show us how, despite mass deportations, alienation, racial abuse and great animosity, Chinese immigrants have always persevered. They have taken the limited opportunities given them and succeeded so wildly that Chinese restaurants and takeaways are now a thriving, essential part of the British experience. The most fascinating aspects of the restaurant menu aren't the exotic names or the specials, but the wonderful time capsules captured by the food and ingredients that make up each dish. Some of the selections you make for your Friday-night treat therefore, are snapshots of my life living in someone else's country.

I

An Ode to the Takeaway Counter

'Here, ah mui.'*

I've just stepped through the glass door to our family takeaway, past the waiting room and through another wooden door next to the giant red-brick counter to get upstairs. Before I can even take my shoes off, Mum springs up seemingly out of nowhere and hands me several packs of spring roll wrappers. I'm twelve years old and have just finished another long day at school. A few of my close friends are in tow, all of us with the hope of gossiping and relaxing for a little while before the takeaway opens for the evening. 'Take one and pass one along to your school friends. Carefully peel and separate each layer. Make sure you don't rip holes in them and when you're done put them back in the packet.'

'Unlucky, mui,' my brother Jacky says, as he barges

---

* Ah mui – Cantonese word for little girl, younger sister or an unmarried girl. It was my family nickname because I was the youngest in the family. I despised it at the time because I found it too cutesy and feminine, but I've grown used to it now.

past me and makes a break for it past the counter and upstairs to our bedroom. My other brother, Keen, follows suit and as he passes snarkily reminds me, 'Well, it *is* your turn.'

I look back up at Mum, who's looking as determined as ever, and I realise there's no point fighting. She forces the wrappers on me and leaves me and my friends (who are now looking slightly bewildered) to get on with it while she goes to the living room down the hallway to put her feet up in front of the TV for a rare five minutes to herself before service.

Typical Mum and her strict Asian parenting, I think to myself. I know lots of parents are strict on their children, but my mum – she was in a league of her own. Her parenting style undoubtedly had its origins in our East Asian heritage. She was overbearing and overprotective; I wasn't allowed over to friends' houses, so brought them back to the shop so we could hang out under Mum's watchful eye; but, *of course*, she unofficially hired kids to work on her illegal production line. At any given opportunity she would rope in everyone around her to help out with the food preparation work. At ages 16 (Keen), 15 (Jacky) and 12 (me), instead of lounging at home with TVs and toys, my brothers and I spent a considerable portion of our childhood working alongside our parents after school. While Mum and Dad were always busy working, we had to find whatever ways we could to entertain ourselves while carrying out the work. We came up with silly prep work achievements such as 'first to find a mushroom that looks like a butt wins' or 'whoever sliced the best-looking char siu gets first dibs to pick their character on Smash Bros. Melee on the GameCube' to make work go by faster.

As much as the takeaway was a place of business, though, the counter was a shrine to me and my brothers. The walls often featured awards my brothers and I got from school, colourful drawings of family members and art decorations, all surrounded by quiet reminders of Hong Kong – shelves filled with imperial guardian lion foo dog ornaments and golden waving lucky cats. Auspicious red and gold decorative fish firecrackers and painted red scrolls with lucky calligraphy phrases adorned the walls. Right behind the counter, hanging proudly front and centre, was the official Lucky Star calendar with 12 cartoon Chinese zodiac animals (only regulars got one for free during Christmas). My parents named our Chinese takeaway Lucky Star after Mum's favourite Cantopop singer Alan Tam's song. It also contained the word 'lucky', and Chinese people love auspicious phrases and take them, well, quite literally. Plus, all the good takeaway names such as 'Lucky Dragon', 'The Gold Lion', 'Happy Gathering' and 'Happy Garden' were already taken by my uncles and aunties who'd settled in neighbouring Welsh villages in the Valleys. The Huis strategically opened Chinese takeaways in South Wales surrounded by a close-knit network of family and friends: near enough to offer an emergency lifeline in case anything were to happen, but not close enough to be fighting over the same customers. Lucky Star, our shining five-point hub, guided our family of five through it all.

The auspiciousness doesn't end there though. More often than not you'll find a jade plant with its bulbous green leaves pushing up against the front window near the entrance of any Chinese takeaway to keep the waiting room lively. Strategically placed in a southeast location for feng shui that brings the owner prosperity and success, the plant reflects vibrant, well-rooted energy. It is vital for newfound money, which is precisely why my parents had two to ensure maximum profits. Our plants sat in gigantic contrasting-pink Chinese rice-pattern ceramic vases, one in the alcove next to the menu board and the other on the right-hand side of the counter.

The plants in the takeaway and on the counter were Mum's prized possessions: cute aubergine-coloured butterfly-like oxalis; a spindly, elegant orchid plant topped with a bright fuchsia flower; and a huge silver bay (Chinese evergreen – another fortune-bringing plant) where its thick oval leaves unfurled outwards and towered over the other plants. Mum could keep any plant alive, even the ones that I nearly killed by overwatering as I 'helped'. Her serious green-fingered skills stemmed from her childhood growing up on a farm in rural China during the Cultural Revolution, where food was scarce and the only way to survive was to learn how to grow your own. In Wales, instead of growing out of necessity, she grew for love and as a stress-reliever. It was always

upsetting to see her hard work destroyed by bored teenagers hanging around waiting for their food, picking off
all the delicate pretty white flowers. There's a familiar
look and feel to most Chinese takeaways up and down
the country in the UK. They all look the same from an
outsider's perspective, but look a little deeper – beyond
the plants, fish tanks, lanterns and menu boards – and
you'll find the people that work behind the counter have
their own stories and personalities that they project into
their business.

The counter was the only space in the house where we
actually had any room to move about without bumping
into one another. It was where my school friends showed
me how to do a handstand against the wall with my feet
rested against the big white menu board. It was here
where we did most of the prep work when there was no
room in the small, cramped kitchen. I actually didn't
mind helping out with the daytime takeaway admin
so much. I only loathed the unsociable hours of service
because that meant a lack of free time to do much else or
hang out with anyone else besides family, which made
me feel awkward and lonely. I found it hard to make new
friends and became a bit of a hermit who kept to myself.
Sometimes the stress of the kitchen going at full force,
the endless waves of customers coming in and out, and
the shouting and swearing from the heated arguments
all became too much, especially for a young child. But
there were advantages to this environment. Prep work
gave me that first opportunity to handle a knife and a

hot pan, the foundations for cooking, learning valuable knife skills, attention to detail for portioning, how to be organised and work efficiently. Frying, peeling, slicing, dicing, whisking and washing – it all kept me off the streets and out of trouble and gave me something to do to pass the time in rural Wales.

When it comes to prep work, obviously some tasks rank higher than others. Quartering white button mushrooms meant a free pass to wield a meat cleaver to slice through stacks of mushrooms sitting in electric-blue plastic trays. Cracking and beating hundreds of raw eggs one at a time with a large novelty-sized whisk in a humongous vat gave me a chance to unleash my inner witch, mixing a bright yellow-orange concoction until homogenous (and, before you ask, yes, I have stuck my (clean) arm in a jug full of eggs to retrieve the accidental broken eggshells that sank to the bottom). Despite the high level of repetition there was something weirdly soothing and therapeutic in beating eggs like in those slime videos.

On the flip side, deveining and deshelling prawns was by far the worst task. The longer you stared at those evil aquatic crustaceans, the weirder they looked. First, twist and rip off its head, then pull off its ten legs, dig your nails under to peel off its hard exoskeleton shell along with the tail, and pass the peeled prawn to Jacky, who had the all-important job of scraping out the digestive poop tract with a knife. Over and over, box after box, until your fingers stung from the fiddly shards of shell and legs stabbing you. We probably got through about 150 prawns in one sitting. The fishy iodine odour also clung to you for days on end afterwards and, no matter how many times Mum washed our clothes, there was always a fishy undertone to our laundry.

But the king of all prep work? Hands down, bagging vats of freshly fried snow-white prawn crackers that are still slightly warm to the touch. Most customers don't give a second's thought about the bag of prawn crackers that arrives in most orders – packaged neatly and portioned exactly by hand. The process involved shovelling the cooked crackers into individual plastic bags, then passing them to Keen, who made a loud whirring noise as he opened and closed the heat sealer. Jacky and I would sneak the odd prawn cracker or two while packing. One for the bag. One for the gob. (Only to realise we'd eaten too many to fill a full one, so we *had to* keep this half-eaten bag aside for ourselves to finish off later.) Like most prep work, it was a never-ending task but a fulfilling one, one where you could see and eat the progress. You did it for the love of the family.

Aside from being an extended space for prep work, the multifunctional counter space and the waiting room was also often an event space that hosted birthday party feasts year after year for every member of our immediate family. Keen and Jacky would fish out the makeshift dining table reserved for bigger gatherings (usually an old door or mahjong table with a tablecloth on) from the garage. Family and friends sat on blue and yellow plastic stools gathered around dishes that filled the table from one corner to the other.

The meals that accompanied these parties were unlike anything that would make it onto the takeaway's menu. We'd have shark fin soup* for starters, divided into small red melamine bowls (the distinctively Chinese-looking ones with the abstract floral design and a smattering of white semicircles in the background), accompanied by a selection of Walker's variety multipack crisps. Cadbury's chocolate fingers and Haribo Starmix sweets would be dotted around in neat little piles on paper plates. For the main course, there'd be glossy sweet-and-sour pork with chunks of green pepper; onion and pineapple chunks; an impressive plate of ginger and spring onion lobster egg noodles, complete with red claws jutting out; a small portable rice cooker filled with piping-hot jasmine rice ready to go on its own plastic stool like a pedestal; a plate of traditional boiled eggs (dyed red† to

---

* Shark fin soup is a traditional Cantonese soup that's popular in Hong Kong and eaten before special occasions, such as weddings and banquets. However, because of the barbaric nature of shark finning, it's now frowned upon and has slowly been phased out. Mum smuggles back imitation shark fin (made from agar agar to look like the real thing) in her suitcase on her annual trips to visit family back in Hong Kong and China.

† Boiled eggs are dyed red and often presented at birthdays, weddings and parties to celebrate one month since a baby's birth. (One month was a significant milestone in pre-modern China, due to high rates of infant mortality.) Eggs are generally auspicious in Chinese culture and so you'll often see them as part of Lunar New Year celebrations dyed red or brown/gold (leaving them white is avoided as this colour is unlucky because it's seen to signify death).

celebrate another trip around the sun); and no banquet was complete without a mountain of gloriously golden homemade spring rolls – light, with a shatteringly crisp skin – sitting on a cooling rack with a tray to catch any excess oil. It all added up to a stunning mishmash fusion fit for a twelve-year-old Chinese girl living in Wales.

The takeaway's counter was therefore a gloriously versatile space. Name me one other room where you can blow out birthday candles, watch a live drunken boxing match between two rowdy customers, enjoy a steam facial from the multiple Boxing Day hot pots bubbling away on portable gas stoves, witness a hen party aftermath where the bride-to-be is sick in the corner, host a high-stakes mahjong tournament with three tables going at once, and hold an unofficial Six Nations rugby viewing where chips and fried rice is strewn everywhere whenever Wales score a try. The range!

I made use of the takeaway as if it was my own home, hanging out wherever I pleased. If you passed by Lucky Star, it was not unusual to see kids playing in the front counter space during the day when the shop was closed. This was where I could play, study, spend time with family and hang out with school friends. If the kitchen is the heart of the home, then the counter was my portal to another dimension – it was the gateway to work life and home life. Besides, I was rarely allowed over to friends' houses as a kid because my parents had the idea that girls shouldn't stay out – it would 'give the wrong idea'. However, being the youngest, I knew how to sweet-talk my parents and try to keep in their good books so I could manipulate some freedom. One of my greatest successes was when we came to a compromise that I was allowed to have friends over after school or on Saturday mornings during my small window of time to let loose.

So I'm standing with the spring roll wrapper packets in my hands after Mum's just shoved them into my possession. As soon as Mum leaves and the coast is clear, I immediately get up, drop the wrappers on the counter and go behind it to take everyone's drink order from the mini-fridge below: two Cokes, one for Lauren and Tasha, one Diet Coke for Lisa, two 7ups for Jane and Louise, and a Tango orange for me. We sit cross-legged on the cool white stone tile floor, in the open-plan space, surrounded by floral cream tiles and red-brick walls under the white artexed ceiling with paint chips peeling off, slurping fizzy drinks and reaching over one another, teaching each other how to peel spring roll wrappers properly, delicately peeling back the layers one by one and chatting about our favourite topic: boys.

'So, Ange. Who do you fancy in school? Cai? Lewis? Or Jake?' asks Lauren with her lilting Welsh accent while accidentally stabbing a hole in the spring roll wrapper pack she's working on.

Lauren is my best friend and she is the leader of our pack. She was the only other girl in my school who didn't have white skin. She was mixed-race, brown, had jet-black curly hair, and I idolised her. She was everything that I was not. She was confident and charismatic whereas I'm shy and introverted. Naturally, we hit it off instantly and became best friends. We were inseparable and stood out like a sore thumb in a sea of white classmates.

'I . . . uhh . . .' I blush furiously and start to feel sweat beading on my forehead, trying to think of someone to respond with. The three hottest and most popular boys in school could never even notice a girl like me, let alone like me, I think to myself.

'C'mon, Ange, you *must* like someone in school?' Lisa presses.

'Well . . . uhh, I kinda like . . . Cai?' I mutter, pretending to concentrate on peeling carefully to hide my embarrassment.

'Ooh! Angie fancies Cai! Angie fancies Cai! Angie fancies Cai!' they all tease in unison.

I sit there flustered, looking down at my spring roll pack and trying not to make eye contact. My cheeks are on fire. Argh. Why did I say Cai of all people? He's the best rugby player in school and looks like a pull-out from a teen magazine, but he doesn't even know I exist. The Chinese girl who constantly stinks of deep-fat-fryer oil with a hint of prawn fancies the hunky, blond, spiky-haired Cai. So silly. They're never going to let me live it down. Why? Why? Wh—

'Aw, c'mon, Ange. Don't be like that. You know we're

only winding you up,' Lauren sympathises, breaking my chain of thought.

'All this work is making me hungry. Do you have any food, Ange?' asks Lisa, putting her pack to one side. She's clearly bored of peeling.

'Yeah, can you sneak us some food?' Jane chimes in, excitedly tearing a wrapper too quickly, ripping off a giant corner. In the back of my mind, I'm already worried about what Mum's going to think of our handiwork – she's going to get pissed off and stop me from seeing the girls if they keep this up.

'Oh! Uh . . . I really shouldn't. I'll get into trouble,' I mumble.

'Oh, go on, Ange!' Tasha piles on.

'C'mon, Ange! Ange! Ange! Ange! We all need fuel to carry on,' they all chant.

'Okay, okay, okay. Hang on, but you all have to carry on peeling! And stop ripping them, Jane!'

I did often wonder whether my friends were actually friends with me or if I'd bought our friendship with free prawn crackers and soft drinks. Did my friends actually like me for who I am? Or did they only like me because my parents owned a Chinese takeaway and that meant free food for them? Either way, I didn't want to find out and be that loner kid in school with no friends. At least I had a group of girls who were still willing to stick around and be friends with me, even though I was unavailable from the hours of 5–11pm, seven days a week.

I get up to find some food, poke my head round the living room to see that Mum has nodded off with the remote in her hand and a Cantonese cooking show blaring out. Now's my chance. I leap across silently, hoping I won't get spotted, snooping around the kitchen, opening and closing storage containers looking for food I can take without Mum and Dad realising that me and my mates are eating into their stock. As I scurry back across carrying bags of poppadoms and prawn crackers Mum suddenly wakes up.

'Ah mui, it's five o'clock! Time to wake Dad and open up!' Mum frantically shouts, dropping the remote and springing into action.

My heart is thumping out of its chest. I can't believe she hasn't noticed my contraband! I've somehow miraculously gotten away with it. What an adrenaline rush – is this why kleptomaniacs steal all the time? However, that dopamine hit doesn't last long, as I now have the dreaded monumental task of prodding a hibernating father bear awake who's potentially going to maul my face off grumpily.

'Uh, okay, Mum! I'm on it!' I yell as I continue to make a break for it towards the counter. The countdown is on and I have so much to do before we open at 5.30pm. Half an hour to get rid of my incriminating stolen freebies, collect the shoddy spring roll wrappers with holes and tears, say goodbye to the girls, kick them out, wash the rice, flick the switch to 'cook' on our ancient rice cooker that's probably been around longer than I have, go upstairs to our room to signal my brothers (who are midway through a Mario Kart tournament race) to get ready for work, put on my work uniform that is an old hand-me-down covered in dried curry sauce and oil splatters, and *finally* wake Dad up. I'm crossing my fingers that he's gotten enough sleep after yesterday's all-nighter at the casino.

I want to shoo the girls out the door as quickly as possible before Dad starts to make his way downstairs. The less my friends interact with my parents the better, because, my God, are they embarrassing, especially Dad. My friends probably think he is an angry little weirdo who only wears white vests and sports branded shorts. Plus, the language barrier means none of my friends really know what they are saying, which causes awkward silences and broken English sentences that involve a lot of nodding and pretending to understand one another. I try my hardest to carve out a boundary between school social life and takeaway work-life to restore some social order. I hate it whenever my Western life and East Asian takeaway life cross paths, it feels wrong and unnatural, like seeing a teacher outside of school.

'Ah mui! Where's Dad? Have you woken him up yet?!' Mum bellows from the kitchen as she puts on an apron to get ready to set up shop. Gah, this woman is so loud! I feel so sorry for our neighbours. I wish she spoke more softly like other mums do when my friends were around. I rush over to the girls, 'Sorry about Mum. Uh, see you tomorrow at school, I guess? Thanks for all your help and have fun later!' I wave them off, holding their plastic stacks of spring roll wrappers.

On their way out of the door, the girls make plans to carry on hanging out and roam the streets mooching around the corner shops with the rugby boys in our year. I feel a pang of jealousy that they are able to do whatever they want without having to consult their parents first on their every move. I sigh. The fear of missing out is always too real and I hate finding out all the gossip the next day at school. I so desperately want to be a part of the action, to know the inside jokes that happen in real-time and to be seen wandering around, but I am always left behind. I don't bother asking Mum for permission to go out and join them because I already know what the answer is going to be. Already, at a young age, I had learned that there was no point getting into a silly tiff over something so trivial before another night of stressful service. Nonetheless, in that moment, I long to escape the confines of these four takeaway walls. Free to do whatever I wish, to go out and play just like the other kids.

There's a tension created by overlapping spaces; the takeaway counter space is both a place of connection and isolation, home and work, playground and business. As a child, I felt trapped and obligated to be at the take-away, but I also recognised the need to help my parents. I would see the two of them on their feet all day and night, working their socks off in order to put food on our table and keep the roof over our heads.

Being surrounded by family members all the time was also a blessing and a curse, building strong family core values from a young age, but also having no life outside of family. The majority of my time was spent there, making it the cornerstone of my life now and for the future I dreamed of. Throughout my childhood, I lived like Cinderella. Whatever I was doing, or wherever I was, I always had to be back and ready to work by 5pm or else my parents would kill me.

Dad luckily wakes up in a good mood for once. He comes down the stairs singing out, 'Let's get this show on the road! Ah mui, ah mui, ah muuui! Flip the open sign and turn the lights on!'

Takeaway kids on the counter like me are hard to miss. The counter is another realm from the outside Western world, a peek inside the East Asian immigrant takeaway world. It's where our regular customers, part-time counter staff and delivery drivers watch my brothers and I grow up behind the counter, like watching exotic zoo animals from behind a partition. The customer: independent and free to do whatever and order whatever. The worker: constrained and chained to the shackles of the takeaway. We're both humans, the only difference is one is standing on one side of the giant plank of wood running across the room and the other behind it. This makes the us-versus-them divide even bigger, and the counter itself is the symbol of otherness. It's the first thing customers see when they enter the takeaway, and the last thing they see when they leave.

I sit at the counter with my head down, trying to do homework without my parents' help, but I'm constantly being pestered by customers with questions. I feel uncomfortable and embarrassed, not knowing what to say; because I can't run or hide anywhere, I just have to sit there and take it.

'Alright, pretty little lady? How's it going, love?' asks a middle-aged male customer who looks old enough to be my grandfather.

'Oh! Uh, I'm okay. You know, the usual. I'm just doing some homework. Nothing much.' I mumble and blush. I duck my head down even further into my books, hoping he'll cotton on that I really am not in the mood to talk.

'Aw, maths, is it? Maybe I can help?' He peers over the counter nosily. 'I'll have you know, not only have I got the looks, I've also got the brains! Bahaha! Stuck, are you? You're Asian, you're supposed to be good at maths, you know.'

'I'm fine, really. Thank you. I don't need any help,' I say sternly, and get up to pretend I'm fetching an order, but in reality I'm going to hide in the kitchen. Annoyingly, I have to run back out the front again because the phone is ringing.

'What's yer name?' he quizzes me, as soon as I put the phone down.

'Angela,' I say bluntly and clearly, busy writing down the phone order, wishing he would leave me alone.

'Angela. Angela. Angela. Such a beautiful name. Angela, my love. Where are you from?' he bellows out in his thick Valleys accent, every word a sing-song.

'I'm from Beddau. Here. In Wales,' I reply, wishing I was anywhere but here and wanting this conversation to end already.

'No, no, no. I mean where are you *really* from?' He continues to cross-examine me and squint at the same time.

'My parents are from Hong Kong and China, if that's what you're asking?' I reply while rolling my eyes so hard they could fall out of my sockets.

'Ohhh, Hong Kong. I've never been and I've always wanted to go. I hear it's meant to be lush there. Hey, if we ever got married maybe we could go together?' he asks cheekily, with a grin.

'But, I'm twelve,' I reply, looking disturbed and feeling uneasy in my seat.

'Angela! Order ready!' shouts Dad from the kitchen. *Oh, thank God*, I think. Saved by Dad. I leap up from my position and sprint to the kitchen.

'Here's your order, sir. I hope you enjoy it.' I smile weakly.

'Well, let me know if you ever want to take me up on my offer. I know where to find you and I'll see you next week.' He winks at me and laughs, raising his white takeaway bag at me as he closes the door.

I shrug it off, thinking that this is normal friendly customer banter and that to reject men's advances is all

30

part and parcel of the job. And so, there I sit on my yellow plastic stool, trying to solve algebra equations, popping up like a meerkat whenever somebody walks through the door. Of course, not forgetting to put on a smile and be polite, because the customer is always right (even if the customer makes me feel shitty and irritated on the inside). Always on the frontlines, dealing with whatever comes at me.

Sometimes I would sit on my own, sometimes I sat next to Keen and sometimes I sat next to Cecilia. Cecilia – an old Welsh lady in her late sixties – was our long-serving counter assistant and she had been working for us for as long as I could remember. She had short frizzy grey hair, wore the thickest brown square glasses, hobbled about on a crutch and smoked like a blast furnace. Plus, she only lived five minutes up the road, which was handy for my parents whenever they needed an extra pair of hands to help out, even on her off-days. Cecilia was attentive and caring, but a hothead. She took me under her wing, fended off the drunken customers and was probably the closest thing I had to a grandma. Of course, I had real biological grandparents, but they either died when my parents were young or I wasn't really that close to them. I would look at Cecilia and often imagine having my distant Nai Nai (Cantonese for paternal grandmother) around instead. She'd be the real brains of this oper-ation; she would boss everyone around and look after us three when Mum and Dad were too busy. I craved the unconditional love of a grandparent, being spoiled without judgement, and Cecilia was the next best thing.

While the takeaway was open, in between phone calls and customers, we would watch *EastEnders* on the small, boxy TV in the corner that was intended for those waiting for their order. Often, I'd juggle takeaway work with school work, squeezing in any reading and writing before opening and in between the lull during service until close. If I had a big project due or exams the next day I'd be spared from sitting at the counter and was allowed to study upstairs in our bedroom, occasionally being called down to lend a helping hand whenever it was busy. Sometimes my brothers or Cecilia would help me with any questions I was stuck on as my parents were too busy and didn't understand. In return, I stubbed out Cecilia's cigarettes when she got up to go into the kitchen to fetch orders (although she didn't often see it as a favour). I couldn't stand the smell of smoke and I was constantly coughing around her, plus I knew they were bad for you. When she would return, she'd look me straight in the eye and sternly accuse me, 'Did you put out my cigarette, Angela?' to which I would stay silent and play dumb, looking around, hoping someone else would fess up despite there being clearly no one else on the counter except us. She'd get pissed off for a few seconds, then light another one and the vicious cycle would go on.

While I did slightly resent the busy service, it was more of a love-hate relationship than I often liked to admit. Despite the clear negatives of a busy night, I actually liked it when we had nonstop customers because time flew by. At least that way you were so busy you didn't have time to think and, before you knew it, it was 11pm and another night of service was over. Being bored during service was the worst. You were left with your own thoughts; awkward silences would fill the room, because the conversation between me and Cecilia inevitably ran dry only an hour into service. We would desperately wait for someone to walk through the door, get annoyed by the clock ticking, long for the phones to ring and become increasingly irked by the fridge under the counter humming on and off. Just waiting for time to go by and wishing our lives away. The harsh, bright fluorescent ceiling lighting and the way the television illuminated my face seemed to put me on show for every passer-by to see, a small black-fringed bobbed head sitting behind the counter next to a smoking white grandma, watching Pat Butcher slapping people to get out of her pub.

Besides Cecilia, there was also Dewi, our delivery driver, in his mid-thirties. He was a lanky, dorky blond Welshman who laughed at his own dad jokes and over-shared stories about what his two baby sons got up to. Often, he'd have the kids in the car strapped in the baby seats in the back while he did his delivery rounds. The nights he didn't have the kids, he'd be standing around reading the papers and watching TV with me and Cecilia, making small talk with me in between orders. This was my version of water-cooler chatter, except it was less gossip about other colleagues and more bitch-ing about customers who didn't answer their doors for deliveries. In a way, they were my extended family. My parents working the woks, my brothers and I on inter-changeable lid and counter duties and Cecilia manning the phones. I probably saw Cecilia and Dewi more than I did my actual blood relatives in Hong Kong and China.

'Okay, so four deliveries. One in Gyriant Gwyrdd, one in Glendale and two in Mansion Chase. I'll prob-ably be about forty-ish minutes? Give me a call if there are more deliveries,' Dewi says.

'Sure, will do. See ya,' I reply. I walk back to the kitchen only to find that Mum has forgotten to include a bag of spring rolls waiting on the sidelines. 'Wait, wait, wait! Dewi, we've forgotten an item for the de-livery order!' I yell and run after him. It's too late, he's already pulling away in his car. We call his mobile phone to see if he'll pick up to tell him to turn around, but no luck.

When news breaks that there is a bag of spring rolls up for grabs left behind on the silver worktop in the kitchen, my brothers and I circle around them like vultures and wait on Mum's orders with bated breath. 'Fine, fine. Yes, you can eat them. I'll make some more when Dewi comes back and add them to the next round of deliveries – can't give them to someone else anyways, they'll go soggy.'

Mum sighs and rolls her eyes. We dive into the white paper bag, claiming a spring roll each, crunching through crispy bronzed cylinders to reveal the steaming tender rainbow-coloured vegetable insides. Rapidly inhaling and exhaling with our lips ajar, the three of us are too hungry to wait for the rolls to cool. There's no greater thing than a forgotten leftover spring roll. At that moment, tearing into a bag of spring rolls, we forget we are in the takeaway and feel like we are at home.

Vegetable Spring Rolls

The ultimate party food that has been there throughout my life: the spring roll. Whether it's the jumbo meat version or the mini vegetarian ones, it's classic ubiquitous finger food. A crisp, paper-thin pastry wrapped in an array of whatever filling you like. From carrots and bean sprouts to shrimp, pork and duck, the humble spring roll is one of the most well-known Chinese takeaway dishes that the UK has taken on. Evidently, it's also one of the first dishes Mum tried to teach me how to make (mainly so I could help her out in the takeaway), but when I'd watch her seamlessly tuck, fold and roll perfectly at lightning-fast speed it was like watching a master at work. Mine always turned out to be wonky or filled with holes, making them susceptible to being greasy and stodgy. By tucking and rolling tightly it results in a crispier roll. Prepare to sacrifice a few ugly ones because practice makes perfect.

Serves: 20 rolls | **Prep time:** 10 mins | **Cook time:** 2–3 minutes

Ingredients:
1 tbsp cornstarch
2 medium onions, thinly sliced (approx. 2mm thick)
2 medium carrots, grated or julienned (approx. 2mm thick)

1 × 300g pack of bean sprouts
A handful of frozen peas
2 cloves of garlic, minced
1 tbsp soy sauce
1 tsp sesame oil
A pinch of chilli powder
A pinch of white pepper
1 pack of 40 sheets (20cm square) spring roll paper
Vegetable oil for deep frying
1 tsp MSG (optional)

Method:

1. In a small bowl, whisk together the cornstarch and two tablespoons of cool water to form a slurry, which will act as the glue to help the rolls stick together. Set aside.

2. Add a tablespoon of vegetable oil to a wok or a pan and stir-fry the onions and carrots for about 2 minutes, then add the bean sprouts and peas. Cook for a further 2 minutes. Add in the garlic, soy sauce, sesame oil, chilli powder, white pepper and season with salt and freshly ground black pepper. Cook for another minute, but only half-cook the vegetables. They should still retain some crunch and bite.

3. Transfer the filling to a large shallow bowl, drain off any excess liquid and let cool. Place the mixture in the refrigerator to cool further for at least one hour. It's important to work with cold filling, so it's easier to handle when wrapping and to ensure there's no standing liquid. If there is any, discard any additional liquid; we want the filling to be relatively dry to prevent soggy spring rolls.

4. Place a spring roll wrapper on a flat surface in a diamond shape with the corner facing towards you, add two spoonfuls of the vegetable mixture and place the filling in the corner of the wrapper about 5cm from the edge. Fold this corner towards the centre, tuck it under the filling and roll it over once. The trick is to roll tightly, but not so overstuffed that it's bursting at the seams or rips the wrapper.

5. Fold the two side corners towards the middle of the wrapper while continuing to roll up. Paint the top edge with the cornstarch slurry mixture and wrap tightly the rest of the way. Make sure all edges are tightly sealed. Place the roll seam-side down.

6. Cover the spring rolls with cling film to avoid drying out and cover the wrappers with a damp tea towel while you're working your way through rolling them out or else the skin will dry out and crack.

7. Pour the vegetable oil into a wok or a large pan to a depth of about 5cm. Heat to 180 degrees Celsius or higher and ensure that the oil is hot before frying by using a thermometer or by inserting a bamboo chopstick in the oil – when bubbles form around it, that's when you know it's ready for frying. Once you start frying the first spring roll, you can adjust the temperature accordingly depending upon how quickly it browns.

8. Slide several spring rolls into the oil and allow

them to cook for 2–3 minutes, turning them over a couple of times to ensure even browning on both sides. Cook until the wrappers are golden brown. Remove the spring rolls onto a cooling rack or paper-towel-covered plate to allow them to drain. Serve hot with optional sweet-and-sour sauce, sweet chilli or any other sauce of choice (personally, I'm a big fan of having them with Heinz salad cream).

9. After rolling the spring rolls (before frying) you can freeze them. If you have baking paper or cling film, line a baking tray with it as it will prevent them from sticking and freezing together. Place the spring rolls in a single layer without touching on the baking tray. Once frozen, transfer to a container or a freezer bag. They keep for up to a month and should be fried from frozen.

2

Weekend Service

– RING RING RING –

The silver-corded phone that sits to the left of the counter, worn from years of being picked up and slammed down, is shrilling again. I hastily pick it up.

'Hello, Lucky Star. How may I help you?' I automatically regurgitate in my sing-song takeaway-order voice. 'A delivery? Sure, can I have your address? Please? 34 Heol-yr-esgob. And what's your phone number in case anything happens and we need to contact you? 0-1-9-0-1. Yep. 2-1-8-9-6-8. Okay. What would you like to order? A special chow mein. Yep, but no prawns? Okay. Black bean beef. Uh-huh. Two bags of chips. Yep. A portion of chicken balls. What sauce would you like with the chicken balls? We do barbecue, curry or sweet-and-sour. Sweet-and-sour sauce. Sure. Anything else with your order? No? That's it? That'll be £17.20, plus the extra pound for delivery. So that's £18.20 in total. Your order will arrive roughly in . . .' I cup the handset with one hand and turn my head round to check the rustic wood-framed clock on the wall: '. . . half an hour to an hour's time? Okay, thank you. Bye.'

As soon as I place the handset down on the receiver . . .

– RING RING RING. RING RING RING –

'Hello, Lucky Star. How may I—'

'Ni Hao!' Followed by barely covered-up sniggers in the background.

'Hello?' I ask tentatively.

'Ching chong ching chong! Hahaha!' There's now a guffawing as the hilarity of the situation seems to be too much to cope with.

'Huh? What?! Wait a minute . . .' It's starting to dawn on me what's happening.

'Egg flied lice, pwease!'

'Come again?' I decide I'll give them one more chance.

'Me so hornee. Me love you long time!'

I slam the chunky handset down and throw it across the counter in rage.

Not again. *If I ever find out who that punk is, I swear I'll look for him, find him and set my dad on him*, I think to myself. This happens every other bloody night and I'm getting really tired of the prank calls. What does 'me love you long time' even mean anyway? I can practically feel my blood boiling and steam coming out of my ears. This is *so* unfair, I think. I don't even want to be doing this shitty job, dealing with these idiots. I just want to go hang out at Lauren's house with the girls and play like all the other kids. I wish I was someplace far, far away from here.

Try as I might, I can't stop thinking about the ignorant dumbass long after he's hung up. Why am I so confused and irritated by this? What have I done to deserve this? Ugh. I hate my life, I hate this stupid job and, most of all, I *hate* being Chinese. Why couldn't I have been born *normal* into a *normal* family? Life would be so much easier. I wouldn't have to deal with this crap. I didn't sign up for this; it wasn't part of the job description. In fact, I didn't even sign up for this job in the first place, but if I refused to do it I'd probably be disowned by my parents and kicked out of the house. As long as I live under this roof, I have to help out with the family business. I guess at least I get some weekly pocket money out of it.

As I walk down the narrow, white artexed hallway and closer to the kitchen, I feel a blast of hot air punch me in the face like opening the door to a chip-grease-fuelled sauna. The air is brimming with enticing smells of aromatic curries, fiery satays, funky black beans and fragrant sweet-and-sours all rolled into one. It's a tight space, made even tighter with five bodies frantically scurrying around trying to get things done without knocking into each other. Red quarry anti-slip tiles on the floor, with an odd cracked tile or two showing signs of wear. We have two stainless-steel silver surfaces, one central island for packing orders, a line of heavy-duty wok burners, a deep-fat-fryer station, a domestic gas cooker that always has bubbling pots of sauces on the hobs, and a giant fridge that is clearly too big for the room. The five of us have to carefully manoeuvre around the fridge whenever the door is open, like in *The Matrix*'s famous slow-mo 'dodging bullets on the rooftop' scene. Our set-up isn't much, or state of the art, but somehow it works, and so do we. I take the paper ticket and yell, 'One special chow mein with no prawns (22), one lemon chicken (10e), one black bean beef (6), two bags of chips (94 × 2), chicken balls with a sweet-and-sour sauce (12),' to my parents over the loud whirring extractor fans, then stub the ticket on the makeshift receipt spike, which Dad made out of a small piece of wood and four nails.

'Okay, lah, ah mui!' Dad shouts back as he effortlessly rocks the steel wok back and forth with his left hand while stirring the lemon chicken with a wok ladle in the right. He grabs a bottle of lemon juice from the wonky white shelf that Mum has fashioned out of old tiles to the left of him and squirts it directly into the wok. As soon as the liquid touches the wok, flames creep up the sides, licking the raw ingredients and bringing a charred smoky addition to the zesty dish. He stands on a flattened cardboard box splayed out on the floor to stop himself from slipping and to help catch fallen grains of fried rice and strands of chow mein, which makes for easier clean-up.

Dad's work station is nestled in the top left-hand corner, surrounded by prepped ingredients all within arm's reach. Sliced chicken, diced char siu, peas and prawns sit in mismatched plastic tubs on a giant tray of ice behind him; jars of spices and sauces in metal bowls on the stainless-steel shelf in front of him. I can hardly hear him, or much else, over the jet-engine-like roar of the water-cooled industrial wok burner range; the clash of the metal spatula; the hiss and sizzle of Mum plunging chicken balls into the scalding hot oil – it's like a war zone in there, but thankfully run with military culinary precision. Organised chaos churning out the orders when it is just another normal Friday night in with the family. We always do the same thing, every night, seven days a week. I feel trapped, and I hate having no social life outside the takeaway. Scratch that, I hate having no life. TGIF? Thank God It's Friday? More like 'Takeaway Graft Is Forever'.

The takeaway has always been a part of my life. According to Mum, when I was a baby, I slept in a cardboard chip box in the pantry storage under the stairs by the kitchen while she worked and occasionally checked in on me during service – how I didn't wake up crying from all the noise I'll never know. I started helping out when I was eight years old. I used to stand on a step stool, reaching over the tall counter to serve customers. My parents taught me and my brothers the ropes as soon as we could walk and talk so that we could help ease the burden and, one day, take over the business when they retired. I couldn't think of anything worse, and neither could Keen and Jacky. Even though my parents made cooking, especially cooking with a wok, look like a piece of cake, in reality it was tiring and repetitive. Using a wok single-handed involves so much strength, plus extensive arm and wrist movement from your non-dominant hand, that I'm surprised bodybuilders don't use them to train. You should see the size of Dad's fore-arms from all that wok action – hench! But their hopes and dreams of me taking over the business were quickly dashed when they saw me pathetically struggle to pick up a wok. I couldn't even pick it up with both hands. That damn thing weighed a ton. Not surprisingly, I was quickly relegated to less labour-intensive roles such as answering phone calls, dealing with customers and lid duty.

What is lid duty, you ask? Well, it's exactly what it sounds like – mindlessly putting lids on aluminium foil trays, pressing down the four corners to secure the hot food contents inside, again and again, like you're on a production line of a packing factory, blitzing through orders until your thumbs are all cut up and your legs are jelly from standing up all night long. To ease the pain of doing the same task day in and day out, Keen, Jacky and I raced each other to see who could seal the containers the fastest – 4.3 seconds was my personal best (now that's a skill I'm proud to endorse myself for on LinkedIn). Finally, I was better than my brothers at *something*. Being the youngest and the only daughter in the family meant my parents compared me to my brothers every chance they got. Chinese families have traditionally favoured sons over daughters because a boy meant a person to carry on the family name and having a girl was wasteful, someone to marry out into someone else's family, so I had to live up to the high standards that my parents set and prove them wrong.

But truth be told, lid duty and telephone answering aside, my parents had always discouraged us from wanting to get too involved with the family business and to take over when they retired because they knew it was backbreaking and unsociable work. My parents didn't open and run a takeaway out of passion and love, they did it in order to fund a higher education for me and my brothers, to be able to study hard and get good jobs. We were their investments and having the next generation to carry on the takeaway legacy was less of a pipe dream for them and more of a blackmail incentive for us to achieve straight As. My parents came to cook, so that we didn't have to.

Lid duty, however, was something that could be fit in alongside schoolwork, and it was only the final part of the well-oiled Hui machine. It was game time, and we were in the zone. We were the living embodiment of 'teamwork makes the dream work'. Mum would pass me the prawn toast to box up. Dad ladled the chicken curry from the wok perfectly without spilling a drop. I folded down the rim of the takeaway container at warp speed, Jacky grabbed a bag of poppadoms and Keen put everything into a bag. Easy-peasy. Job done.

The customer comes in to collect his order. He isn't

sniggering or looking at me funny, so I don't think he is the prank caller. Too old. While Cecilia sits next to me puffing away on her bar stool, I lean back on my plastic yellow stool against the wall and continue catching Pokémon on my Game Boy to decompress before the next onslaught of orders comes through.

Three minutes later, the same man reappears at the door. Approaching the counter, he gestures towards the bag. 'This isn't my order. I ordered fried rice, chips, sweet-and-sour duck and curry sauce.'

Uh-oh. Dad's going to kill me. I walk back into the kitchen with the returned white plastic bag and break the bad news to my parents. As suspected, Dad flips out and starts shouting at me. His angry voice commands the entire house; it's so loud that customers waiting in the front room don't know whether to flee for their lives or cower in the corner confused. Who knew such a small pot-bellied man could yell so loud? Mum tries to defuse the situation by calmly telling me it is okay, and that they'll remake the order and throw in a bag of prawn crackers as an apology, despite it being the second time I've gotten an order wrong today. Two out of a hundred orders a day isn't bad in my book, but I don't want to get smacked for backchat. It's exhausting.

'I'm sorry . . . I—'

'Ah mui, you're so useless and stupid! Be more careful next time and always read back the order to customers to prevent mistakes.'

Despite all my efforts, I can't seem to physically stop

the tears that are welling up inside me and a few sobs come out as I desperately try to sniff them away.

'Uh-oh, here we go again. Here come the waterworks. You're such a ham bao.* Crying won't get you anywhere.'

I hate it when Dad shouts at me, he makes me feel so low – like I will never amount to anything – and I always feel so guilty for messing up. Unfortunately, the pressures of the kitchen mean Dad screams and shouts at me almost every day. Of course, I didn't mean to mess up. Can't Dad see that? What more can I do if I've tried my best? It wasn't *my* fault, I think. Stupid customer. *He* should've been the one to check. While I would never say this to Dad, I never understand why getting an order wrong is such a big deal to him, freaking out over the minute details that, in the grand scheme of things, don't really matter. I don't have time to dwell on this or get too upset though, because the next round of customers is coming in thick and fast.

'A little help, please!' shouts Cecilia from the front counter in between the symphony of high-pitched phone rings.

I wipe my tears on my sleeve and try to compose myself. I run out to see the waiting room has suddenly filled out, with customers packed in like sardines. I grab a notepad and pen and put on my biggest smile.

'Sorry about the mix-up, sir. We're redoing your order

---

* Ham bao is the Cantonese word for cry-baby and my other unofficial nickname, because I'm a sensitive soul and cry a *lot*.

now, which won't take long, and we'll throw a bag of prawn crackers in too,' I tell the customer, then turn my attention to the next person in line. 'Hiya, sorry for the wait. What would you like to order, ma'am?'

I run back into the kitchen, trying to reel off the order above the din and stub the paper ticket on to a nail along with the backlog of other tickets piling up.

'That order's ready, mui. It's the one we got wrong earlier.' Jacky points to the lonely white bag waiting on the sidelines without looking up from pressing the container lid of another order down. 'Make sure everything's in there this time and don't forget the prawn crackers.'

I take the order, hurry back to the counter, hand over the customer's food and apologise profusely before moving on to serve the next customer. I return to the kitchen, recite dishes off by heart and add another paper ticket to the pile. While I'm there, I grab an empty cardboard chip box from the stack sitting next to the fridge, place it on top of the silver worktop and start to fill the box. Carefully placing silver-foil boxes filled with barbecue spare ribs, fried rice, noodles and chop suey, brown-paper-wrapped polystyrene cups of amber-hued curry sauce and bags of chips,* ticking off items on the order like a game of bingo. I close the flaps on the box and carefully carry the big order (almost bigger than me)

---

* Many Chinese families took over old fish-and-chip shops, which may be why chips – often with curry sauce – became a fixture on menus. Chinese takeaways serving chips has become a British tradition.

back out to the front. Cecilia is coming straight at me with a paper ticket but jumps aside at the last minute to avoid a spillage catastrophe.

'Sorry! I couldn't see you!' I shout back at Cecilia while she's already down the hallway leaving another ticket in the kitchen. At the counter, I call out 'Okay, we have ticket number 32. Number 32, anyone?'

A couple comes forward to the counter with their ticket. I hoist the heavy box of food up, repeat their order back to them to double-check everything is there and hope they'll enjoy their meal.

'Alright. Has anyone else not been served? Who's ne–'
– RING RING RING –
The phone starts to rock in its cradle again.

'I'm coming, I've got it!' Cecilia shouts as she slowly hobbles back round the corner.

'Is Dewi here for delivery yet? Where is he?' Keen yells faintly from the kitchen. 'Give him another call. We've got loads of delivery orders sitting here waiting!'

It's relentless. The line of customers seems never-ending and the phone lines are ringing off the hook. Back and forth carrying orders, up and down the hall-way repeatedly, as if I'm in a *Benny Hill* sketch until service is over and my legs nearly give way from being on my feet all night.

As soon as the closed sign is flipped at 11pm, after a gruelling 14-hour day, we bolt upstairs to get in line to wash off the night's work and get ready for bed just before midnight while my parents carry on deep-cleaning the kitchen. As soon as the chores are finished Dad grabs his jacket and storms out of the house. 'I'll be back later. I'm going out.' He doesn't need to tell us where he's going. It's obvious. Casinos are the first port of call for Dad, and many others in the Chinese community, including many of my aunties, uncles and cousins, because they're the only places open in the early hours of the morning.

It's been a bad day but it would be made worse the next morning when it became apparent that Dad has gambled and lost all of yesterday's earnings playing mahjong at the casino. When Mum finds out, she goes ballistic – and she rarely loses her cool. My brothers and I, in our shared bedroom next door to theirs, can hear them at each other's throats when Dad creeps in at 5am, the three of us lying in our beds, silently awake, wishing the arguing would stop, but the yelling only gets louder. Eventually, I resort to banging on the walls to finally shut them up.

'SHUT UP! Some of us are trying to sleep. I hate this stupid house and I hate both of you!' I scream, as I pound the walls with my fist from my bed.

It wasn't always like this. It depended on the previous night's winnings. Today is a walking-on-eggshells kind of day. I detested any form of gambling because I associated it with the root of all our problems: if only Dad didn't gamble, we wouldn't have to work twice as hard; if only Dad didn't gamble, maybe he wouldn't shout at us all the time; if only Dad didn't gamble, maybe he would stop making me cry. He'd regularly miss the majority of the morning to catch up on sleep while poor Mum silently picked up the slack of prep work for the takeaway, housework and looking after us three – always without complaining. Why she put up with him I don't know. Why any of us put up with him I don't know.

The next morning, everyone is in a foul mood. I hate my parents, I hate my life and I need to get out.

I slam the front door, immediately sprint upstairs and sling my school bag into our bedroom to avoid any further confrontation. I'm physically and emotionally exhausted from the stress of last night. My mind is foggy and my stomach growls. *I'm starving.* I barely ate anything at school, too anxiety-ridden replaying yesterday's events over in my head. Plus, I hate everything they have on the school canteen menu, and when the dinner ladies try to force me to eat a plate of lumpy mash with baked beans for lunch, inevitably most of it ends up in the bin. I nag Keen or Jacky to go downstairs to get some food for me but neither brother's brave enough to venture downstairs because they're also taking refuge. Instead, they're busy beating each other as Link and Kirby in the middle of a Smash Bros. match, fighting one another to blow off steam before another night of service.

I sneak back downstairs into the kitchen to try to get a snack without being noticed. Mum and Dad are in the kitchen and have their backs to me. I pause in the doorway and watch them quietly work away making our pre-service family dinner, mesmerised, but also crushed that I'd told them I hated them yesterday. I know everything they do, they are doing for us, by whatever means possible.

Contrary to popular belief, we rarely eat the food we serve customers. Mum deems fried foods as 'yeet hay', a Cantonese phrase that means 'unhealthy' and literally translates to 'hot air'. In Chinese culture, certain foods are believed to cause an imbalance in the body's energy levels; too much hot or 'heaty' foods such as sneakily nabbing a chip or two during service would result in breakouts, sore throats and lethargy. Chinese takeaway food should be reserved for a weekly treat, and you don't need me to tell you it's not good for you if eaten every day. Although Dad would never apologise for his behaviour and outbursts like the previous night, nor be able to make up for the money he lost, watching the tenderness with which he and Mum prepare our family meal* shows me how much they care about us, and each other. I seldom see the soft side of my parents, particularly Dad, but maybe this is his way of reaching out. Somehow, without telling us, he is trying to make it up to us and win back our love.

Dad lifts the lid of the rice cooker like a magician performing a spectacular illusion and disappears behind

---

* In hospitality, family meal means a group meal that a restaurant serves its staff outside peak business hours, usually just before opening. Typically the meal is served to the entire staff at once, with all staff being treated equally, like a 'family', but I guess in this instance we are literally family.

a plume of rising steam. I'm instantly hit with the smell of jasmine rice's almost buttery popcorn-like sweet, floral aroma intertwined with the delectable smoky-sweet fragrance of lap cheong (Chinese sausage) and lap yuk (Chinese cured pork belly). Dad plucks the steamed Chinese charcuterie out with his asbestos fingers, places it on the wooden circular chopping board and begins slicing it into bite-size pieces before returning it to the pot.

– CHOP –
I'M
– CHOP –
SORRY
– CHOP –
PLEASE
– CHOP –
FORGIVE
– CHOP CHOP CHOP –
ME

You could have sworn he was hacking down a tree rather than slicing. The banging of the cleaver is so loud it echoes all the way through to the front counter. He scoops up the chopped meat with his cleaver in one swift motion and splays it decoratively on top of the rice. Mum appears by his side, she drizzles the dark soy sauce mixture and sprinkles the spring onions in. Dad vigorously mixes everything together with a rice paddle to fluff up and to ensure each grain is coated in the sauce, and specks of rice go flying everywhere like mini firework sparks.

He looks over his shoulder and spots me hovering around.

'Ah mui! Ah mui! Ah muiii! I've made your favourite bo zai fan,' Dad chuckles. (Bo zai fan is claypot rice.) 'Call your brothers down to sik fan*.' My mouth's watering just looking at the fluffy, steamed rice studded with maroon and white marbled pieces of sweet-savoury Chinese sausage and dark-brown cubes of Chinese cured pork belly flecked with bright-green spring onions; I've forgotten all about the snack.

I know Dad's ulterior motive and what he is doing. He often conveniently 'forgot' any of the previous night's events even happened. My parents have so much pride that they'd rather hide how they really feel, especially Dad, and after years of repressing emotions instead of discussing them, it gets harder and harder for them to admit mistakes. They stubbornly stick to their justifications, and I have to pick my battles. I'm so used to Dad's rampant inability to apologise that I start making excuses for him to friends, family and customers, and have convinced myself that he'll simply apologise in other

---

* Sik fan means to eat dinner or eat rice in Cantonese. It's probably the most important Cantonese phrase. Rice influences nearly every facet of life. A meal isn't a meal without rice and this is something that echoes far and wide in many parts of East and Southeast Asia. Rice acts as a neutral component to the meal and it gives one a sense of fullness, which is why it's so important.

ways that are no less valid. This flavourful bowl of rich, savoury rice goodness, lovingly prepared by my parents in front of me, might be a delicious peace treaty and an act of love, but just once I wish Dad felt comfortable enough to be apologetic. Baby steps. I'm sure one day we'll get there. I grab a bowl excitedly before I can dig in to appreciate this elaborate family meal . . .

– RING RING RING –

An over-eager customer calls in their order ahead, before we've even opened.

– RING RING RING – RING RING RING –

'I've got it!' I shout at the phone as if it can hear me. I huffily put down my bowl of rice to rush up and get the phone call in time.

'Heeell-loooo! Tynant Lucky Star! How may I help you?'

There's silence on the other end of the line.

'Hello?'

'Me wan the noo-doo pwease! Hahah!'

Oh great. Him again.

Bo Zai Fan / Claypot rice with lap cheong (Chinese sausage) and lap yuk (Chinese cured pork belly)

A soothing and satisfying meal before (or during) hectic service that's effective for feeding many mouths with very little effort. If you want the classic crispy, crunchy rice base, then I'd recommend cooking in a clay pot directly on the hob or an open flame for the best results. If you're short on time like my mother was on most days, then let the rice cooker do all the work for you, as it's an ideal 'leave-and-forget-about-it' dish. Seeing plumes of steam rise and escape from the pot and breathing in the intoxicating smell of the aromatic, fatty cured meats mixed with the fragrant rice always makes me giddy with anticipation. Sometimes Mum would let me be in charge of the rice paddle and gave me the most important (and fun) task of mixing everything together. It's an exciting interactive dish to do with kids, where they can see the white rice turn a lovely golden colour as each grain is coated in the sauce.

Serves: 4 | **Prep time:** 15 mins | **Soak time:** 30 mins | **Cook time:** 12–15 mins

Ingredients:
- 2 cups (400g) jasmine white rice
- 2 cups (500ml) water
- 2–3 links of lap cheong Chinese dried sausage

58

7.5cm piece of lap yuk Chinese cured pork belly
2 spring onions, diced

For the sauce:
2 tbsp light soy sauce
½ tbsp dark soy sauce
1 tbsp fish sauce
1 tsp sesame oil
1 tbsp Shaoxing wine
¼ tsp sugar
¼ tsp white pepper

Method:
1. Start by washing the rice. Put the rice into a bowl, add enough water to cover, then use your hand to agitate the rice and swirl the grains. You'll see the water go cloudy; discard the cloudy water, fill up with clean water and repeat at least three times until the water runs clear. Add 500ml of water and soak the rice for 30 minutes. It's important not to miss the soaking step as this helps the rice cook through evenly.
2. Next, make the sauce. In a small bowl, mix all the sauce ingredients together. Set aside.
3. You can either make this dish in a clay pot or a rice cooker. Place the meat on top of the washed, un-cooked rice, press the button, and cook normally. By cooking the meat and rice together, the fat from the meat seeps into the rice.

4. For those using a saucepan or clay pot, bring the rice to a boil on high heat and cover with a lid. Once bubbling, turn the flame down to the lowest setting possible and cook for 12 minutes. Switch off the heat and let the rice stand for 1 minute with the lid still on. Once steamed, take the meat out and slice it.

5. Fluff the rice, return the meat to the rice along with the sauce, spring onions and an extra drizzle of sesame oil. Have fun stirring the rice and make a glorious mess together. Serve with greens or choi or eat as is.

3

Language Barrier

'What is it, mui? Come on, spit it out,' Dad asks, half listening while he's busy frying poppadoms.

'Oh! I . . . Uh . . . Don't worry about it. It's not important,' I say, as I help lower the dried rice-flour discs into the vat of bubbling hot oil after school, still in my uniform.

'Tsk. Stop wasting my time. You know I'm busy and have got a million things to do before service,' Dad yells above the din of the extractor fan and sputtering noises of bubbles coming from the bottom of the tank. Furrowing his brows, he carefully presses the poppadom down with a wire strainer to ensure it is submerged and, after a few seconds, they magically puff up and double in size into crispy, bubbly, yellow UFOs.

I want to open up to Dad and ask him for advice on what to do because someone in school is bullying me. A girl in my class threw my new shoes in the bin today. No one helped me and everyone rushed off to class because the bell had rung and I had to fish them out of the bin and now they were sticky, covered in fizzy red pop and gunk from the other kids' leftover food. I silently sobbed in the toilets alone, trying to wash them out in the sinks and dabbing them dry with toilet paper. Should I confront this person? Should I retaliate? Should I tell the teacher? But if I dob on them, would that make me a grass? Worse, even more unpopular than I am now? As always, whenever I try to muster enough courage to call for Dad's attention or try to speak to him, I always chicken out and pretend everything's fine.

My parents were supposed to be my protectors. We're taught as children that we're supposed to have this unbreakable, close bond, but every time I tried talking to them it was like walking through a field of landmines. Any words or actions could trigger an explosion and, more often than not, it would end in tears or frustration because of miscommunication. Because my parents' mother tongues were Cantonese and mine was English, our conversations always relied on poor translations using a dictionary or Google, which meant nuances, slang and cultural references were often lost. I was comfortable and spoke English at ease with friends and teachers at school, but this meant I bottled up my anxiety only to release it at home. It was exhausting leading a double life; being a different person depending on who I was with. I had nowhere to channel my fury and confusion, and so I took it out on my parents and blamed them for not being able to speak the same language and for not being bilingual too.

My brothers and I would gang up on them. We could converse easily because we spoke Chinglish; a mix of English and Cantonese. We gossiped about our parents behind their backs or told each other things about the shop in secret, knowing full well that they couldn't understand us. It was a mean bullying tactic whenever we purposely spoke back in English against them. Mum could always tell when we were badmouthing her, and she often followed up our conversations with 'I don't understand what you're saying. Stop speaking in English to each other. What are you saying? We're a Chinese household, we speak in Cantonese.'

Not speaking the same languages fluently meant that, alongside general misunderstandings, I never had a heart-to-heart with my parents. Those deep conversations, where you stay up all night talking for hours, meaningful discussions about anything and everything. My relationship with my parents was so challenging due to the language barrier that we ultimately didn't know each other because we couldn't understand each other – almost all of our conversations were surface-level, like whether I'd eaten, or being told to be back promptly at 5pm for shop opening.

On top of an actual language barrier, my parents didn't have the luxury to give time for 'smaller' issues as they were focused on the takeaway, our livelihoods and feeding the family. I wanted to talk to them about stuff that mattered, such as the bullying, my anxiety, career prospects, my identity crisis and going through puberty.

But what would my parents make of me being bullied in school, if they knew what was happening? Would they step in to help? Would they kick up a fuss? Probably not. They'd most likely tell me to stop being so over-dramatic, fight back and get over it. Chinese culture is a very black and white concept where feelings of sadness and hopelessness are believed to be one's own fault for not trying hard enough. Depression, anxiety and other mental health issues do not hold the same significance in other cultures as they do in Western societies. So, on top of trying to grapple with the linguistic and inevitable generational divide, there was also a cultural divide that meant we never saw eye to eye.

Growing up, I would have loved to learn more about them, their backstory, as I didn't know anything about my parents' lives before they had us. Why did they choose the South Wales Valleys to settle, of all places? What was it like selling noodles from a cart where they grew up in Hong Kong? What was growing up on a farm in China like? I rarely got the chance to ask these questions because the struggle to stay afloat and to put food on the table was more important. Not finding the right words to say to each other resulted in a hint of loss, perhaps, or unexpected distance. Wealth may bring comfort and security, but time is life's greatest asset, and we never seemed to have enough of it. No time for each other and no time to meaningfully be with family. Working less, though, was not an option for low-paying, self-employed businesses like ourselves.

It wasn't just talking properly with each other that we found tricky, I've also never hugged my parents unless it's for big life events such as birthdays, graduations or someone leaving. If blood makes us related and loyalty makes us family, then why did my parents feel like acquaintances? It's a strange feeling. When I was with my parents I felt like I could never let my guard down, to fully be myself and just 'be'. Spending time with them felt unnatural and I was never at ease. It was as if I was trying to find a comfortable sleeping position, but ended up wriggling around all night and never finding a sweet spot.

After a while, the anxiety from not being able to communicate with my parents and having to switch between two languages – and two versions of myself – led to a spiral of behavioural change. Outside the takeaway: chirpy, bright and friendly Welsh Angela; during service: anxious, sulky and miserable Chinese Angela. This was most evident when I was around my parents, and I constantly felt weary at home. Quietly stressed out and often sucked into a vacuum of overthinking, I didn't have the tools to process my fears, insecurities and desires. I wasn't conscious of the impact of my mood on others, especially my parents. I kept all those swirling thoughts and feelings bottled up inside me, my inner voice repeatedly telling me that I was better at being alone. There was no need to confide in others; my problems were insignificant and I'm strong enough to solve them on my own. I felt like I was stuck in a vicious destructive cycle and my mind was like a well, starting off empty and with every incident I couldn't get my words out or anytime I couldn't express myself my mental well gradually filled up and overflowed. I became fixated on scenes in my mind, obsessed over things I wished I could have said or done and found it difficult to regulate big emotions.

Due to my emotionality, I cried a lot between the ages of five and, well, now at 30. It's why family members unofficially dubbed me ham bao mui, a cry-baby, because I used to cry all the time. I cried when I accidentally got burnt from the hot oil splatters from the deep-fat fryer. I cried when I couldn't sit next to Lauren in class. I cried when my parents scolded me over a bad grade. I cried when I couldn't beat my brothers at Mario Kart. It was so common, my school teachers permanently kept a box of tissues on my desk because of all the waterworks. If crying was an Olympic sport I would get gold. Crying was my way of reaching out; I stuck my head down and silently sobbed.

It was frustrating having to rack my brain to try and find the right vocabulary to tell my parents how I felt, and so I built up a mental barrier to block the Cantonese words in my mind, and it became a struggle to string together Chinese sentences. Our conversations then became an awkward dance that would take twice as long. I would suddenly pause mid-sentence and ask, what's the Chinese word for calendar? Nostalgia? Melon? And Mum would answer patiently. Most of the time what came out of my mouth was some crappy Chinese boiled down and stripped back to the bare basic units of meaning. 'I don't feel well,' when what I really meant was that my brain was so cloudy and I was so anxious that I had gnawed my fingernails off and I didn't have the energy to get out of bed. To which Mum would suggest a physical antidote: 'Stop being lazy. There's nothing wrong with you. Here, drink some tong (Cantonese soup) – it'll help make you feel better.' While it did feel like a hug from inside out – and I was grateful for someone to provide me with comforting herbal healing Chinese soups – it didn't make me feel better mentally. There was no way around it: I spoke English and my parents spoke Cantonese (to make things even more confusing, they also speak Hakka and Dapeng dialects).

Funnily enough, when I started nursery school, all I spoke was Cantonese and I couldn't speak a word of English. I was notoriously shy, so much so that my teachers and parents sought help on how to manage my affliction. They enrolled me on a speech-language therapy course to give me a helping hand to learn English and to better communicate with others. Soon, English replaced Cantonese and Mum was worried that I'd lose my native tongue, so she also enrolled (well, forced, more like) me and my brothers in Chinese school on Sundays from the age of five. Eventually Mum also signed up for her own English lessons to try and help bridge the gap that was beginning to grow. We started learning each other's language together, but it didn't take long until things went awry.

My interest in reading and writing Chinese quickly waned because I wanted to detach myself from anything Chinese-related in a bid to fit in with my Welsh surroundings. I had internalised a lot of shame about where my family came from. Kids in my class demanded I translate words they put in front of me or asked me to write their names in Chinese as if I was some exotic translation parrot squawking back answers to them. I found anything Chinese embarrassing and I so desperately wanted to fit in, I shunned my mother tongue. Mum's demands of work and motherhood forced her to drop English classes and Dad didn't even bother to try. Ever since they immigrated, he'd spent the majority of his time in the UK surrounded by Chinese speakers (working in the takeaway with us, watching Chinese TV, spending his free time in casinos with extended family and going back to Hong Kong every summer), so he never developed an understanding of English other than swear words, which were reserved for top-tier level of anger.

By age six, I was sparring with Mum every weekend because I was hell-bent against going to Chinese school and she was adamant we should be bilingual in Wales. I threw tantrums, only to be coaxed into learning by the promise of dim sum before lessons. This kept going until I was 16, hobbling over the finish line to finally achieve a B in Chinese at GCSE level. Much to my dismay, my brothers both got As and I didn't hear the end of it. I felt proud I'd managed to even get this far and regarded the GCSE as the light at the end of the tunnel. Mum, however, nagged me to keep going and learn Mandarin too for her sake. I carried on for another year or two, but eventually dropped learning Chinese, ostensibly due to time constraints and preparing for university. In reality, I always struggled to see the point of Cantonese because it served no purpose for me other than for helping in the takeaway or when going back to see family in Hong Kong. We lived in Wales, an English-speaking country, everyone in my life spoke English, so why would I need to speak any other language?

Looking back, I regret not studying harder and not continuing with my Chinese studies. I made the conscious decision to disassociate myself from my language and community. Most immigrants (often subconsciously) make a choice at some point to embrace the host country's culture and language while dismissing or rejecting their heritage. I realise, in retrospect, the importance of learning my ancestral tongue. Not just to stay connected with my family's heritage, but as something that's intertwined with my identity, memories and sense of self. I am thankful that Mum forced me to hold on to Chinese, it was a reminder to not forget who I was and to take ownership of a culture and language that could have been potentially lost. At least I can speak and hold conversations fluently with friends and family (albeit at the proficiency level of an eight-year-old), and I'm glad to be a slightly rusty native speaker. First-language attrition, the process of forgetting a first or native language, is not a badge of shame but a symbol of perseverance, and this adaptability should be seen as celebratory – it's proof of our inventiveness as humans.

Mental colonisation happens among immigrants. There's a currency in growing up in a hostile, white homogenous society and losing your previous accent. My parents' goal of moving to another country for a better life and assimilation was precious enough to make the sacrifice worthwhile, but for the next generation of immigrants like me, societal cohesion is not considered important enough. We live in tribes now. Mum and Dad's refusal to learn the primary language of a country that they've been living in for three decades meant Keen, Jacky and I were the middlemen for any translation work between my parents, staff and customers. On top of our schoolwork, we took on day-to-day takeaway and life admin such as reading and translating important letters my parents didn't understand, paying bills and taxes, renewing insurance, liaising with health inspectors whenever they did a surprise food hygiene check, and many other things to keep business and life ticking over. We were the parents to our parents, and we had to look after them – it was a huge strain on our relationship and my life. Losing fluency in your native language is a gradual process and you don't notice until it's almost too late. While we now sort of speak the same language, we still cannot communicate properly. Sometimes, the barrier is more than just the words.

*

The Valleys is a place unlike any other. For somewhere that doesn't have a lot going for it, it makes up for it in character and all the larger-than-life mischievous personalities that reside there. The happy-go-lucky pensioners, the lads shoplifting in corner shops and the woman at the local caff serving you a greasy fry-up with a cigarette hanging out of her mouth – this is the place that I called home as a child and I had a constant love-hate relationship with it growing up. Beddau sits in the dip of what feels like a million peaks and troughs of the mountainous valleys. During summer, when the sun shines its glistening golden rays on the rows of grey pebble-dash terraced houses that hug the scraggy hillsides and the towering derelict coke works, it's a fine line between beautiful and bleak. On a hot August day, the small town smells like rubbish and asphalt mixed with the scent of freshly cut grass wafting in from the main rugby field at the top of the hill. I guess I should be grateful for whenever the perpetually wet Wales gets any sunshine at all or experiences temperatures like this because they only come once in a blue moon, but I hate the summer here because that's when the kitchen is at its worst. It's unbearable. In an already hot kitchen – and one without a decent ventilation system – the temperature often reaches highs of 35 degrees Celsius. Unmoving, sweltering dead air fills the room, while we're all stuck indoors with no air conditioning behind a row of deafening woks shooting flames from the burner underneath like a dragon breathing and spitting flames from its cave.

'Ah mui, I've run out of sliced green peppers. Can you fetch me some from the other fridge?' Dad requests as he stands behind his workstation, topless in a black and white striped apron, Nike sports shorts and red flip-flops, trying to beat the heat while he works. The red-hot glow warms his face while he churns out orders of shredded crispy chilli beef. With every flick of the wrist, a rattle of a ladle against the woks and the hiss of steam. The smells of garlic, ginger, five spice, chilli powder, sweet-and-sour sauce and about a dozen other aromatics waft from Dad's direction. It's a smell that has a physical aura, one that is felt as it fills the sinuses and shuffles down the throat. Soon the chaotic sounds of the takeaway become background noise. I imagine a visible wiggly scent trail that turns into a hand beckoning you to come, like they do in cartoons where Jerry the mouse from *Tom and Jerry* would use his nose to follow the smell blindly in the hope of finding something delicious at the other end.

'Earth to muiii!' Dad repeats. 'Get the peppers.'

I stop daydreaming and snap back to reality, realising I'm in the middle of busy service. 'Okay, Dad! On it!'

I rush to the other fridge in the utility room to the left of the kitchen, an old – cold in the winter, but roasting hot in the summer – lean-to that's covered in the same white tiles on the walls as the kitchen. A narrow slither of a space that somehow my parents managed to use every inch of, squeezing in a sink, washing machine and a secondary fridge to store more prepped ingredients.

They certainly put the 'utilise' in the utility room. It's so compact in there that the fridge door doesn't fully open, so in order to get what you need you have to carefully manoeuvre your arm at an angle and feel your way around. I return with a cucumber and hand it over to Dad. A growing puzzled look spreads across his silent, stern face that reads, 'How could I have possibly raised such a slow twelve-year-old daughter?'

'No, no, no. Not a cucumber! A green pepper! They're on the bottom shelf next to the blue trays of mushrooms and your Sunny Delight orange juice cartons.' Dad raises his voice and furrows his brows, growing more impatient with every wok toss. 'Hurry! Get a move on. I need it now for this dish and the order is waiting on them.'

The Cantonese word for cucumber and green pepper – cheng gwaa and cheng jiu – sound *very* similar and I often get the two mixed up. Both are green. Both are essential ingredients for the takeaway (one's used for a salad decoration to go with the prawn toast, the other is used for black bean and sweet-and-sour dishes). Both are the bane of my life. I run back to the lean-to with the cucumber and try again. After much panic rummaging and frantically looking through every fridge shelf like I'm on *Supermarket Sweep*, I can't find the green peppers. I face defeat, take a big gulp and fear the worst. My heart skips a few beats faster and sweat starts to bead on my forehead as I return empty-handed, awaiting Dad's wrath.

'Are you kidding me?! Why can't you follow simple instructions? Faster to do it myself,' Dad shouts, and rolls his eyes. He slams the wok down, shuffles out of his corner from the wok range, and shoves Mum out of the way to get past. My brothers and I all take a step back, knowing full well not to interfere and to move far away enough from Dad when he is raging on his warpath. Miraculously, he swiftly returns with a tray of sliced green peppers. How do Asian parents seem to automatically know where everything is at all times? The house and takeaway is cluttered and filled to the brim with so much stuff. Yet, they just know. Is this their sixth sense?

'See! Green peppers!' Dad waves the tray in the air mockingly. 'Now, that wasn't so hard, was it? Honestly, so useless. What's the point of giving birth to children if they can't do anything right?'

I hate it when Dad is like this. His bad attitude rubs off on us all, his moodiness drags us all down with him and his snide comments pierce my heart like a metal arrow lodged uncomfortably. I want to retreat further into myself, stick my head down, not cause any further trouble and be invisible. My internal mental well spilling out, mind reaching a critical mass and feeling too overwhelmed and afraid to speak out. *Useless, useless, useless:* my internal monologue berates me and swirls around my head. I feel hot tears start to prick and water droplets start to form in the corners of my eyes. Then Mum's soothing, kind, gentle words lift me out from myself.

'Don't be so hard on her,' Mum reasons with Dad, trying to calm him down. 'She's trying.' Mum lifts the thin strips of fried beef from the sizzling deep-fat fryer, carefully shakes the frying basket to get rid of the excess oil and dumps it into Dad's wok.

'Mm,' Dad grunts, while he works quickly to combine the bright-red viscous sauce with the deep-fried strips of beef. His left hand tosses the wok back and forth and his right hand turns the spatula quickly, folding in the spicy sweet-and-sour sauce together with the meat until every single piece is coated with a light, glossy sheen. He turns around, grabs a shiny silver container from the stacks of food packaging sitting on top of the worktop and scoops the shredded crispy chilli beef into the tray. Jacky grabs a white poly-board lid and presses down the four corners while Keen pulls a white plastic bag hanging from a metal hook, begins packing and takes the order out to the front. Without saying anything, Dad gets another silver container, spoons the remnants of his chilli beef from the wok and scrapes the leftovers in. He slides the extra portion over the silver worktop in our direction. My brothers are rolling up their sleeves ready to dive in to claim first dibs. Dad silently shakes his head at them, nods at me, indicating that this is specifically for me, and smirks.

'Thanks, Dad.' I give him a smile, wiping the tears from my eyes.

Before we can cherish this rare father-daughter moment, Cecilia interrupts and walks back into the kitchen holding the same white bag we've just sent out moments ago.

'The customer just checked his food and found carrots, onions and peppers in the shredded crispy beef. Did you remember to cook it plain?' Cecilia asks as she starts to unpack the bag on the table and opens the silver container to show proof of Dad's mistake.

Mum and Dad turn around; they both have a bewildered look on their faces, not quite grasping what's going on in this situation.

'Dad, the customer asked for no vegetables,' I explain in Cantonese, and point to the paper ticket that reads: '59 – No V'.

His brow furrows and he squints his eyes as he picks up the paper ticket for a closer look. 'I can't fucking read English. I don't know what "V" means,' Dad grumbles confusingly.

'"V" stands for vegetables. "V" means choi,' Mum repeats. 'Haiya*, read the order carefully!'

'It's okay, Cecilia,' I say. 'Thanks for telling us, my parents said they're sorry for the mix-up and will quickly remake it now.' I falsely translate back to her.

Those green peppers. Bane of my life. Bane of our lives.

*

---

* Haiya is a Chinese interjection similar to 'ah' or 'shoot' in English and can be used as an expression of sadness, anger, shock or disappointment. Unsurprisingly, my parents used this phrase a lot when talking to me and my brothers.

Though words don't come easy to us, our language is food and we mainly only interact around food. In Chinese culture, we don't greet each other by saying 'hello', we ask whether 'Sik jor fan mei ah?' (食咗飯未呀?), which means 'Have you eaten yet?' Probably one of the most important phrases in the Chinese language. Food has a basic meaning, but there's also an underlying message: eating well and eating properly are two very important things in Chinese culture. It's a symbiotic and easily parsed relationship that expresses concern for whether somebody else has eaten, and it's equivalent to expressing care, concern and protection for their well-being. Mum used to fill my bowl with huge portions of food, encouraging me to eat up then scorning me for eating too much and I'd almost always make a fuss about it, complaining that I was bored of eating Chinese food, I wanted to eat what my white friends ate. Plus, I didn't want to eat so much, as I was trying to watch my figure for fear of being scorned by the weight police, also known as the aunties, uncles and my extended family members. Instead of trying to understand her actions, I pushed her away and rejected her food.

Mum and Dad have always tried to indulge me – it was their dearest expression of love. When Mum was a child, food was the most precious thing she had (or, more accurately, lacked). She was born at the height of the Great Chinese Famine. Instead of fluffy white rice and an abundance of fresh vegetables, she ate over-watery congee (a type of rice porridge) bulked out with rotting sweet potato to make the meal last for the week. People were so hungry in her village they ate leaves, tree bark and, in worst-case scenarios, there were also general reports of cannibalism that occurred during the famine. Dad grew up with nine cousins and siblings under one roof, so there was never enough food on the table and my dad, being the runt of the litter, was always left with scraps after fighting his family over food. My parents therefore always gave me the best-looking portions while eating the undesirable leftovers themselves. It only dawned on me later on in life why eating all your food was such a big deal to my parents. Not because it was wasteful to leave food behind, but for them to have lived through famine and experienced the hardships of not having enough, now being able to put food on the table and offer their kids extra nourishment must've felt like a dream. A real achievement. It must've been painful for them to experience my refusal to eat what they put in front of me day after day and requesting to eat Western food instead. To my parents, food is love and food symbolises family.

There was something mesmerising about watching my parents make our pre-service family dinner. I often silently observed on the sidelines of the kitchen after school, trying my best to not be in the way, but close enough so I could peek at what was coming for dinner. Mum finely dicing garlic and ginger with a gigantic meat cleaver (her and Dad's number-one knife preference), while on the next burner over Dad is precariously balancing a gigantic two-tier stainless-steel steamer on a metal rack above a wok filled with a bubbling bath of water. The visible mist escapes through the holes: it's steam time.

Mum gently adds the finely chopped garlic and ginger into the wok to bao heung or 'explode into aroma', as they say in Cantonese – the process of tempering, gently dry-roasting the aromatics to release their natural flavour. The kitchen is now filled with wonderful, intoxicating smells of fresh vibrant herbs and spices. Next, she adds the morning glory, stir-frying it quickly until it wilts slightly before adding a pinch of sugar, salt, white pepper, oyster sauce and a splash of water. Bite-sized pork ribs marinated in fragrant fermented black bean sauce are placed on the bottom shelf of the steamer, but the top layer is reserved for the pièce de résistance: sea bass.

Whole steamed sea bass is a regular feature across many Chinese families' dinner tables. The word 'fish' sounds like the word for 'abundance' in Cantonese and traditionally the fish is served whole with its head and tail on to represent family togetherness and unity. Mum picks up her huge silver cleaver and finely slices more ginger and spring onion with micro-precision. I gawp as she covers the fish with the matchstick aromatics, delicately placing it in the steamer and putting the lid on.

Dad's busy chopping pieces of pork into bite-sized pieces, which he passes to Mum, who mixes them in the fermented black beans, red chillies, ginger, garlic,

Shaoxing wine and soy sauce with a pair of chopsticks, setting the meat aside to soak up all the savoury goodness before putting them in the bottom of the steamer under the fish. Dad's in charge of the final step. I'm in awe of their teamwork, how they lean over each other, grabbing bits of ingredients and sharp knives from here and there, seamlessly without a word; a culinary ballet, a lifetime of work, a marriage. A kitchen Capoeira dance battle without ever knocking into each other. Using a spatula, Dad places a ladleful of oil in the bottom of the wok. The oil starts to bubble and he rotates his wrist in a clockwise motion so it swirls around just below the lip of the wok, where flames climb up the sides, providing fuel for the grand finale.

'Waaah!' he shouts as he turns around with the wok. 'Stand back or you'll get burnt!' With one hand, he pours the hot oil all over the fish. The moment the hot oil hits the fish, something magical happens. There's an instant crackle of sizzling and spitting noises. The fragrant aromas from the oil fill the air and signal it's time to eat up.

Without fail, we always eat together every night. All this effort for a family dinner is a Chinese parent's way of saying: 'I love you'. Although our feelings are rarely discussed and mental wellbeing is a concept that simply doesn't exist in their book, cooking is a silent act of love because you are nurturing the people you feed and putting in the time and labour to nourish someone's soul as well as their body. Food is the key to our hearts. No matter how busy my parents are, they always carve time out of their busy schedules to ensure we eat together every night. Having a home-cooked family meal is important to them. Eating dinner together is the adhesive that binds us together as a family. There is something special about setting aside time every night to do this small act. It requires very little of us, just 45 minutes away from our usual quotidian distractions. Sometimes it feels like a chore to endure forced quality family time, yet it is invariably one of the happiest parts of my day.

For family meal, the five of us gather around the newspaper-covered square coffee table crammed in the makeshift living-room space, sitting on the floor and mismatched sofas. There's never a dull moment when the five of us are together. 'Sik fan,' we all eagerly say in unison before clambering over each other with chopsticks to get first dibs on dishes. With the blaring television playing the Hong Kong TVB (one of Hong Kong's biggest TV channels) news jingles in the background, me and Jacky are locked in a chopstick war fighting over the same piece of pork while Mum sneakily scoops more succulent pieces of fish into our bowls, insisting we should eat more fish because it'll make our skin smoother.

I turn to Mum and Dad, chopsticks and bowl in hand. 'The fish is so silky and fresh,' I say.

'Of course!' Mum smiles at me. 'I steamed it just right and not a minute over. It took me ages to pick the right fish at the market, too.'

'Don't forget to eat some of the pork,' Dad says, picking up a piece with his chopsticks and putting some in my bowl. 'Eat up.'

My dad prides himself on his cooking. Mum is on another level though. Not a day goes by when she's *not* cooking something. She lives and breathes food and is always pottering about in the kitchen and constantly whipping up something new for us, giving out creations she's made for relatives as gifts or going back to perfect her tried-and-tested recipes. Cooking and eating is a way of life in our family. It's central to who we are and it's the concrete pillar that props us up, but really it's Mum who's the foundation and who holds this dysfunctional family together.

Steamed fish is an aroma closely associated with my family – with safety and with affection. I speak in recipes, bond over quantities and taste ingredients that remind me of home. Perhaps this is why food and family are so inherently part of me, as a child and grandchild of immigrants. Maybe I'm desperate to cling on to these last ties to my culture; maybe food is a particularly strong language for immigrant children. To me, it symbolises a home that I've never even lived in. One foot firmly in the deep Welsh Valleys where I was born, the other in the island of Hong Kong, a 12-hour flight away on the other side of the world – my second home.

As the great American cook and author James Beard observed in his 1974 book, *Beard on Food*, 'Food is the common ground, a universal experience.' No matter our home country or culture, food is something we share for enjoyment and survival. Food can convey so much of our heritage, our history and our family. While this is certainly true – food does bring us together – it can also be the very thing that drives us apart. For years, I'd resented Mum for not sticking to her language courses and Dad for not even making an effort. It would've made life a whole lot easier if they spoke English, spoke the same language as us kids, and we might've understood each other a bit better rather than speaking in tongues through the language of food. My parents and I never seemed to be in sync and danced to each other's offbeats. I pinned the blame on them, for not learning, for not trying, for their laziness, but now I realise how deeply hypocritical that was. Mum and Dad had always shown up for us in their own way. They did things for me and my brothers despite their limited English skills. I'd spent a good part of my life pushing away from them, but I was really pushing away from my own guilt and frustration. We're still learning to sync up, but that's okay. As a family, we've learned to dance to the beat of our drum.

Steamed Sea Bass with Ginger and Spring Onion

Tell someone how much you love them by steaming a whole fish. You can steam almost any firm-fleshed fish such as cod, sea bream, trout, grouper or salmon, but sea bass is one of the most common fish used for steaming in Chinese cooking. This is a straightforward healthy centrepiece dish that can be left to its own devices. In Cantonese, 'yu' (魚), the word for fish, shares the same pronunciation with the word 'yu' (余), which means surplus, going hand-in-hand with 'leen leen yow yu' (年年有余) – a common Cantonese expression used during the Lunar New Year meaning to wish people abundance, wealth and surplus every year. This makes fish a must-have dish on Chinese dining tables every New Year or for family meal. For bonus luck points, the fish should be served whole, with head and tail attached, which symbolises a good beginning and ending for the coming year (explaining why this dish is a must for Lunar New Year celebrations). A word of warning, though: an old superstition says it's a big no-no to flip the fish while eating, as this symbolises 'belly's up', or in Chinese, 'fan tow' – a capsizing boat, or death. Don't be intimidated by using the whole fish: in fact, the cheeks and eyes are the best bit. Mum claims that eating fish-eyes boosts Omega 3, which is essential for achieving straight As (or Bs in my case).

The hardest part of this recipe is simply figuring out how you're going to steam it. Once you have your steaming arrangement worked out, it's plain sailing and delicious times.

Serves: 4 | **Prep time:** 10 mins | **Cook time:** 15–20 mins (depending on fish size)

Ingredients:
1 whole sea bass, gutted and descaled (you can ask the fishmonger to do this for you, if needed)
1 thumb-sized piece of fresh ginger, peeled and finely sliced into matchsticks (julienned)
2 spring onions, finely sliced into matchsticks (julienned)
1 handful of fresh coriander, roughly chopped
2 tbsp light soy sauce
¼ tsp sugar
2 tbsp vegetable oil, for drizzling
Steamed rice, to serve

Method:
Preparing the fish:
1. Remove any scales from your fish using a fork. Pay particular attention to the belly area and the edges of the fish, including the top, near the dorsal fins, and the head. There's nothing worse than having to pick out scales while you're having dinner.

2. Give the fish a final rinse, shake off the excess water, pat dry with a kitchen towel and transfer to a heat-proof plate for steaming.

Steaming/Cooking:

1. Peel the ginger with a spoon. Finely slice the ginger and spring onions into matchsticks. You can either use a wok and metal steam rack or, if you don't have those, you can place the fish, ginger and spring onion (reserve half for garnish) in a foil parcel in a steamer or on a baking tray in a 200°C (180°C fan)/ gas mark 6 pre-heated oven. Evenly sprinkle with sugar to bring out the natural flavour of the fish and steam for 15–20 minutes depending on the size of the fish.

2. Use a butter knife to peek at the meat and check if the fish is cooked through. The meat should be opaque down to the bone, but the bone should be slightly translucent and not fully cooked. That's when you'll know it's done.

3. Carefully pour off all the liquid accumulated during steaming and transfer to a plate (if using foil method). Scatter the other half of ginger, spring onion and coriander over the fish.

4. Drizzle over soy sauce.

5. Heat a pan or wok with vegetable oil until the oil starts to bubble and smoke slightly.

6. Carefully drizzle the hot oil over the fish. Be sure to stand back, as it will sizzle and potentially spit. Serve with rice to soak up all the sauce.

4

Super Sunday Ritual

Sundays are a weird thing. You're either savouring the last remnants of the weekend or preparing for the week ahead, but when you work in hospitality there is no weekend. The days bleed into nights and the late nights carry over into the next day. A sense of time is destroyed, with no boundaries or visual markers to remind us that another day has ended. Whatever rare window of free time we had, it was slotted in between doing other things, but our time off somehow always revolved around the takeaway. To pass the time we folded boxes of pistachio-green paper menus ready to hand out with every meal and spent Saturday mornings posting them through neighbours' letterboxes in the hope of drumming up more business. Unbearable ennui resulted in refilling cans of soft drinks and bottles of water in the mini-fridge under the counter. Piles of unread important letters that my parents were unable to understand needed my attention. There were plenty of ways to be productive when living and working in the same establishment. No matter how much I complained about being bored and having nowhere to go in a sleepy, isolated ex-mining village (because the bus drivers operated on a 'once whenever they feel like it' service), there was always something to do at home. An endless green-light loop stuck on go.

As a takeaway family, we work when people are celebrating: weekends, nights and holidays. Our opening hours were between 5pm and 11pm but, in reality, conventional takeaway hours come with caveats where we are required to have the ability to perform daytime audit duties on top of the already long hours. Shuffled and disordered, like a giant blur; a dream state, or perhaps a nightmare. For many, Sunday is a day of rest, but not for the Hui family – it was our super Sunday ritual. Our one day of the week to break out of our perpetual state of timelessness to venture out of the village and to our closest city, Cardiff, to stock up on goods for the business. This also meant enduring quality family time over dim sum at Happy Gathering, one of two banquet-hall type Cantonese restaurants in town, and going to Chinese school.

Mum rushes us out the door impatiently as we have a busy day ahead of us and we're already running behind schedule. The five of us clamber into our clunky old forest-green Rover R8 (Dad's prized possession) and I'm always squished in the middle because, being the youngest and smallest, I don't take up as much room. Dad puts his foot down, hogs the right-hand lane and pelts it down the motorway. It's overcast, everything grey, no shadows. I watch the undeveloped scrubland and trees zoom by and disappear behind us in the window as we spend the next half-hour of the journey listening to Dad's carefully recorded Cantopop mega mixtape on cassette, blaring out all the big names such as Anita Mui, Aaron Kwok, Faye Wong, Beyond, Danny Chan, Jacky Cheung, Sam Hui and Andy Lau on the highest volume. My brothers collectively groan, and I sink lower into the black leather car seat, hoping that any passers-by aren't able to hear this embarrassing show of tunes.

Driving past the Cardiff City football stadium, the city centre never ceases to amaze me. The smooth pavements, towering streetlights, tall buildings, white modern studio flats and apartments in the distance overlooking Cardiff Bay; a glistening man-made blue seafront. Despite being less than 15 miles down the road, the capital offers something different and something aspirational. Everything feels new, with a buzz in the air, and it's exciting to be able to break free from our rural confines of Beddau.

Our first port of call: the cash-and-carry wholesalers. As our car rolls up in an industrial estate in Grange-town – a diverse working-class area with a significant Somali, Asian and mixed-race community – the sky starts to clear up and the sun starts to peek through, as if welcoming us into the city. Global Foods cash-and-carry is a mecca. From the outside, it doesn't look like much – dark-blue corrugated roof held up by a red steel frame and a giant white 'Global Foods' banner with a little globe logo – but on the inside, it's a different story. Floor-to-ceiling shelves of hyper-organised, neatly la-belled products. From jumbo tubs of herbs to multipack tins of sauces and boxes of savoury snacks, you'll find everything you could possibly need under one roof that comes in catering size and can only be bought in bulk. I feel the full effects of the *Alice in Wonderland* syndrome, realising my tiny ant-like presence in a vast warehouse packed to the brim with comically large items.

The place is bustling full of people, rushing around scouring the shelves; everyone has a different story but has also somehow ended up in South Wales. An Indian man in a pink shirt rocking a mighty grey moustache is on his Nokia 3330 phone, pulling his cart full of plastic tubs of rainbow Haribo pick-and-mix sweets. A Somali man and his wife, who is wearing a black niqab, browse the condiments and spices. Another Chinese man, wearing a red polo top, Diadora tracksuit bottoms and a navy bum bag, hauls a massive orange nylon netted sack of white onions over his shoulder. Who are these people? Why are they here? What are they buying? Where have they travelled from? Do they own shops like we do? What type of food do they sell? I stare at the strangers for too long, intrigued about their backstories, but never daring to ask or speak to someone. Besides, we're all too busy carting our blue flatbed warehouse nesting trolleys, snaking up and down the long aisles, narrowly passing the workers in hi-vis jackets operating forklift trucks stacking more crates of multipack bottles of Coca-Cola, extending to reach the higher shelves. I didn't understand at the time, but as I grew older I realised we were all there for the same reason. We were all immigrants with immigrant food-businesses trying to make a living, trying to provide for our families and trying to stay afloat. We would bring back our hauls, car boots jammed full, to our tiny rural corner shops, delis, newsagents, takeaways and restaurants – we would stock up our 'foreign' pantries, refill shop shelves with 'ethnic' brands and cook exotic dishes that couldn't be made without that journey to the wholesalers, because what we're looking for isn't accessible or available any-where else in local Western supermarkets like Tesco, Sainsburys or ASDA.

I eagerly take my position sitting on the end of the trolley, feeling buzzed about my new surroundings. Either that, or I'm getting a sugar rush from eating too many of the Haw flakes* Mum gave me as a snack in the car to keep quiet. Dad pulls the cart with me on it through the see-through PVC strip curtain and into the walk-in fridge. A huge white room, filled with a maze of metal shelves stocked with an array of cheeses in alphabetical order, multicoloured tubs of bell peppers, blue plastic trays of mushrooms, oversized plastic bags of bean sprouts and vats of milk. We scoot over to the

---

* Haw flakes – Chinese sweets made from the fruit of the Chinese haw-thorn. A dark-pink disc-shaped candy that tastes sweet and slightly tart.

neat Jenga tower of cardboard chip boxes in the corner of the room. On the ceiling, four fans are pumping out gusts of cold air, so cold you can physically see the plumes of breezy air coming out. This is what I'd imagine spending time in an actual igloo would be like. Jacky gives Dad a helping hand loading up the trolley with heavy chip boxes while Keen feebly tries to carry the big bags of bean sprouts one at a time. Mum has already disappeared and split off somewhere else to cover more ground (most likely to be found in the East and Southeast Asian aisles stocking up on soy sauce, oils and noodles). She always complains about the lack of full range here; that you can't get certain ingredients, even though in my eyes this place is a Disneyland that supplies it all. The trolley is starting to get heavier as we accumulate more items and Dad can't wheel it with me any more, so kicks me off while I run amok towards the snack aisle looking for Mum (and more snacks). I sneak Ginbis Dream seaweed animal biscuits, Want Want Senbei rice crackers, Calbee shrimp chips and strawberry Pocky into the trolley without my parents knowing.

On the truly special occasions, once quarterly, we ventured further afield than Cardiff, making the two-hour-plus pilgrimage from Wales to Wing Yip in Birmingham – at the time it was our nearest large Asian supermarket – for the sole purpose of stockpiling Chinese groceries. Cardiff has more of a 'China street' rather than a 'Chinatown', featuring only two Asian grocery stores, which only stock a fraction of the items my parents are looking for. The majestic sight of Wing Yip with its bright-green curve-tiled roof on red stilts and its contrasting yellow sign sticks out like a sore thumb among a grey web of roundabouts, welcoming you in as you drive through into the carpark. Our trips were not leisurely grocery shopping trips, they were bargain-hunting supermarket sweeps that resemble blood sport. I'd wearily slog up the aisles struggling to keep up and push a gargantuan trolley behind Mum. I'm slowly being weighed down by the growing boxes of instant Nissin Demae ramen, bags of wriggling fresh lobsters plucked from the fish tanks trying to escape and bottles of Mum's favourite brand of Shaoxing wine. Eventually I have to tag out and pass the baton to give the trolley-driving duties to my brothers, because it gets too heavy and I'm unable to push anymore. I was deep in the trenches of an Asian wonderland; it was a sensory overload and I loved every second of it. If Mum was in a good mood, we'd be rewarded with one final stop to the on-site bakery to bag end-of-day discount baked goods such as pork floss spring onion rolls, pineapple buns, dan tart (egg tarts), coconut cream buns, pandan cake, char siu puffs and my absolute favourite: steamed Chinese sausage buns. The sugary, floury smells of cakes and Asian breads were intoxicating, filling the entire store and lingering in the air to entice you to buy more. We bought everything we couldn't get our hands on back in Wales to stockpile until the next big trip, like squirrels hoarding food for the winter. We didn't do family day trips to the seaside like the other Welsh families; cash-and-carry wholesalers were the only tropical paradises we needed.

'Don't be rude. Greet your family members,' Dad whispers and elbows me.

I can feel my stomach drop and the cogs in my head turning, trying to calculate the next crucial string of words I'm supposed to say. I'm frantically jogging my memory to try and remember what to call each family member. This is it, fight or flight. Do or die. I *hate* being put on the spot or anything to do with the limelight.

'Uh ... uh ... hi, saam baak (third eldest paternal uncle, Uncle George), saam baak niang (third paternal aunt, Auntie Sarah), Kyle biu gor (older male cousin), Nina biu jie (older female cousin), Maria biu jie (older female cousin), Sally biu jie (older female cousin),' I stutter and panic. I'm unsure if I'm actually addressing any of them correctly, stumbling my way through the names, listing them off one-by-one like I'm in some exam I'm destined to fail.

'Mm, okay, lah. Gwaai.* Gwaai. Sit, sit, sit.' Uncle George gestures for us to sit on the high-back ruby-red velvet dining chairs and join their table covered in crisply ironed red tablecloths that give a certain

---

* Gwaai, meaning a good, obedient child. Something I am clearly not because I always fell into my family's bad books.

formality, and rightly so because dim sum eating is serious business.

Phew. I've passed the test. Another week of not feeling the wrath of the extended Hui family for messing up someone's name. Chinese uses a different kinship system than English. The Chinese kinship system is classified as a descriptive kinship system, which means referring to each of my family tree by a different kin term (there are at least eight different terms just to refer to the many, many cousins I have, and that's only on my Dad's side of the family). In short, it's confusing as hell to wrap your head around and if you don't call your second cousin twice removed the correct term, you'll be damned for all eternity and extended family members will gossip for weeks on end about how bad your Chinese is or brand you for being rude.

With the weekly shopping list ticked off, it's time for my favourite part of Sunday. Yum cha,* a traditional, weekly get-together taking place during prime-time brunch hours. Happy Gathering was our church, where we held tea drinking and dim sum eating rituals, and we prayed at the altar of steaming bamboo baskets. Happy Gathering is my happy place. A two-storey restaurant in Canton on Cowbridge Road East, a long stretch of road that connects to the city centre. It's one of the most ethnically diverse of Cardiff's suburbs, dotted with

---

* Yum cha – to 'drink tea' in Cantonese, yum cha is a traditional brunch involving Chinese tea and dim sum. Also, the best meal of the day.

butchers, greengrocers, Italian pizza parlours, Welsh greasy spoons, Greek hairdressers and Indian takeaways. On the inside, the establishment is an opulent sight to behold – a grand piano in the centre of the room surrounded by dozens upon dozens of large, circular tables seating entire families. Servers dash quickly between them, zipping from the kitchen to the hungry masses and back again. Red paper lanterns hang from the ceiling, red napkins on tables, there are tropical fish tanks embedded in the walls and a maroon short-pile carpet. An overwhelming red colour scheme runs throughout the restaurant to symbolise luck, joy and happiness: the three stages of the dim sum eating experience. There are two round 'top tables' on a raised platform at the back of the room, which is the centrepiece of the restaurant, positioned in front of two golden mythical creatures: a mighty phoenix on the left and a fierce dragon on the right. They face each other, locked in an intense battle over the double happiness symbol '囍' in between them, a Chinese symbol of joy and happiness, commonly used as a decoration for love and marriage. For many of the extended Hui clan, it's a rite of passage to have your wedding banquet at Happy Gathering. It's one of the few places for traditional Chinese weddings in South Wales. We've been coming here for years, decades even, and the entire staff has watched us grow up.

Sunday lunch is always a sell-out when Cardiff's Chinese community descends on the place en masse and others come from miles away to enjoy the array of tantalising morsels and to catch up. I feel both at ease and on edge to be surrounded by Chinese friends, family and strangers. Is this what it feels like to be a majority rather than a minority? To not stand out like a sore thumb, but to also blend in, looking like everyone else? My mind vacillates between confusion and comfort from taking a seat at the table, joining the other Chinese people who look like me. Our day-to-day life is an isolated bubble, and it's all too easy to forget that life outside the takeaway world exists. For a brief moment in time on Sunday, all of us coming together to sit around a table breaking bread means nothing else matters, it's our safe space.

I often wonder what life would have been like if my parents had stayed in Hong Kong instead of settling in the UK. How would my brothers and I have turned out? I can't imagine what I'd sound like without my Welsh twang, or picture Jacky listening to anything else but Iron Maiden, System of a Down and Limp Bizkit, or Keen reading something other than Final Fantasy video-game strategy guides in English. If we'd been brought up on the other side of the world, would we even know what these things are? Dress the way we do? Or act the way we do? Maybe in an alternate universe, but I'll never know.

Keen picks up the white porcelain teapot, stands up and pours pu'erh tea into tiny white cups sitting on the glass lazy Susan in the centre of the table. Scents of sweet, dried fruits and honey, followed by the earthy notes of a forest, fill the air with every pour as the cups spin around. My parents, aunt and uncle knock their fingers on the table twice as they carry on talking without breaking conversation. It's a sign of thanks to the tea-pourer, a Chinese mannerism and part of the yum cha etiquette that's been passed down for generations and is said to have originated with Emperor Qianlong of the Qing dynasty. We spend hours drinking pu'erh Chinese leaf tea at a snail's pace, sharing stories old and new, recounted over a table full of towering stacks of steel and bamboo baskets that hold a variety of delectable small bites that encompass everything from delicate golden-brown ham sui gok (fried glutinous rice dumplings) to silky cheung fun (rice rolls) and fluffy cloud-like char siu bao (steamed BBQ pork buns). Every time the waiter brings out more food, he stamps our paper ticket, like a game of dim sum bingo waiting for all our numbers to be dabbed off.

I stand up and pluck a har gow dumpling with my chopsticks, but it's stuck to the paper underneath and the other dumplings in the basket. I try my best to shake it and break it free. Jacky comes to my rescue with his chopsticks and pulls the round parchment down to release everything. I place the dumpling in my bowl, squeeze the prawn filling out and slip it into Jacky's bowl. There's something about the iodine fishy scent and taste of prawns I'm not a fan of, but I absolutely adored eating the bouncy, chewy translucent wheat and tapioca crystal skin.

'Where did you learn to hold chopsticks like that? Didn't your parents teach you properly?' Auntie Sarah scolds, and points her chopsticks at me. 'Also, why aren't you eating the prawns? They're the best, most valuable bit!'

'Uh . . . uh. I never . . .' I break eye contact and mutter into my lonely bowl of har gow skin.

'It doesn't matter, as long as she can pick food up and enjoy food whatever way it's fine.' Mum always defends me. She picks up the slippery char siu cheung fun with her chopsticks like a pro and slides it into my bowl. 'Here, mui, try the cheung fun, it's leng leng waat waat (beautiful and smooth) today.'

Before Auntie Sarah can comment and pick on something else wrong with me, the next flurry of dishes are flying out the kitchen. Steamy fresh aromas of beef, chicken, coriander, duck, pork, prawn and turnip seeping through the covered bamboo baskets alongside other Cantonese staples: a trio of Cantonese roast meats on a bed of jasmine white rice and pak choi, beef ho fun, a bowl of pork and century egg congee. Waiters keep coming through, steamers keep piling up; the taller the tower, the higher the accomplishment, and the more satisfied we become.

'So, how's school going?' Auntie Sarah asks while chewing her way noisily through a piece of braised chicken's foot. 'Do you have a boyfriend yet, mui?'

'Yeah, mui, do you have a *boy*friend?' Keen mimics, as he peeks in between the bamboo towers.

'Ngo mo nam pung yow!' (I don't have a boyfriend) I huff loudly above the noisy background chatter coming in from all directions.

The Chinese that comes out of my mouth is so juvenile, my extended family mockingly call us younger generation kids 'hoeng ziu jan' – a banana person. It's a Cantonese label used to describe someone who is yellow on the outside and white on the inside. Basically, an overseas-born Chinese person with Westernised values who can't speak the ancestral tongue. I realise, in these moments, that I don't have an easy relationship with my parents or with my extended family for that matter, and I often worry our language barrier might prevent us from ever truly understanding each other.

'I should set you up with Michael,' Mum blurts out with a mouth full of food, pointing her chopsticks at me. 'You know the twins? Aunt Chamomile's sons. Find you a nice Chinese boy to marry.'

'Yeah, ah mui. He's a leng jai*, we'll introduce you,' Aunt Sarah sniggers, as she sips some more tea.

I roll my eyes. I hate it whenever Mum tries to force her pushy maternal matchmaking on me. I'm only twelve and she's already exerting pressure on me by trying to pawn me off. My parents, aunties and uncles always try to uphold a traditional dating style for us in Wales. This is because they have a long-idealised tradition of continuing family lineage, which is very important within

---

* leng jai – a good-looking/attractive boy.

Chinese culture, but finding a suitable spouse, finding love and getting married are so far off my radar that in my eyes men are well and truly from Mars. I need to get out of being interrogated.

'Ngor yew hoei mau ci!' (I need to go to the toilet) I blurt out, trying to excuse myself to leave.

'It's not mau ci, it's sai sau gan (restroom),' Maria laughs. 'Sor mui (silly girl), mau ci is an old saying that no one uses any more.'

'Someone's been watching too many old Chinese period dramas on TV,' Nina teases. 'You should probably pay more attention at Chinese school.'

I am bored of listening to my relatives talk about school, work and gossiping about relationships. My brothers and I, along with the kids from the other tables, all slip away to wander around the restaurant, mess about with the cigarette vending machine in the corner and play hide and seek. If you hover around the kitchen watching the dim sum chefs in their whites folding dumplings long enough, they'll eventually give you free After Eight mint chocolates.

'Mai dan mm goi!' (Cheque, please!) Dad raises his hand, beckoning a waiter to come over.

No one can leave the table because the adults are at war fighting over the bill, yanking the paper slip back and forth between them, an intense game of tug-of-war. When Chinese parents fight for the bill, it's no laughing matter. It's a whole song-and-dance.

'Stop it, it's my turn to pay!' Uncle George nags.

'No, no, no. I'm not having it,' Dad protests with a slight annoyed tone in his voice.

'Come on, let go of the ticket. We'll pay,' Auntie Sarah tuts.

'Just let us pay, we're in a hurry to get to Chinese school,' Mum reasons.

'Haiya, stop being like this. I refuse. Older brother should pay for his younger brother.' Uncle George resists and the look on his face shows he is getting increasingly rattled over this debate.

'Haiya, okay, okay, okay, lah. You win, I give up. Next time I pay.' Dad lets out an exasperated sigh and releases the ticket, but secretly stuffs some cash in Uncle George's pockets without him realising.

Not long after, they end up laughing, patting each other on the back and wagging their fingers at each other, like footballers do after a good game. Next time, next time, lah. I'll get you next time.

Our car pulls up to a grey and red grid-block building, down the road from Happy Gathering, hidden among tree-lined cul-de-sacs and semi-detached homes with cars on driveways. The grey clouds have started to form again, surely a bad omen that we have to endure two hours of Cantonese lessons at Chinese school. The school itself is rented out from another Welsh comprehensive school on weekends. During the time we're studying, my parents go to a nearby local park and meet other Chinese parents. Dad plays a friendly game of football with the other Chinese uncles from neighbouring take-aways and Mum does Tai Chi in the park with all the other Chinese aunties.

'Repeat after me. Yat. Yih. Saam. Sei. Ngh,' (One, two, three, four, five) chants Mrs Li, our Chinese teacher, a slim, lanky woman rocking a perfect box-dyed copper bob with a stern, serious face.

'Yat. Yih. Saam. Sei. Ngh,' reply the whole class in a collective monotonous drone. I look around my class of 30 Chinese kids roughly the same age as me, who all look bored half to death. My brothers and I aren't in the same room because they're older and in a more advanced class. We all sit in an alien geography classroom surrounded by maps of Cardiff, world globes and students' homemade volcano sculptures. On my table, I sit with three girls who are also Welsh-born Chinese takeaway kids like me. I wouldn't say that we are particularly close or best friends for life now, more like passing acquaintances who bump into each other on the street and say, 'We should catch up some time,' but never do. They are all older than me by a year. Kate is the mature, kind, motherly type whose dark-brown shoulder-length hair complements her soft round face; Gina has stunning elf-like features, a prominent forehead and widely spaced eyes; and Julie, the joker of the group, sports jet-black Rapunzel hair down to her hip, which I am insanely jealous of. Despite looking nothing alike or acting in any way similar, in a way they remind me of my Western girlfriends back in my village. I have two circles of friends and they never cross paths. They are very separate, and I feel like I'm leading a double life, a debilitating pattern of putting on different faces for different people. It's exhausting. I feel like I have to expend a lot more energy trying to keep them apart and I'm jealous of others who don't have to do this. I'd like a seamless relationship with all circles of friends without having to explain myself and where I could be unapologetically myself.

'Okay, good. Now write out each character to fill a page of your exercise book and write slowly to practise the correct strokes,' Mrs Li instructs, while pressing a button on her black digital stopwatch.

For the next 15 minutes we all stick our heads down and work in silence. It's so eerily quiet that you can physically hear the concentration of the room. The sound of pencils scribbling on paper, the faint voices of my fellow students quietly murmuring the characters as they write them and Mrs Li's heels clacking around the classroom in time to the ticking of the clock above her desk.

'Try to keep within the lines of the square box,' I faintly hear Mrs Li instructing a classmate on the other side of the room. 'The stroke is wrong, it should go from left then right.'

– BEEP BEEP –

'Everyone done? Okay, moving on,' Mrs Li announces, walking back to the front of her desk and pressing the button of her stopwatch again to reset the timer, like a dedicated running coach recording split times. 'So, who here can tell me what the seasons are?'

Her question is met with blank stares and uncomfortable silence.

'Anyone?' Mrs Li prompts. 'Surely, someone must know.'

I look around and shoot my hand up, as if my arm has a life of its own, because this is something I would never normally do. I have a gut feeling that I am 100 per cent sure of this answer. I stand up and start to smugly list off all the ingredients from our best-selling signature Lucky Star takeaway dish, also called Four Seasons: ngau yuk (beef), gai (chicken), char siu (char siu pork), tai haa (king prawns), zuk seon (bamboo shoots), maa tai (water chestnuts), gnaa choi (bean sprouts), sai kan (celery), joeng chung (onions) and, finally, ceng dau (peas).

No one answers. At this point the silence is deafening, but seconds later the room erupts into laughter that seems to go on forever. Blood starts to rush to my cheeks, visibly burning my face red to the point you could fry an egg on it, and my heart starts to race a couple of beats faster. I'm a laughing stock. *Oh God, I said the wrong thing, didn't I?* Crap, I thought, and I stand there in front of the class wishing the ground would open up and swallow me. The one time I pluck up enough courage to actually speak out and people make fun of me.

'Alright, alright, alright. Settle down, everyone.' Mrs Li furrows her brow and an annoyed look covers her face. She gestures her hands to quieten the room down.

'As delicious as that sounds, I'm sorry, but that's not right. Sit down, Angela. I meant the four seasons in the year, the change in weather and the plants. Anyone else want to have a go?'

Kate sheepishly puts her hand up, stands up and recites: 'Chun teen (spring), ha teen (summer), chow teen (autumn) and doong teen (winter).'

'Good, very good, Kate. Now let's move on to different celebrations in the calendar. Repeat after me . . .'

Before Mrs Li can say another word, her stopwatch goes off again to indicate it's time for a much-needed half-hour break.

Chatter starts to fill the room; some get up to go for a toilet break and others immediately whip out their handheld Nintendo Advance games consoles, linking up with one another to squeeze in a quick Pokémon battle before the lesson restarts. Even though the public humiliation I've just experienced seems to be largely forgotten about and everyone else has moved on, my shoulders are still feeling tense and a fatigue washes over me. I'm wiped out.

Julie puts her hand on my shoulder to bring me back into the room again. 'Hey, Angie, what you said was so funny, such a great joke,' she sniggers. 'You should've seen the look on Mrs Li's face, priceless.'

'Ha, ha. Yeah, I'm joking. I got you all, didn't I?' I nod and fake-laugh awkwardly, pretending that that was the plan all along.

'Sorry, Angie, didn't mean to show you up. Mrs Li

can be a real stickler and super-strict,' Kate reassures me with her gentle voice. 'No hard feelings?'

Gina doesn't say anything as she is busy concentrating on drawing manga cartoon characters that look like they could be straight out of a book. The level of detail and skill, that girl has serious talent. To pass the rest of our break time, I draw Sailor Moon manga girls and try to copy Gina, but mine look like badly drawn stick figures with big wonky eyes and straw hair compared to hers.

– BEEP BEEP –

'Okay! Quiet please. Back to your seats, people.' Mrs Li claps her hands to command the room once again. 'Now, where were we?'

The next hour of class is a blur. Soon, we are all walking in a single file to leave the building. I spot my brothers who are already outside, waiting in the car park congregating with a group of their Chinese friends, dancing from one foot to the next, trying to keep warm while waiting for our parents to pick us up. The clouds have started to turn to an angry shade of grey, sharp icy winds slice through me and the temperature has dropped. After such a big day, I'm ready to retreat into my bubble and go home. Plus, I'm *freezing* and I've had enough. I can see Dad's dark-green car at a distance hurtling towards us and almost drifting to our location. He's wearing his football gear covered in mud and as he swings open the car doors Cantopop is blasting out from the speakers again.

'Quick, quick, quick. Get in. Get in. Get in! We don't have time and I'm desperate for a shower. I'm stinking.' Dad rushes us impatiently as we say our goodbyes. My classmates and their families go their separate ways in their cars, swimming upstream to the valleys and beyond, hurrying back to our takeaways in white suburban communities in time to open the shop at 5pm.

Four Seasons

Four Seasons was our take on the ubiquitous chop suey, but with added extras. It was the signature special dish at Lucky Star and the first number on our menu, which had it all and represented all the elements: land, sea and air. Char siu pork, chicken, prawn and beef mixed with veggies such as carrots, water chestnuts, bamboo shoots and celery. It's bound in a starch-thickened sauce that clings on and coats everything in this stir-fried harmonious dish. Chop suey is probably the most adapted cuisine in the world – this style of Chinese food is the history of survival, ingenuity and cultural identity. It is a British Chinese takeaway classic created and tailored for Western palates. Just don't mistake it for the actual four seasons like I did.

Serves: 2 | **Prep time:** 10 mins | **Cook time:** 10–15 mins

Ingredients:
For the silky chicken marinade
1   chicken breast
1   tsp sesame oil
1   tbsp Shaoxing wine
1   tsp light soy sauce
¼ tbsp sugar

1 tbsp cornflour
Salt and pepper

For the Four Seasons stir-fry
2 cloves of garlic, smacked and diced
3 slices of ginger, smacked and diced
½ onion, peeled and cut into chunks
A small handful of soaked and rehydrated wood ear
    mushrooms
2 broccoli florets, halved
A small handful of bamboo shoot slices
2 water chestnuts
4 baby corn sliced into quarters
¼ carrot, sliced into circles on a diagonal
2 white button mushrooms, quartered
1 Chinese leaf, quartered into chunks
¼ of each green, yellow and red pepper, sliced into
    chunks
5 cooked duck slices
5 cooked char siu slices
5 king prawns, deshelled and deveined
White pepper, sprinkle
2 tbsp oyster sauce
1 tsp sesame oil, to serve
1 tsp MSG (optional)

For cornflour slurry
1 tbsp cornflour and 1 tbsp water mixed together
    until a thick liquid and no flour remains

Method:

1. First make the marinated chicken. Slice the chicken into chunks. In a bowl, combine the chicken with the marinade ingredients and set aside for at least 10 minutes while you work on preparing and cutting the rest of the ingredients. This technique is called velveting and takes stir-fries to the next level. The cornflour and Shaoxing wine help tenderise the protein and make for juicy and silky meat.

2. In a large pan add a cup of water and bring to a boil. Add the marinated chicken to poach. Cook for 2–3 minutes until the chicken has changed colour and it's no longer raw. You want to cook the chicken slightly under and sieve it out. Reserve the liquid for the sauce and stock for later.

3. In another pan, add 1 tbsp of vegetable oil. Cook the aromatics (garlic, ginger and onion) to explode into aroma to release its flavour. Cook for 1–2 minutes.

4. Add about half of the liquid back in. Add the wood ear mushrooms, broccoli, bamboo shoots and water chestnuts. Cook for 1–2 minutes.

5. Add the rest of the vegetables and cook for 1–2 minutes.

6. Add all of the meat, king prawns and chicken in. Cook for 3–5 minutes or until the prawns have changed colour.

7. Add cornflour slurry to thicken the liquid into a sauce. Give everything a mix to ensure everything is coated. Season with white pepper and more oyster sauce if needed. Drizzle sesame oil before serving.

5

We're All Going on a Summer Holiday

The first thing I notice about Hong Kong in the summer is the heat. The moment I step off the plane I'm hit with heavy subtropical air. It's off-the-charts high levels of humidity, as if the atmosphere is tightening its grip, plunging me headfirst into a hot, steamy, sticky shower. Five minutes outside in this sweltering June weather and it's unbearable. My shirt is already soaked to the bone and uncomfortably clinging to my form; sweat doesn't cool in this situation, it only rolls off. The second thing I notice about Hong Kong in the summer is the cold, the intensity of the air conditioning inside airports, public transport, shopping malls, restaurants and relatives' homes blasting out an arctic breeze to combat the high temperatures. It's a much-needed initial sweet relief, but five minutes inside in this sweltering June weather, it's excruciating. I feel each goosebump on my skin pop up, the bristling hairs on the back of my neck protruding and sending little shivers down the back of my spine. Despite being 30-plus degrees Celsius outside, I still have to bring a cardigan or a jacket to brave the artificial blizzards and then strip off layers to cope with the blistering UV rays. I face an eternal struggle between hot and cold, never fully comfortable in either environment, inside or outside, here in Hong Kong or back in Wales.

I've been taking trips back and forth to the motherland since I was three years old to visit friends and family, but also to restock on equipment and ingredients for the takeaway. We'd close the shop for one to two months at a time and we didn't have anyone to deputise to keep it open. All this annual toing and froing to Hong Kong wreaks havoc on my identity. A bifurcated reality, where I'm forever balancing multiple societies in my head and heart at the same time: trying to forge a life in a place that I was lucky to be born in, but also dreaming of a place I should've been born in. As a child of immigrants, I often associate my native land with my actual mother and father (and all the baggage therein), and coming and going between countries traps me in suspended adolescence. Too Western for my motherland, too Eastern for my homeland.

My parents helped me apply for my Hong Kong permanent identity card and I've been working my way up towards three-star status all my life. The stars indicate if you are a Chinese citizen or not, and therefore entitled to a HKSAR (Hong Kong Special Administrative Region) passport. However, if I don't visit Hong Kong for more than three years, I'll lose my right of abode, meaning I'll lose the power to vote, lose access to public financial assistance and participation in government programmes. Plus, without those three stars they have the right to deport me. Whenever I visit Hong Kong, I imagine a mobile phone top-up card where you have to top up your balance when you're running low on credit. I go back to top up my Chineseness; if I don't return, I am effectively making the decision to renounce everything that my parents have worked so hard for.

Now that I'm thirteen, and entering my teenage years, I always feel like a tourist who's not on holiday, unable to fully absorb the meaning of these journeys. It's one of those places where you end up more tired and stressed out rather than relaxed. Just before the six-week summer school holidays roll around, Mum convinces – well, bullies – my teachers into allowing my brothers and me to take time off school during term time, a few weeks leading up to the summer holidays (definitely not allowed today and my parents would probably be bankrupt from all the fines). My teachers prepare a massive A4 ring binder full of homework, exercises, revision notes and tests for me to do while I spend my summer on the other side of the world. We don't have our permanent home to call our own in Hong Kong, so we often stay at various relatives' flats and houses. This year, we're staying at my Ayi's (Mum's older sister, whose actual name I don't know because I've always called her Ayi, which is the Chinese word for aunt) sky-high 19th-floor shoebox flat in Wong Tai Sin looking up at Lion Rock Hill, a granite mountain covered sparsely by shrubs. It's one of the tallest mountains in Hong Kong and a popular hiking spot for a panoramic view of the city. Together with my family, Ayi and my three cousins – Beyond (25), Sammy (23) and Sean (18) – it's a tight squeeze. There's nine of us in a three-bedroom flat. They used to babysit me and my brothers whenever my parents or auntie weren't available, but we gained rare independence once my brothers hit comprehensive school. White walls coupled with white tiled floor, as a cooling antidote to the stiflingly hot summers, topping and tailing in grey built-in storage bunk beds in different rooms, plus sofa beds, all sharing one bathroom and a tiny green kitchen that's only big enough for one person to enter at a time. Having space on this island is somewhat of a luxury.

Like its war between outside heat and inside freezing air-con, Hong Kong is yin and yang. It's a mix of old and new, British and Chinese. A 12-hour flight to the other side of the world will show you that life in Hong Kong is the complete opposite of the South Wales Valleys. This cluster of mountainous islands makes up an autonomous territory that was a former British colony until 1997. Freedom of speech and living standards have been drastically deteriorating over the past decade, but Hong Kong remains one of the most densely populated cities in the world, with 7.4 million people packed into row upon row of prefab apartment blocks, a far cry from Beddau's 4,000-odd population. This in-your-face Asian metropolis is like a kaleidoscope – you never know what you might see next. It's colourful, chaotic, and loud

– really, really loud. Hongkongers aren't afraid to tell it how it is, in fact they sound like they're shouting all the time – but that's just their normal volume. They're forced to speak up above the din of the crowds and traffic while navigating through a mishmash of narrow streets. On the first night of our arrival after dropping our luggage off at the flat, we all head out for dinner and sit on flimsy, green plastic stools around a folding round wooden table in the street, dabbing our clammy foreheads with pocket-sized packets of Tempo tissue over dinner at a dai pai dong*, a traditional open-air restaurant near our flat that specialises in seafood; it's packed with a wonderful diversity of clientele. After-work bankers in their unbuttoned suits mingle with bare and tan-bellied grandpas drinking Blue Girl beer. Sean tells me that he could tell from a mile off that I was not a Hongkonger because I was too polite.

'You need to be angrier, outspoken and more cyun (cocky),' Sean instructs. His box-dyed spiky red hair and dangly ear piercings move about as he expressively moves his accordion player hands. 'Repeat after me. Puk gai!† But say it with heart and vigour.'

---

* Dai pai dong – a 'stall with a big licence plate' in Cantonese. These outdoor hawker stalls are affordable and open-air restaurants serve some of the city's best no-frills food. There used to be one on every street corner but, sadly, they're a dying breed due to the Hong Kong government removing them from public streets.

† Puk gai, or P.K for short – Cantonese swear word that translates to 'falling onto street', which means to drop dead; sometimes used as a noun to refer to an annoying person that roughly means a 'prick'.

I take a deep breath and bellow out with everything I have, 'Puk gai!'

The low hum of conversation coming from neighbouring tables suddenly stops and they turn their heads around and shoot us a confused, worried look. Rolling their eyes and tutting under their breaths, muttering 'on gau' (stupid), they resume clinking beer bottles, eating and smoking.

'Haiya! Stop teaching her swear words. She's only a kid,' Ayi scolds us with a stern side-eye, as she gets up to pluck a juicy razor clam loaded with garlic and vermicelli noodles with her hands from the centre of the table. She places it into my bowl, working her way round the table and feeding herself last to ensure everyone has a piece. It freaks me out how much Ayi and my mother look and sound alike: the same round face, chubby freckled cheeks and button nose, the only difference is Ayi is darker-skinned and has longer black hair with more grey strands running through. 'We haven't seen each other in so long and *this* is what you chat about? Swear words?'

'She needs to know these things if she's to get by and be a true Hongkonger!' Sean insists with a goofy lop-sided smirk, and he takes a swig from the bright-green Schweppes Cream Soda can. 'Now say it again, but with more emphasis and meaning.'

'Mm hai ma? Gum mo liu!' (Are you kidding me? So stupid!) Sammy crosses her arms and shakes her head disapprovingly, but chuckles. Her middle-parted straight jet-black hair swishes about as she moves. Sammy always has her head screwed on and always knows the right words to say. 'She doesn't need to learn swear words to fit in. Don't listen to him, mui. What you really need to learn is how to haggle.'

'Yes! Totally agree. Haggling is Hong Kong 101. What you want to say is, "Ha, gum gwai?!" (so expensive?) and "pang D la" (cheaper!).' Beyond excitedly butts in and has the biggest Cheshire cat-like smile. She wags her finger at me and knocks over a can of Coke, tipping brown fizzy liquid on the table. Even though Beyond is the oldest, she never acts like it. She's ditzy, but lovable.

'You want to say both these phrases with real disdain and disgust,' she carries on while dabbing up the spilled mess she'd just made with a tissue. 'You want to really drive it home and bag that bargain.'

Despite being a few years younger than my cousins and only communicating through broken Cantonese, we always have a laugh during the short amount of time we're together. But, no matter what my family have tried to teach me or my best efforts to fit in, I've never felt like a real Hongkonger, always on the outside looking in. Looks, mannerisms and politics are not what solely defines the Hongkonger. I don't wish to identify myself strictly in national terms – the duality and complexity of my British and Hong Kong identity is something I've grappled with all my life. There is no simple answer to what constitutes a Hongkonger. I realise that identity is not binary, it's malleable and accumulative, constructed by family backgrounds, life experiences, social interactions and continuous learning; it's not something that happens overnight. After this trip, classmates and teachers back in Wales will ask me how my summer holiday in Hong Kong was. I will bring back gifts and tell stories about how unique my home city is and how I always feel a sense of pride, but pride is actually the wrong word here, because how can I be proud of something that I'm born into? It's about being unapologetically me and unapologetically Welsh-Chinese, because that's who I am. It's about celebrating your culture, your heritage and revelling in it. Either that, or I'll tell everyone I've successfully managed to pull off a bargain like a pro at the market trying to haggle a couple of hundred dollars off a knock-off designer handbag or the latest Pokémon game, which turned out to be fake. Maybe that's the real badge of Hong Kong honour.

The next morning, my parents go to Sai Kung (Dad's birthplace and where his childhood home is) bright and early to catch up with old friends they haven't seen in years, while Ayi and my cousins are busy working. Like the majority of the population, they work on Hong Kong Island, where most of the offices, skyscrapers and shopping centres are. My brothers and I are left alone in the flat to slowly work our way through our homework ring-binder assignments and plonked ourselves in front of the TV watching Chinese cartoons like *Dragon Ball Z*, *Sailor Moon*, *Doraemon* and *Chibi Maruko-chan*, with the gentle hum of the air-con blowing a cooling gust in the background.

When cramped living conditions, being stuck indoors and boredom took its toll, my brothers and I decided to sneak off to escape homework and walk to the nearby Wong Tai Sin Temple. Wong Tai Sin is Hong Kong's only landlocked district and it's home to an intriguing mix of commotion and calm. This Taoist temple is where people go to pray for good fortune, light incense sticks and have their palms and fortune read from the side stalls. It may be a place of worship, but really this is our playground. Whenever my extended family members weren't working often my cousins would babysit the three of us when my parents or auntie weren't available, but we gained rare independence once my brothers were old enough and they started comprehensive school. Other times, we were left to our own devices because our parents are always busy either having yum cha catching up with old friends and relatives they haven't seen for years, dealing with private family stuff they refuse to tell us about, or shopping for things for the takeaway. We know not to tag along with our parents, or to do adult things, because we know we'd be bored out of our minds being dragged around by them and listening to them gossip about trivial things, like how so-and-so's son has gone off the rails and is sleeping around. The three of us therefore spend our time throwing spare change in the koi ponds trying to hit the fish, climbing on the zodiac-shaped stone statues and getting lost in the gardens, a much-needed moment of calm in a hectic city. A green zen surrounded by multicoloured high-rises as far as the eye can see in every direction, towering visual markers of today's emphatically urban society. It's a quintessentially heady mix.

We stop by a 7-Eleven convenience store to pick up some drinks. I open the fridge and fetch us three bottles of Pocari Sweat, a popular blue and white Japanese sports drink that replenishes water and electrolytes, ideal for this muggy climate. I accidentally drop them all, then more fall out from the fridge, causing a chaotic pile-up in aisle two.

'Haiya! Nei day gaau gaau zan, mou bong can!' (Stop mucking about at the store and not buy anything!) the store keeper yells at us for messing things up and causing trouble.

'Deoi m zyu!' (Sorry!) Jacky quickly picks up the drinks and puts them back. He taps his orange Octopus card* on the machine and scampers out of there sharpish. 'God, mui, so leon zun (clumsy).' He teases and playfully punches my arm.

'It wasn't my fault! They all fell out!' I protest, and poke my tongue out at him while struggling to open my bottled drink.

Keen's mobile phone rings; he answers and holds the phone between his shoulder and ear. Before I can even

---

* Octopus card – a Hong Kong travel card that helps you get around the city and can also be used to buy things in local shops.

ask, Keen takes the drink out of my hand, opens it and gives it back to me. Mum asks where we are and tells us to meet them in Sai Kung. Here, in Hong Kong, I feel free, I can be myself and do what I want without scrutiny. Mainly because I'm under my brothers' supervision rather than my parents' iron grip, but it's such a beautiful thing to walk around being the majority, knowing that most people aren't wondering 'What are you?' because I don't look so different any more.

We split our time between Wong Tai Sin and Sai Kung, a fishing village on a peninsula and roughly an hour away from central Kowloon. The eastern part of the island within the new territories feels a lot more disconnected than the rest of the city because there isn't a nearby MTR (mass transit railway) or rail station and it's only accessible by bus on long, winding roads that curve around mountains and coastline. The three of us wave down a green 16-seater light bus, scan our Octopus cards, hop on and cling on for dear life as we race down Clear Water Bay Road and Hiram's Highway, the two main roads going in and out of Sai Kung. We're bombing it down the road, fast speeds hurtling well over 80km/h, the red warning light flashes nonstop indicating we are well over the speed limit and the speedometer flashes and squeals. I look around at my fellow passengers perched on padded plastic leather seats: Chinese students in uniform gossiping, Filipino maids chatting on the phone and Australian tourists who look just as terrified as we are. Some buses don't come equipped with seatbelts, but if you're lucky enough to have them, very few people put them on anyway. The best thing to do is clutch on to the metal bars on the side, or hold on to the plastic handles on the back of each seat or anything else that's useful for when the bus swings around a corner at high speed to save yourself from flying out of your seat. There are no stop buttons and to get off passengers have to call out their stops by street name or landmarks like the police station, temple or hospital, while those unfamiliar with the route shout out 'yau lok' or 'ha yat jaam', which simply means get off or next stop. The driver gestures with his left hand to confirm he's heard the instruction, before swerving frighteningly across the road and skidding to a stop. An hour later, we made it in one piece after our white-knuckle ride.

You can tell you're not in the city any more because in the rural New Territories the cicadas' deafening shrieks are so loud they rattle and drone high up hidden in trees all day. Cicadas are the soundtrack to my summer; every time I hear one I feel like I'm hearing a heat wave. Depending on where there is room for the five of us to stay, we sometimes stay at my grandmother's old place in Sai Kung. After my grandmother passed away, my dad and uncles inherited the place together, each with their own room for their family to use. A shared Hui hub. We reach our grandmother's old house, skipping over the elevated doorstep (an old tradition to keep ghosts out) and through a big metal-gated door. Before we can even wipe off the sweat and take our shoes off, Mum presents us with three ready-lit yellow and red incense joss sticks. The glowing ember smoulders and releases a smoky, woody fragrance. They stink, and I hate the way they smell.

I see dusty family memorabilia still adorning the place: old baby photos and a rare group photo of the extended Hui family at a local Chinese restaurant in Sai Kung for grandma's 81st birthday in the glass TV cabinet. I didn't really know her that well and only met her a handful of times, mostly I was too young to remember much, but I knew she was brash and frugal. Dad and his seven brothers and sisters lived in this house in the 1960s, and he had a scrappy childhood, getting into fights with other kids in the neighbourhood and fighting with siblings over food. I distract myself by looking at the line of straight-faced black-and-white passport-style portraits of my deceased grandparents and uncles in the top right-hand corner of the room, their straight blank expressions looking down on us. On the north wall of the living room, a red and gold ances-tral shrine with two red bulbs flanking either side emits a warm crimson glow. In front of it is a small statue of Kwun Yum* (Hong Kong's Mother Goddess), three small red cups of wine, a plate of tangerines with their leaves still attached to them and an incense burner with

---

* Kwun Yum – the ultimate spiritual goddess of mercy and bodhisattva. In Hong Kong, she is worshipped above the rest. The universal god-dess is an enduring symbol of the adaptability and inclusiveness of the Chinese spirit.

a light dusting of ash from old burnt-out incense sticks.

'We've returned home!' my brothers and I chant together in unison, and bow our heads down to pray and shake our joss sticks up and down three times before placing the sticks on the burner to pay our respects. 'Please look after us and protect us!'

I wasn't entirely sure why we did this back then, it was something that we were told to automatically do without question. Ancestor veneration is based on a long-held belief to respect, honour and look after ancestors; in turn, they watch over us, give us wisdom, guidance and assistance from the afterlife. The souls of the departed are informed of all important events in the family, like who's married or has given birth, and who comes and goes.

I head upstairs to the top floor for a quick lie down because I was still feeling tired and jetlagged before we all go back out to explore the city and have dinner. I flick the switch, and the bulb flickers on and off with excitement like a disco. Dust and cockroaches. Even though it's more spacious here in Sai Kung and we're surrounded by verdant trees and pristine beaches, I've always preferred to stay at Ayi's cramped place due to its centrality, being surrounded by loved ones and, of course, having access to the internet. Plus, there are no cockroaches and mosquitoes in Wong Tai Sin, the damn mosquitoes. In Sai Kung, there's always a mosquito trying to find its way to me, lured in by the scent of my sweet blood and caressing my skin. Annoying minuscule black dots hover near me and are terrible flyers. They try to battle the air-con fan's typhoon-like winds, struggling to land on me, as I fail to swat them away. By the end of the trip my arms and legs will be covered in bright-red mosquito bites (even with Mopidick, Hong Kong's number-one mosquito lotion that reeks of menthol), which swell into itchy, painful boils that keep me up all night scratching uncontrollably. I rest my head on a pillow that's as flat as a pancake and a hard bed in pink Hello Kitty bedsheets. The rackety air-con system that's probably older than me sounds like it's on its last legs and vibrates loudly, mimicking the deafening cicadas outside. I lie there half-awake in a shared room with my brothers who had the same idea for a quick rest, despite it only being the afternoon, and are already fast asleep in foetal positions with their backs against each other on a double bed, with no duvet because it's too hot. I watch their bodies rise and fall as they breathe soundly in their sleep. The room smells musty and unused, like wood, lotus oil and old people. The fan's friendly wind beckons me to join them. I tried to stay awake for as long as possible, but ended up conking out and the five of us accidentally sleep through the night. It takes us a couple of days to break out of jet-lag mode and sync up into the groove of Hong Kong.

The next day I woke up groggy and confused, realising that we've probably messed up our body clocks from that nap. I cannot believe we slept for 12 hours. Dad and I are the only ones wide awake at 4am. We wander through

the quiet, dark streets together and check out the shut-
tered shops and restaurants. Dad points out all his old
haunts where he grew up hanging out, how much the
area's changed and what has stayed the same. There are
benefits to waking up before the sunrise. The cool, warm
weather is at its optimum: not too hot and not too cold. I
know that'll change, as soaring temperatures are immi-
nent, but I enjoy it while it lasts. We walk through the
park where old ladies start to gather to illegally gamble
playing zi pai (cards) and do a morning meditation class.
Hong Kong's elderly are very active: they jog, they swim
in the sea and they rule the roost here. Eventually, we
arrive at Sai Kung pier where fishermen have already set
up camp and are throwing their rods back and forth in
hope of catching something. I can start to see the golden
light of daybreak bringing glimmers of warmth. The sun
softly caresses the seafront and ignites the birds into a
chorus of melodies. We perch on the barrier and stand
there in silence taking in the sights and sounds, as the
tides gently crawl to the shore and waves crash against
the concrete before sloshing back, forming foam and
froth. Dad produces a fishing line from out of his pockets, crouches down and ties an angler's loop knot. He
hooks a piece of dried shrimp to the other end and plops
it into the crystal-blue waters below. We peer over the
edge of the pier, watch our bait sink and wiggle the line
around, not doing much. After five minutes baby black
tadpole-like fishes start to dart towards us, nibbling away
and retreating. Quietly observing from above, waiting

and watching sea creatures go about their daily lives, I never knew calm like this existed underneath the ocean. In fact, I never knew calm like this existed outside the busy, hectic kitchen.

By 7.30am it's already 26 degrees. We duck into a cha chaan teng (tea house lounge) for breakfast and to take advantage of their ceiling fans. It's hard to build up an appetite when the weather is as hot as it is. It's no surprise that most of us alter our dining habits in the summertime. In general, we all eat a little less and choose dishes that are not as heavy. Palates tend to gravitate towards refreshing lighter foods like ice cream, fruits and salads. Being in Hong Kong, food is never a simple matter, you automatically have a cultural or national interest in food, which is why no matter the season, noodles will always reign supreme. Inside this humble Canto-Western diner, there's an eclectic charm to its vintage decor. Colourful tiled walls, intimate private booth seats and square tables packed in close together. Sun-damaged pink plastic containers containing melamine chopsticks and silverware atop every table. A group of tourists and fresh-off-the-plane expats come through the door and sit at the table next to us. The servers put water out on their tables and they started sipping them. Dad chuckles and shakes his head and mutters, 'What a bunch of amateurs.' He starts washing our cutlery in the cup of hot water on our own table. The only way to determine whether or not someone is a true Hongkonger is not judging them by what they order, but by whether or not they drink the water on the table that's intended for cleaning. We read from laminated menus, order two set meals and they come out almost immediately. The lightning-fast curt service and quick preparation ensures you're in and out with minimum fuss. I have my go-to order: a big blue melamine bowl of snow cabbage vermicelli noodles topped with minced pork in a gravy-like sauce alongside a crustless fried egg white bread sandwich on a little plate. It's an underrated noodle dish that doesn't get as much recognition as it deserves. Salty, fatty pork with hints of sweet-tang from the pickled snow cabbage. With every molten slurp, I can feel my internal heat rise up and out of my skin, each molecule of water settling on my skin and sinuses clearing up. I choke it down greedily, spluttering sodium-rich broth everywhere because I try to fit too many noodles in my mouth in one go. I urgently grab a serviette from the dispenser to cover my mouth and cough into it.

'Woah, woah, woah. Careful. What's the big hurry?' Dad asks with concern, stopping midway through eating his instant ramen with Spam and egg. 'You okay? Slow down when eating. We're in no rush.'

Slow down? SLOW DOWN? NO RUSH? I scream inside my head and heart. I don't think I've ever heard Dad say this string of words together in my life. He is not a patient man, he's permanently stuck on fast-forward and wants things done immediately in a takeaway setting. Outside of the shop, I barely recognise him. For him to tell me not to hurry is him telling me to go steady, enjoy this moment, you've earned it. It's as if Hong Kong Dad and takeaway Dad are two separate people. Who knew there was a peaceful and patient side to Dad? His demeanour mellows out and his hunched shoulders, a tightly wound ball of stress from all the years of manning his station, finally relax. The two of us sit opposite each other in a miniature orange booth, heads bowed over, scooping noodles into our mouths. Listening to people chat, laugh and joke. I sip on a glass of iced Ovaltine, a malted milk drink, to wash down my food; for Dad, his favourite, a refreshing tall glass of lemon iced tea. Eating and drinking without a care in the world.

Tropical cyclones are a common occurrence here. Instead of being named after people's names like they do in the West, typhoons are named after fruits like Manghukt, Rumbia, Pulasan and Krathon. I gaze out through the window grille and look down below at the yew trees swaying in one direction, flailing their branches, and the ant-sized people trying to navigate around Lion Rock. They must be incredibly brave or stupid to go out in this weather, I think. Just typical, our last full day here and there's a predicted typhoon warning symbol number three (T3) coming in our direction. Despite the torrential weather, there is something so soothing and satisfying about being stuck indoors. Safe inside Ayi's apartment tower, where we were protected from gale-force winds, the sounds of howling wails and the angry-looking large pillows of clouds that are starting to blot out the sun.

'AHHH!' Mum cries from the bedroom. She's packing our suitcase ready for our afternoon flight back home tomorrow. I immediately rush over to the bedroom to check if everything's okay.

'What, what, what? Are you okay? Are you hurt?' I ask flustered.

'Haiya, I've forgotten to buy so many things!' Mum shrieks, and puts her hands on her head in a state of panic. 'We have to head out to Mong Kok to stock up on some last-minute things. Let's go now, it's not raining yet!'

Mong Kok in Cantonese means 'crowded corner'. True to its name, it's the busiest and most densely populated area in the city. It offers everything from trendy multistorey shopping malls reaching the skies to unpretentious market stalls hidden away on dark alleys, the busy streets filled with crowds, neon lights and signs.

'Wei, wei leng lui (hey, hey pretty lady).' Mum lifts up a wok for the takeaway and squawks across the store at the si tau por.* 'Jo mo pang D lah ma? (Can I get it cheaper?)'

'Mo ar! Juy peng ga la! Jung peng d ngor sik boon!' (No way! That's the cheapest I can do otherwise I'm out

---

* Si tau por – a boss lady/store owner. They're fierce and strong. They are a true example of what makes Hong Kong a special place to people who keep it dear to their hearts.

of pocket.) She argues back like a shouting tennis match from one side of the room to the other.

'Gum gwai! (So expensive!) What if I buy multiple items? I want to buy this spatula and fry basket too,' Mum demands while raising more items in view for the storekeeper to see.

'Haiya, okay, okay, lah. You're twisting my arm. I can do $400 for the lot? It would've been $500!' the woman protests.

'That's a deal. Good. Bag it up!' Mum shuffles over towards the till carrying all the cookware, trying her best not to knock anything down between the narrow aisles stacked floor to ceiling with pots and pans.

I start to hear heavy plops of rain drumming off the roof of the kitchenware store. Uh-oh. Red rain.* For a brief moment, I think that we might be doomed adventurers, trapped and destined to get swept away in a mighty flood. In Hong Kong, it doesn't rain, it pours.

The sky starts to cough out great bouts of water and chuck buckets of sopping moisture everywhere. People flee to find shelter and safety. It teems down in a biblical deluge, the floodgates in the sky have been opened and no one is there to close them back up, it seems. We have no choice but to brave the weather with our feeble umbrellas, carrying all our goods. Soon, my hair is doused

---

* Red rain – in Hong Kong they have rain indicators on how heavy the rain is. Red is a warning signal that's likely to bring serious road flooding and traffic congestion.

like sad, dripping noodles. Saturated T-shirts cling to our bodies, broken umbrellas flip inside out, more nuisance than help, and squelchy feet in flip-flops try not to slip with every step. Our plastic shopping bags slowly collect water, meaning we're weighed down even more while trying to make it out alive. The rain is as hot as a hellcat's spit, bitter and stinging, blurring my vision. There's nothing quite like being outside in the rain during a typhoon. An intense power shower washing away the stickiness, leaving you feeling renewed, but also very, very wet. I laugh at the silliness of the situation. We're no cleverer than those hikers on Lion Rock I mocked earlier. When we get in, I shower off the storm and sleep deeply through a night of heavy rains, frenzied whipping winds and kinked lightning that wriggles from the sky and fizzles down on the city below with a golden sheen. Ayi and my cousins cross their fingers, hoping for the typhoon to be upgraded to a signal number eight (T8), because that means a day off work, their version of a snow day.

The following day, we finally make it to the airport with only five hours to spare. It's 11.30am and our flight is at 4.30pm. The summer sky is neon-blue and vibrant, made even brighter by the previous night's storm. I know that my Chinese parents are extremely cautious when it comes to certain circumstances in my life, but overexaggerating a minor situation like ensuring there's enough time for the airport and turning it into a mini life crisis is just another thing my brothers and I have to contend with. We immediately make a beeline towards the check-in baggage area, weaving our way up and down through the maze of retractable queue barriers with our luggage trolley.

'Good morning, sir, ma'am, how are you? And where are you flying with us today? May I see your passports, please?' the lady from Cathay Pacific behind the desk asks. 'How many pieces of luggage would you like to check in today?'

Before she can even finish her sentence, Dad and Mum are already loading up cases on the scales to weigh their suitcases. The digital scale reads: 30.6kg.

The woman taps away on her computer and politely says, 'I'm afraid it's too heavy and you will have to pay for excess baggage. How would you like to pay today?'

'No, no, no. It's okay. I can take stuff out to lighten the load and we can all carry it by hand-carry,' Mum says with a flustered panic, waving her hand. 'Hold on.'

Mum had overdone it with the shopping for the takeaway and now everything she's bought for the hold luggage is splayed out everywhere on the airport floor. We're holding up the queue and onlookers behind us are gawping in amazement and fear at just how much stuff there is. Towel-wrapped meat cleavers, bags of rice, woks, a rice cooker, chopping boards, packets of lap cheong, bags of dried seafood and metal fry baskets. Mary Poppins' magic handbag has got nothing on my mother's suitcase.

'Here, Keen. Take the dried shrimp and carry. Jacky,

shove the lap cheong in your backpack. Mui, put the bags of rice in your suitcase,' Mum orders without looking up at us, trying frantically to even the load and avoid paying extra.

So embarrassing, I think. I try to bury my face in my hands to hide my embarrassment. I guess holiday mode is officially over and it's back to normality.

Pickled Cabbage with Minced Pork Vermicelli Noodle Soup

This is my go-to cha chaan teng order. It's an underrated dish overshadowed by the other more popular options like wonton egg noodles, macaroni soup with ham or instant ramen with Spam and egg, but in my opinion this dish is worthy of the same hype and respect. It might not be as filling as your typical soup-based noodle dish because of the thin rice vermicelli noodles, but it's a lighter dish that doesn't send you to sleep straight after eating. It's also equally satisfying. The thick pork and pickled cabbage is cooked in a thick, salty, umami sauce that sits on top of the noodles and slowly melts into the noodles and clear broth. It coats each noodle strand and seasons the soup. The more you eat, the more flavoursome it becomes. It comes together quickly and easily, doesn't require a lot of effort and uses a lot of staple pantry items you might already have. Regardless of whatever time of day, season or temperature, it's something comforting that can be eaten whenever the mood hits. Slurp it up, choke up in excitement and make a splattering mess. No judgement here.

Serves: 2 | **Prep time:** 10 mins |
Cook time: 10–15 mins

Ingredients:

For the noodle and soup base:

½ packet of thin vermicelli rice noodles

1 litre chicken stock or vegetable stock

½ tbsp soy sauce

½ tsp white pepper powder

¼ tsp sesame oil

1 tsp white or red miso paste (optional)

For the pork and cabbage sauce topping:

1 tbsp vegetable oil

½ (200g) pack of pork mince (or can use veggie/ vegan mince)

1 tin snow/pickled cabbage (available from most Asian supermarkets; my favourite brand is Ma Ling, the yellow label one), drained and soaked for at least an hour before using to rinse off excess salt. If you don't have time, be sure to at least give the pickled veg a quick rinse)

3 tbsp oyster sauce

¼ tsp sugar

½ tsp Shaoxing wine

¼ tsp white pepper

½ tsp sesame oil

Cornflour slurry (1 tbsp water and 1 tbsp cornflour)

1 spring onion, chopped (optional)

1 tbsp chilli oil (optional)

Method:

1. Bring a pot of water to a boil. Add noodles and cook for 2-3 minutes or until soft. Use chopsticks to break up and constantly move noodles to prevent clumping and sticking together.

2. Once cooked, shut off the heat and drain noodles. Run under cold water or soak in ice water to stop further cooking. Set aside.

3. Heat a separate pot of chicken or veggie stock. Season with soy sauce, white pepper and sesame oil. If using, add miso paste for a deeper and more umami flavour. Bring everything to a low simmer.

4. While the soup base is heating up, work on the meaty topping. Add a tablespoon of vegetable oil to your wok or frying pan over high heat and rotate to ensure an even non-stick layer. Add the mince and stir-fry for 4–5 minutes until the meat has browned and no pink, raw meat remains. Add the pickled cabbage to stir-fry for 1–2 minutes until wilted slightly. Add oyster sauce, sugar, Shaoxing wine, white pepper and sesame oil. Give everything another stir to ensure it is mixed together evenly. Depending on how you like the consistency, play around with the water and cornflour ratio. Add the slurry to the pork and cabbage sauce mixture to thicken and the sauce should start to come together. You want to aim for a thick ketchup consistency.

5. Add stock to bowl, add noodles and top with pork and cabbage mixture. Optionally, add a small

handful of chopped spring onions and a big dollop of chilli oil.

6

Troubled Youths

There are certain times of the year when running a Chinese takeaway is hell: bank holidays; Christmas; New Year; and whenever Wales win a rugby match. But Halloween was the worst of all. As a child, I had no idea why Halloween was such a big thing or why we celebrated it over here; I always associated it as an American import. A consumerism-focused, man-made holiday that gives us the excuse to dress up in scary costumes and go around trick-or-treating. However, Halloween also gave the kids in our neighbourhood the excuse to play pranks – and sometimes worse – on the nights in the lead-up to the holiday. While these could vary from the fairly harmless moving of people's garden furniture to more serious vandalism and even deadly arson, the most common acts of mischief that occur on this night tend to be the egging and/or toilet-papering of houses. I hated Halloween.

I'm 14, I've never dressed up for Halloween nor have I ever knocked door to door asking for sweets. I don't see the point of it, because Chinese people don't normally celebrate Halloween. Instead we commemorate traditional days of the dead spread across the Chinese calendar year, such as Hungry Ghost Festival, Qing Ming Festival and the Double Ninth Festival. Still, even though I don't see the point of it, I would like to experience dressing up just once and get free sweets. All my friends are hanging out together, roaming the streets wearing witch hats and cat ears. It's 5.30pm, Saturday night, we had just opened our doors for service. It's an unusually balmy dry autumn evening. From where I sit behind the counter with Cecilia, I can see a beautiful sunset peeping through the shop's windows where the sky's orange gold hues stretch far and wide, the colours of fire hearths and tangerine hues are truly beautiful. Just a shame that I can't go outside to enjoy it in all its glory and have to admire it from afar behind a glass.

From the corner of my eye, I can see the front door open a crack. I automatically shoot up, ready to serve whoever has just walked through.

'CHING CHONG CHINAMAN!' a stocky, freckled ginger teenage boy who I don't recognise shrills, and slams the door shut again in defiance. The slam is so loud it reverberates through the house, and I can see the windows physically shaking from the forceful motion. He runs off laughing to join his group of mates who are loitering on the sidelines. I'm gobsmacked and everything happens so quickly that I don't even have a chance to react or say anything. I huff and roll my eyes so hard that I think they are going to fall out of my skull.

'Tsk, those pesky kids,' Cecilia replies apathetically while sitting on her barstool in the corner behind me. She looks up from reading the newspaper that is meant for customers, then carries on as normal reading again. 'Pay no attention to them.'

I sit back down on my yellow plastic stool, slumped on the counter, resting my face in my palms, and carry on watching whatever is on TV without actually absorbing anything that's on. My mind is going at a hundred miles per hour. I know they were just bored teens with nothing better to do with their spare time, but it still sits with me uncomfortably. I feel tiny paper cuts shredding my insides. Do I say anything? Do I tell Mum and Dad? Why didn't Cecilia kick up a bigger fuss? Why didn't she do something to protect me? Should I have gotten up and gone after them? Why am I so annoyed over such a silly thing? It's completely caught me off-guard and I can't stop thinking about it. I know I probably won't stop thinking about it until the end of service. I remain quiet, clench my jaw, get up and stomp to the kitchen to blow off some steam.

'Hey, mui, order?' Keen asks, looking up from playing Pokémon on his Game Boy Advance during the down-time. He's sitting on the silver worktop waiting on the sidelines for more customers.

I shake my head and scooch up next to him. I peer my head over to silently watch Keen fight a gym leader. I always find it relaxing to watch him play video games.

There's something calming about observing him and seeing his excitement at getting lost in another world, as he advances through the levels trying to beat the bosses.

'A little help, please!' Cecilia yells from the front.

I hear a lot of murmuring, hollering and whooping going on. I spring into action and run out to the front to see what all the commotion is about. The counter is filled with a big group of lads, who all look roughly the same age as me. The seven of them are strewn across the waiting area, lying down on the bench, rummaging through the glass bowl of sweets we've left out for the trick-or-treaters. They're throwing chocolate bars at each other like they own the place. I always feel on edge whenever there is a gang hanging around and I can feel my heart stumbling over its own rhythms, and my stomach starting to contract into a tight ball. I get a sudden stab of anxiety in my gut that something bad is about to happen or something is going to go down. A short skinhead kid wearing a grey and navy Diadora tracksuit with his hood up marches straight up to me at the counter.

'Oh, butt. Wor can I ger for 50p?' he demands, and slides a silver coin across to me.

'Uh . . . One poppadom or else a chicken ball?' I nervously glance at the menu board to double-check. 'And that's about it?'

He turns around to the rest of his mates. 'Oh, boys. Lend me a couple of quid, will ya? I want some egg fried rice, curry and chips.'

They all lunge forward towards me at the same time. I feel my body seize up. After a few minutes of scrambling around in pockets looking for loose change, the counter is littered with buttons, keys, receipts and pennies. Coins clink and slide against the wooden countertop as the boys stick their heads down to sort their money to see if they collectively have enough.

'Okay . . . That's a pound . . . Two pound . . . twenty . . . fifty. Two pounds and seventy pence. There.' He slides all the coins over to me. 'A large egg fried rice, curry and chips, ta.'

I quickly jot his order down on the ticket pad:

$$
\left.\begin{array}{l}
20L \\
89 \\
94
\end{array}\right\} \underline{£2.70}
$$

I rip off the bottom of the paper stub and give him the number 34. I cup my left hand under the counter and slide the coins into my hand with my right. I go to the till to key in the numbers and the tray of money pops out. Coins clack and ping as I drop pieces of silvers and coppers into their individual holes.

I hurry back to the kitchen, call out the order, stub the ticket on the nail and return to my post out front. Cecilia is busy serving a lanky, brunette boy from the group.

'That's two pounds fifty, please,' Cecilia requests. She takes their money, shuffles past me and over to the till.

We've had previous incidents where customers have leaned over the counter to steal things while Cecilia has her back turned, so I keep my eye on everyone in case they get up to no good. I think to myself, it's seven against two. Surely, me and Cecilia could take them on? Okay, Cecilia may be old, but she could fend them off with her crutch? We have backup, too. Keen and Jacky can come out from the kitchen to help. This could work. Wait, what the *hell* is wrong with me? These are a bunch of kids no older than 14. I'm sure they mean no harm.

Another customer walks in, an older lady with heavy fake tan and blonde hair.

'Hiya, love, you alright? Can I get a chicken curry, small, with no peas. Beef chow mein, no bean sprouts and onions, and shredded crispy chicken and beef with no carrots or peppers,' she barks melodically in her thick Valleys accent. 'How long issit gonna be? I'm gonna nip out to pop to the Co-op next door.'

We live on a long main shopping street with a bakery, newsagent, pharmacy, supermarket, fish-and-chip shop, Indian takeaway and a hairdresser. Being in a prime, busy location has its advantages and its disadvantages. For the most part, it's a lovely, supportive community and from time to time we'll borrow eggs or tomatoes in a pinch from the Indian takeaway whenever we run out of vital ingredients and vice versa, but being on a busy main strip also means competition and it attracts a lot of trouble.

'It'll be about five to ten minutes,' I call out with my

back turned to the customer as I type the keys in the till and give the lady her change.

'Alri, I'll be back now in a minute,' she yells across the room, and closes the door behind her. I go to the kitchen, bellow out the order and repeat her preferences.

'Haiya! Maa faan! (annoying!)' Dad protests, as he turns around from his station to take a closer look at the ticket. 'No bean sprouts, no onions, no carrot, no pepper. No nothing! So fussy!'

I can still hear the boys messing about over the ear-splitting noises of metal spatulas scraping against woks and the droning fan blades. Cecilia pops her head round and calls out, 'Dewi's here!'

My brothers start to scramble around rushing to get the pre-prepped orders for delivery ready, grabbing plastic bags hanging from the silver worktop island, putting lids on polystyrene sauce cups and wrapping them in brown bags. Mum hands Keen a bag of chips.

I rush back out front to fetch the red nylon insulated delivery bag from Dewi. I can feel that there is something off and the atmosphere is uncomfortable. Dewi shifts awkwardly in the corner, glancing at the boys messing about trying to wrestle each other on the bench. There's an uneasy heavy silence coupled with occasional shrieks of 'GER OFF ME, MUN' and the Cheese Strings advert blaring on the TV in the background. You can see eyes darting around the room and momentary looks of discomfort cross our faces. I have a gut feeling that something is about to go down, like the moment of calm before a quick-draw shootout, but before anyone can say anything . . .

'Is the rice, chips and curry open or closed?!!' Jacky shouts, trying to compete with the rowdy kitchen. The boys can clearly hear him out in front, but I repeat it anyway.

'Do you want your food wrapped or opened?' I ask the group of boys, who now have each other in a headlock.

'Open, please.' The kid with a buzzcut wriggles free and sits up properly.

I poke my head round the corner to shout back to the kitchen, 'OPEN!!!'

Mum comes out to the front and appears with a steaming hot silver container tray filled to the brim with fluffy egg fried rice, chips and curry sauce. Wisps of steam radiate from it and the smells are divine. Greasy, aromatic and fragrant.

'Careful, it hot,' she warns in English with a thick Cantonese accent, then hands it over to me, as I give her the red delivery bag and she returns to the kitchen.

I place the tray with some newspapers underneath and present the tray of food on the top counter in view of the customers. I can hear the boys mimicking and laughing at my mum's English while I have my head down. I pretend I don't hear and feel more tiny paper cuts inside.

'Number 34!' I yell. The buzzcut kid comes forward and gives me his ticket, which is now a crumpled piece of paper. 'Salt and vinegar?' I ask.

'Yer, go'own, en,' he says.

I place a plastic fork, white salt-shaker and a bottle of brown Sarson's vinegar in front of him and instantly realise my mistake. He begins shaking both bottles at the same time, making an absolute mess. Little white salt crystals scatter and blobs of brown vinegar sloshes all over the wood countertop. The acidic odour stings my nostrils. He sits back down on the bench while his mates wait for their food, shovelling rice and chips into his mouth, exhaling every now and then because the food is too hot. Little mountains of rice and splotches of curry sauce fall to the floor and around him on the bench, missing his mouth and going everywhere.

'Cecilia, please!' Keen shouts from the kitchen.

I stay out to guard the front while Cecilia hobbles to the back. She returns with a tray of egg fried rice and barbecue sauce, a piping-hot rice dome that's managed to still retain its shape from Dad's wok ladle, covered in a viscous dark-brown barbecue sauce nestled in its silver container. It looks too perfect to eat. Cecilia places it on some newspaper and grabs a small plastic spoon to give to the lanky, brunette kid she served.

He gets up and stabs the rice dome with his spoon, dropping grains of rice and sauce on the counter. He grabs his food and shouts, 'C'mon, boys. Let's go to Badger's Point.'*

---

* Badger's Point – three benches at the end of the street next to the phone box and opposite the bus stop. It was a hotspot for a lot of kids to hang out while having a drink and a smoke.

They all follow him out the door, one by one, and shut the door behind them, leaving the counter and waiting room in a right state; a whirlwind of mess for us to clean up afterwards. Everyone rests easier and probably thinks, *Thank God, they've left*. Whenever something like this happens, it's as if we're all waiting with bated breath, holding our breath for as long as possible until we're out of the woods. However, we aren't quite out of the woods yet because I can still see them loitering around outside through the window. I feel like a curtain-twitcher, spying on their every move. Being the face of the takeaway and bearing the brunt of whatever comes our way, I've subconsciously taken on a hypervigilant role. It's making me paranoid and I'm indulging in my busybody vices. I can see them eating and dropping more food on the floor outside like Hansel and Gretel leaving a trail of crumbs behind. When the boys finally move on, everyone on the other side of the window lets out a collective heavy sigh of relief, as if unbuckling our belts to stop breathing in and letting everything hang loose. False alarm. I can feel the tension leave my body. At least it wasn't anything more serious.

Jacky comes out with the red delivery bag and places it on the counter. 'There's two deliveries, Dewi. One in Pentref Capel and the other is in Efail y Clwyd. We'll give you a call if there's any more deliveries.' He instructs. 'Ah mui, has that lady come back yet? Her food is ready.'

I shake my head. We wait and wait, but the lady

never comes back for her food. Lonely silver containers sit on the metal shelf growing cold above the woks and a simmering pot of master stock, desperately trying to keep warm. I never understand why people do this. What a waste. The waiting room falls silent again with the sound of Cecilia sparking up, filling the air with cigarette smoke; I can feel the pollution in my lungs. I stand up and unlock the counter door to get into the waiting room to pick up the mangled, littered sweets and trodden chips while listening to *Coronation Street*'s mournful coronet theme tune blaring on the TV. A quick breather to ourselves before diving deep into another round of manic orders again.

I look up at the wall clock and can't believe it's 10pm already. Time has flown by today and I haven't even had the chance to sit down. My legs are tender and my feet are throbbing. Only an hour left, and I'm so done with today.

'Angieee!' Lauren squeals, bursting through the door wearing a pointy black witch hat, with the rest of the girls in tow.

The girls have come to visit me in the shop, and they're dressed in their Halloween get-up. I light up and beam. I'm so glad to see familiar friendly faces after such a horrendously busy and frightfully frantic night, but internally I still feel weirded out whenever non-Asian friends or someone I know from school comes to see me while I'm working. Mainly, this is out of fear of being seen as different, strange or wrong. Either that, or because I look disgusting with my greasy hair in plaits, stained long-sleeved top with dried flaky white batter splatters and my apron covered with flecks of oil-seeped blotches in random patches. I'm so glad that they have taken time out to see me, but the last thing I want is to have visitors when I look like this.

Some of the rugby boys from my year have followed in behind them. There is Squid, Dai Dog, Danny lanky (tall chap), AJ, Smiley (real name Jonny) and, of course, Cai. I'm not sure why men in South Wales always have ridiculous nicknames, but everyone around these parts knows someone, or knows *of* someone, with a stupid name – it's the unofficial Welsh law.

'S'appening, Ange butt,' Cai leans on the counter and casually asks me.

My insides melt. I cannot believe Cai is talking to me. *Me*. In the flesh! Of all people! I look like I've just crawled out of a bog while he looks picture-perfect with his soft blond highlighted spikes framing his cute boy-next-door looks and his lopsided grin that could melt butter. Unfair.

'Uh . . . hi,' I stammer, my cheeks instantly turning rosy. I wish I didn't blush so fast, that I had some ability to keep my emotions to myself. I feel like an open book where everyone can see my feelings as if I've written them in little love notes and handed them out.

Jacky sticks his head round from the kitchen to peek out to the counter to observe what's going on. I turn around and notice his floating head, I shake my head at him, and he understands our silent language that the female customer from earlier still hasn't returned. I can overhear my brother relay the message to my parents in the kitchen that there aren't any customers and the lady still hasn't come back yet, it's just Angela's friends.

'Ah mui! Tell your friends to stop taking over the counter, there's nowhere for customers to sit,' Dad shouts from the kitchen out to the front. 'Tell them to get lost and hang out elsewhere, we're busy working.'

'What did your Dad say? Is he okay?' Cai asks, genuinely concerned. 'He sounds angry.'

'Hahahaha. Oh, fine. He's fine,' I reply, the flush of colour now scorching my cheeks, as I wave my hands to dispel the worry that anything is the matter. 'Nothing's wrong. That's just how he is.' I ignore Dad. I just want five minutes to myself to chat to my mates and hang out, like a normal kid. Except there is nothing normal about this scenario, a group of fourteen-year-olds dressed in mishmash shoddy Halloween outfits sitting in a Chinese takeaway.

'Soooo . . . How was your night? What have you been up to?' I ask, putting my palms on my cheeks trying to act cutesy, but also to try to cool my cheeks down. *My God.* I'm acting like a lovestruck puppy, throwing myself at him. I disgust myself. Play it cool, I think. I flash my biggest smile at him, showing off my pink and black metal braces. *Nice one, dork,* my brain echoed.

'Ohhh, it's such a laugh tonight,' Lisa butts in, wearing fluffy devil horns on her head and a black crop top from Tammy Girl that says 'miss chieveous' in glitter writing and a devil motif, which skims her new belly bar complete with hanging diamanté Playboy bunny. Her attempt at dressing up.

'Yeah, Ange. I wish you were out with us, you should've seen the state of the house we just TP-ed on the top of the rugby field by the phone box,' Jane says, a little spider painted on her face. Her eyes wide with excitement, she grabs a lollipop from the bowl, unwraps it and hands me the rubbish. 'Absolutely covered in bog roll.'

They all snigger and laugh, so in tune that it resembles canned laughter from an American TV sitcom. An old, male customer with a great big white beard and a bulbous red nose has just waltzed in from the pub, Cecilia gets up to serve him.

Jacky comes back out to check again because he's heard the door open and yells back to the kitchen, 'The woman's still not here, but Angela's friends are still here.'

Dad grows frustrated over the no-show and wasted food. He takes it out on me and my friends. He raises his voice louder than ever before, but this time in a terrifying tone, 'DIU*, AH MUI. Tell your friends to go! That's an order! Now!'

---

* Diu – Cantonese word for fuck, which coincidentally is Dad's favourite word.

'Er . . . I think your Dad is calling you,' Lauren says sheepishly.

'We should probably go,' Tasha suggests, but I can't take her seriously as she's wearing little black cat ears. 'We'll see you around.'

'See ya, Ange!' They all wave and call back in unison, with one foot already out the door.

'Er, bye,' Cai calls out bashfully. He waves one hand in the air. 'See you around!'

Aaaargh. This is so mortifying. I can't believe Dad has scared off my friends. Thank God they couldn't understand what he was shouting about, they would've run a mile off ages ago and would probably never want to see me again because of my psychotic, embarrassing father. This is exactly why I feel on edge when people I know come to visit during service, never mind introducing my parents to my Welsh friends properly. My two circles should always be kept separate, and it should stay that way, even though I'm so worn out having to act like a completely different person around my family, with the debilitating pattern of putting on a different face every time. I look up at the clock and it's ten to eleven and I'm tired and exhausted, and not just because I'm coming to the end of my shift. The waves of customers start to trickle down and service is winding down. The sky is pitch black now, the street has fallen silent and there seems to be no sign of life outside. Cecilia and Dewi are busy at the till calculating tonight's earnings, ready to go home after a hard night's work.

– SPLAT –

I freeze. My muscles tense and are the mirror of my anxiety, each one feeding into the other.

– THUD THUD –

The thuds start to match the beat of my heart, getting increasingly faster and louder. The force of the mysterious objects rattle our windows and the sound of whatever it was hitting and breaking on impact echo in the empty waiting room. I'm terrified and my mind is going into overdrive. What if it's stones and our windows break? Or worse, someone trying to set our shop on fire with us inside? It's scary knowing our home is under attack.

My initial reaction is to call the police, but I know my parents would never allow it. Too much hassle, and it would be a complete waste of time because my parents know it would always amount to nothing. I know my parents aren't alone in thinking this. Many immigrant communities are reluctant to report any crime. Always better to take it upon ourselves to resolve whatever the issue is, because the police never believe us and we don't want to kick up a fuss or rely on others. We're taught not to speak out, not to rock the boat, keep our heads down and to fit in for fear of attracting unwanted attention on ourselves and our family. For my parents, silence is a form of protection, and dealing with matters on our own means safety. They see the mistreatment as the price of doing business and just another obstacle they have to overcome.

I cower behind the counter and duck down, so I'm

not in view in case anything serious is going to hit me. I slowly peep back over to try to get a better look at what's happening and to try and catch whoever is throwing stuff at us in the act. I can see drooling yellow splatters all over our windows, with specks of crunchy white and brown shells. We're being egged.

– THUNK THUNK –

Another two eggs smash against our glass windows. I can't see anything or anyone throwing, just flying eggs hurtling at us, exploding on impact. My family rush out to the front. Dad never leaves his kitchen position unless he goes out to do the deliveries on the days when Dewi isn't working. You know it's serious when Dad comes to the counter to take a look.

Dad roars obscenities in both English and Cantonese and flings the front door wide open to try to see who it is, but it's too dark. He raises a fist in the air, hears giggling, and a group of kids scurry off into the distance. He screams into the abyss and the sleepy quiet street echoes with his piercing words. I can see a visible, angry vein popping out of his neck.

Dad slams the door. The whole house shakes like a mini-earthquake. He walks away cursing, exasperated, and goes to the kitchen to grab a broom to get ready for closing. He then comes back out, locks the front door so no more customers can get in, and flips the closed sign.

Cecilia gets up to turn off the outside takeaway signage light and hangs around the till awkwardly, waiting to get paid. Dad puts the broom to one side, grumbles, muttering swear words under his breath, and double-checks tonight's earnings. He pays Dewi and Cecilia cash in hand and walks them out the door.

'Good night, Angela, good night, Jin, and er, good night, Gary!' Cecilia says softly, using my parents' Western names, with a hint of terror in her voice.

'Good night, Cecilia! See you tomorrow!' Mum bellows from the lean-to, already elbow-deep washing up all the pots, pans and woks.

Dad doesn't say another word. He turns around and starts sweeping the floor. Jacky shoots upstairs and gets first dibs in the bathroom to wash off the night's work, but mostly to avoid cleaning and confrontation.

'Haiya, such a mess. Stupid kids,' Dad grumbles, and shouts at no one in particular while he has his head down sweeping. 'Why is there so much rubbish? Whose candy wrapper is this? Why is there so much rice? It's absolutely everywhere. Stupid.'

Keen and I grab a bucket of soapy water and sponge each from Mum. We carefully tiptoe to the counter, trying to avoid Dad and not knock into him. The mood in the takeaway is charged, combustible. It feels like he might detonate at any moment. Keen unlocks the front door and starts working on cleaning the egg-splattered windows. I wipe down the counter, trying to scrub off stubborn sauce stains and pick up flecks of leftover rice in silence.

I look at the wasted rice dotted across the counter and sigh. Mum has always instilled the importance of not wasting food into us and she taught me how each grain of rice represents hard work, grit and resilience. Rice is used to resist racial barriers and forms a common ground that can bind us together. To love cultures, no matter how we clash and intersect. I look up and gaze outside into the darkness and up at the sky. A rural blackness, where the streetlights are few and the starlight goes unchallenged. I can just make out a stunning constellation from the window and a shooting star swoops across the sky. I'm trying to get through the night, and I wish for a better tomorrow.

Egg Fried Rice

The egg fried rice was one of our bestselling dishes and almost every order had this dish. We sold huge vats of the stuff and often sold out before the end of the night. It was the gateway food item to help Westerners understand East Asians better, because even in the South Wales Valleys people knew what egg fried rice was. Kids wouldn't get freaked out over it because the locals had grown accustomed to the rice dish and it was our peace offering. When Mum forgot or didn't have enough money for a school lunch ticket for the canteen she'd quickly whip up some egg fried rice in a flask for me for lunch at school. I never really had a 'lunchbox moment' at school where other kids picked on you for what you ate. Instead, my classmates queued up with cupped hands asking for some egg fried rice like in a scene from *Oliver Twist*. That's how powerful a connector egg fried rice is. There are a million different variations and methods of cooking egg fried rice, but this is a plain version that's similar to what we served at the takeaway. Feel free to experiment and add more to this simple base.

Serves: 4 | **Prep time:** 10 mins | **Cook time:** 25 mins

Ingredients:
3 large eggs, whisked
3 tbsp vegetable oil

1 cup (200g) cooked rice (I cannot stress this enough, but use day-old rice or completely cooled rice, otherwise it'll turn to mush and stick to your pan or wok)
1 teaspoon salt
A pinch of white pepper
Splash of light soy sauce
Splash of dark soy sauce
A drizzle of sesame oil to finish

Optional:
1 large handful of frozen peas
½ tin of Spam, diced
2 spring onions, chopped

Method:
1. Beat three eggs in one bowl. Heat a wok over medium-high heat, and add 2 tablespoons of oil and scramble them. Once cooked, remove them from the wok and set aside.
2. Heat a wok or frying pan over a high heat and add a tablespoon of oil. Tilting the wok or pan to ensure an even oiled surface, add the rice, using a wooden spoon or spatula to flatten out and break up any rice clumps into individual grains; stir-fry for 2 minutes. Next, add the cooked eggs back in with the rice, season and stir-fry for about 1 minute, until the egg is evenly distributed.
3. If using, add the peas and Spam and stir-fry

continuously for another 2–3 minutes. Next sprinkle salt and white pepper over the rice and mix for another minute.

4. Drizzle the soy sauces and ensure each grain is coated. You should now see some steam coming off the rice, which means it is heated through.

5. If the rice looks a little dry, feel free to sprinkle in some water or chicken stock. Adding some liquid directly to any remaining clumps of rice will also help to break them up. Mix in the scrambled eggs and spring onions, if using, and serve.

7

In Serious Trouble with Youths

I'm walking home from school; it's a bright and fresh June day. The weather is unusually warm enough to walk around in only a shirt and a jumper tied around my waist, rare for a usually rainy Wales. I'm carrying my Year 9 pink A4 ring-binder folder and my baby-blue Kookaï school bag, which is actually too small to carry everything I need, but all the other girls in my year have one so I nagged and begged Mum for one until she eventually gave in (but scolded me for opting for style over practicality). As I approach my takeaway's front door, I see a stream of bright-purple liquid shoot across the air at me.

'Fuck you!' Samuel laughs, squeezing an entire bottle of Robinsons Fruit Shoot at me and spraying it all across my blue shirt uniform. He legs it back inside his house next door and slams the door shut. Samuel is my neighbour who lives in the same street as the shop. He's a couple of years younger than me and in all my years, I don't think I've ever seen his parents around. All I see is Samuel and his older brother, their floppy platinum hair and condescending smirks hanging about the front, as if they're waiting to attack me. I stand there gawking with my mouth open for a couple of seconds. Unsure what to do, frozen, standing there like a Sim waiting on instructions. Most days he'd be loitering around in the street playing football or waiting for me to finish school. Whenever I'm near my street I always hold my breath, hoping I won't bump into him. I try to make myself small to stay quiet and avoid being seen or cause any confrontation. I don't want any fuss, I just want to go home. Some days it's just verbal abuse and other days it's tiny stones he has collected from around the street, which he then throws at me. I'm just lucky that today isn't stones, at least I can wash this off whereas bruises, not so much. I look down to see the damage, and I'm covered with pinky-purple splotches. I'm cold, my hair's dripping wet with fruity squash, which is starting to become sticky from all the sugar, but at least I smell like a sweet blackcurrant. I try to wipe off the liquid and rub my hands on my black polyester school trousers. I feel a hot sting at the back of my eyes; my vision is blurring and my nose has started sniffing in an attempt to stop myself from crying. I brush away my tears, hang my head down in shame and stomp inside the shop.

I hate you. I hate you. I hate you. Stupid. Stupid. I mutter under my breath while locking the door quietly behind me, wincing when the door clicks, trying my best to not make a noise. I don't want anyone to find out about this or kick up a fuss, especially Mum. I formulate a plan in my head to bolt it through the waiting room, past the counter and upstairs so I can get out of these wet clothes and have a bath without anyone noticing. Maybe if I'm lucky enough, I can have a quick MSN messenger session before service on the family computer upstairs, talking to my school friends who I've just spent the entire day with. I creep in, take one step and —

'Ah mui! Is that you? Come here!' Mum shouts from the living room down the hall. How did she know? I was super-quiet coming in, it's like she can feel my presence nearby.

Argh. If she sees me like this, she'll ask questions. I'm not in the mood to explain what has happened. I put down my folder and bag on the bench, untie my school jumper from around my waist and cover myself up to try and hide the evidence.

'Ah muiii! You there?' Mum calls again. I can hear the faint sounds of the Chinese channel with comical sound effects and catchy jingles. Mum's most likely taking five minutes for herself in front of the TV before service.

'I'm here!' I poke my head round the door. My hair is still visibly wet. 'What's up?'

'How was school?' she asks while lying down on the sofa, pointing the remote at the TV to turn the volume down so she can hear me better.

'Oh, you know. Fine,' I lie.

'Why is your hair wet? Is it raining outside?' she asks,

and sits up in a panic that her laundry out the back is getting wet. 'Quick, take the clothes in!'

I didn't have the heart to tell her that it wasn't actually raining, so I quickly sprint to the garden to take the clothes off the line. Mum gets up to lend a helping hand and follows behind me, hurrying me through the kitchen to the lean-to and out back. I wouldn't say what we have behind the takeaway is a garden, it's more of a concrete patch with long brick planters on either side that Mum has shoddily made herself. The garden leads on to a grey concrete-block garage that is used as a storage room, housing floor-to-ceiling metal storage racks for more packaging and three chest freezers filled to the brim with prepped items such as spring rolls and prawn toast, next to our Mini Milks and tubs of Ben and Jerry's. One of the freezers is reserved for Mum's Chinese smuggled goods that she's accumulated over the years, things like dried scallops, prawns, salted egg yolks and Chinese medicinal ingredients that I don't quite understand the name of, or their use.

Shark fin melons* adorn the entrance of the garage and on the left-hand side of the garden. They're everywhere. Their thick climbing vines and big fig-like leaves cover the homemade wooden trellis arch Mum has fashioned out of bamboo sticks and old planks of wood she's scavenged from God knows where. Hidden underneath

---

* Shark fin melon – also known as Figleaf gourd is named after shark fin because of its fibrous flesh akin to shark fin.

all the foliage, mottled dark green and white, cylindrical oblong fruits hang heavy and they swell to the size of a large rugby ball. Mum has also caringly made little wicker baskets and nets to support their weight. We move the laundry inside the garage to prevent it from being rained upon, even though it's blue skies.

Together we admire her green-fingered handiwork. I've never seen produce this big and fresh, nothing like what you would get in the supermarkets. In fact, I've never even seen this Asian green growing out of our garden before; Mum has probably smuggled the seeds back from China. Despite its namesake, they resemble squash more than a melon, but there's definitely a hint of melon in their smell, which confuses me greatly. I didn't think it was possible for anything to flourish at all in this small, shabby patch of land that's mainly used as a dumping space for empty vegetable-oil drums and sodden flattened cardboard boxes.

'Twelve . . . Thirteen . . . Fourteen. Look how many there are!' Mum excitedly inspects her pumpkin-marrow hybrid children. I love how animated Mum gets when talking about gardening. She always tells me stories of her growing up on a farm in rural China over family meal. How one day she'd like to go back to the simple life looking after chickens and tending to crops, sur-rounded by fields as far as the eye can see.

'Such a good harvest this year. They're not quite ready yet. Maybe another month or so.' Mum says, inspecting another.

Later that evening during service, at 6pm, Keen is manning the front counter and has his head buried in a new Legend of Zelda game on his Game Boy. The summer days are longer and the nights are mild and temperate, which means there are more kids wandering around on the streets than usual. On the road in front of the shop, through the window we can see a group of teenagers playing football in the street.

'Here you go, sir,' Mum says to the lonely customer sitting on the bench waiting, giving him his bag of food. 'Keen, why didn't you come collect the order when I called your name? You know I'm busy in the kitchen.'

Keen doesn't answer and ignores her. Too fixated on trying to solve his dungeon level. Business is slow on a Monday night, the quietest night of the week. My parents don't bother hiring extra counter staff early in the week, as the older we get the more we can handle helping out. Plus, Dad says hiring someone to sit out front doing nothing all night is like pouring money down the drain. Customers trickle in and out, while the kitchen stops and starts like a revving engine but never quite fully takes off. Mum hovers about front looking over Keen's shoulder, observing his game and glancing outside to see the kids playing.

'What are those kwaai jais* doing?' she asks, speaking to no one in particular. 'Wait . . .'

---

* Kwaai jai/mui – normally, any antisocial behaviour was deemed as kwaai. Hooligans, bad or naughty kids can also be referred to as kwaai.

She squints and sees that the football they're kicking about is actually not a football. It's green and rugby-ball shaped – it is one of her melons.

'My melons!' she says loudly, and throws her hands in the air. Her voice echoes in the empty counter and waiting room. She unlocks the counter door to get a closer look and kneels on the bench. Mum bangs on the window to tell the kids off. Keen stops playing and looks up like a meerkat from behind the counter. I'm on lid duty in the kitchen, but hear Mum call out and I run to the counter to check if everything's alright.

The kids all look in our direction and laugh. We see them glance at one another, nodding as if this was their plan all along. They wanted to get our attention, so we'd have front-row seats to see what is about to happen next. Soon, they start to pelt a barrage of melons at our windows. Green and white stringy flesh explodes like fireworks and the melons' white round seeds bounce off the glass. Before we can act, the kids have already run off. It's a nightmare trying to hold kids accountable because it's impossible to prove that they're guilty and, besides, despite having lived and worked in Wales for 15 years, we were still outsiders in this community, it would always be our word against theirs. Unlike Dad, Mum doesn't believe in causing a commotion and raising her voice, because shouting only makes matters worse, and it certainly isn't going to bring back her melons. Mum's tough childhood living through one of China's bloodiest eras in history meant she became self-reliant and had to fight to survive. Calling for the police to step in to help is a sign of weakness in her mind, and so it's the last thing my parents ever want to do. Plus, they're too busy working to be slowly dragged through the lengthy, painful process to report antisocial behaviour, which they thought was pointless and would amount to nothing.

'Tsk, those kwaai jais,' she sighs heavily with her hands held behind her back. She zones out and continues to stare at the shattered melons lying on the tarmac and pavement outside, long after the kids have legged it. Keen and I look at each other confused and shrug, not sure what to say or do in this situation to make it better. Suddenly, something pings inside Mum. She remembers to rush out back to check on the rest of her prized possessions. The kids in the neighbourhood had broken in. Half of her melons have been stolen and months of hard work instantly destroyed. She unlocks the wooden gate that opens out to a private back road, which is filled with cracks and potholes. More smashed-up shark fin melons are littered everywhere. She silently walks back into the kitchen to grab a broom and dustpan.

'Are you alright, Mum?' I ask, worried. 'Do you need help cleaning?'

'I'm fine, they're just plants. It's okay, they'll grow back,' she says. I can sense the frustration and sadness in her tone – I know she'll never tell us how she really feels. She always tries to put on a brave face in front of us and carries the weight of the world on her shoulders because I know she's too proud. It's as if we were the shark fin melons. An immigrant family in a foreign country trying to sprout and flourish in an alien environment. Working twice as hard just to make something of ourselves in a place where we don't belong, there'll be things that'll stunt or squash our growth along the way. Hopefully, we'll grow back stronger, thicker-skinned and even more vibrant the following year.

'I managed to salvage some. I can still make soup for tomorrow's family meal,' Mum chuckles softly when she comes back in after sweeping up the mess outside for what seems like hours. She's carrying two bulging melons under each arm. 'I've had to pick them early, but I'm sure they'll still be just as delicious.'

She leaves them in the lean-to on top of the washing machine. My brothers and I smile at her, but groan together behind her back. We *hate* drinking soup. (Mainly because it was healthy, and anything that was good for you, we didn't want or appreciate at the time.) Whatever the weather, Mum makes soup. There's always a pot on the hob slowly simmering away for hours in the day to draw out and deepen the flavour, a warm and caring caress from a loving mother. Today's soup of the day: shark fin melon soup with pork ribs. She constantly tries a myriad of different tricks and techniques to force a variety of clear, clean broths down us. In Guangdong culture, drinking soup before or after a meal helps cleanse the palate, aids digestion and contains a multitude of health benefits. More often than not, I'm last to leave the table after family meal, sullenly sitting alone with my unfinished bowl of soup, long after the dishes have been washed and everyone else is already prepping for the night's service.

'Hurry up and down it. The sooner you drink it, the sooner it'll be over.' Mum stands over me with her arms crossed to ensure I drink every last drop of her shark fin melon soup. I glare at the tiny red rice-pattern melamine bowl, now a lukewarm bowl, staring back at me. I brainstorm ways of surreptitiously disposing of its contents like I have done in the past, contemplating whether in the houseplants or down the sink is the safest option. This time, I have no option but to neck it to get it over and done with.

This clear pork broth has all the elements and is a delicate, light balance between savoury and sweetness. I love that the shark fin melon strands are dispersed throughout the soup, they resemble spaghetti or its namesake, shark fin. In fact, this one isn't too bad, but I can't let Mum know I actually like soup, otherwise she'll force even more mysterious mixtures on me, so I moan and stick my tongue out in defiance. It reminds me that drinking soup is not just a bowl of soup, it's an expression of my parents' love, using the language of food, which sometimes I unthinkingly throw away and take for granted. They came to this country with very little, managed to make something out of nothing and sacrificed everything for the three of us. Even if their love does sometimes come with some blunt, snarky back-handed comments: 'You're too yeet hay'; 'You have too many spots on your face and you need to drink more soup'; 'You've gained some weight – you need to eat less rice'. Mum and Dad have taken great pains to instil strong Chinese values in us and a steadfast appreciation for community, family, food and ancestry.

Tonight's service is a real slog. There are barely any customers. I get so bored standing around the kitchen, I go out to pester Keen to keep him company on the counter. I watch the silver wall clock tick away, the second hand feels like a minute, and the minute hand seems like an hour. Time's moving so slowly that it's only coming up to nine o'clock and it's still light out. From dusk skies come the prettiest blush of a rose petal and glorious crimson flames melting into one, stretching out with sepia tones below. Everyone is busy outside lapping up the good weather, having tinnies in the park and barbecues in their gardens, rather than being cooped up inside. It's an unspoken law of the takeaway that whenever the weather is good, business is slow.

A group of teenagers walk through the door and order a half-and-half (a curry, plus a half-tray of rice and a half-tray of chips) between them. We work through the order slowly, as there's no one else, so we can give it our full undivided attention. When they leave we resume our bored positions on standby, waiting our lives away. Five minutes later the teens return. One of them marches straight up to the counter and demands to see the manager, which is Mum. He presents his nearly finished tray of food and complains.

'Look, there's a bee in my food!' He points to his tray of food, looking disgusted. 'I want my money back!'

He has clearly caught a bee, or found it on the pavement, from outside and buried it in the rice. Mum, Keen and I peer to take a closer look. You can see its little legs still wriggling and its wings trying to move.

Mum protests and argues, 'If we cooked it, surely the bee would be deep-fried as well? Plus, I can still see it moving on the chips.'

Another boy chimes in to back up his mate, 'Nah, I can't believe you'd cook bees like tha. Absolutely buzzin' that is.'

She stands her ground and refuses to budge. There's no way we're giving them a refund after they've gotten their fill, eating most of their food. It's obvious that they're trying their luck to get their money back for a free meal, but neither party wants to back down. Mum's determination is etched on her face – it's scrunched up and her tone of voice is harsh, which is so unlike her, as she's always so soft-spoken. She *has* to win this intense standoff because Mum is stubborn as a mule and hates nothing more than being underestimated and bullied into submission. Eventually, she wins the battle and shoos them away.

The following day, while the shop is closed, my brothers and I are in school, Mum has gone out to town for her adult English language classes and Dad is napping, the same group of teenage boys return. In retaliation for the standoff the previous night, they break the wooden back door to gain access into our garden and steal all of our green wheelie bins. They then wheel them over to the empty garage at the end of the street and set them on fire. We didn't actually see the teenagers set them on fire, but Mum is convinced it's them as we haven't wronged anyone else in the village and can't think of anyone else who would do this to us. When Dad finally wakes up for prep work around midday, he walks out back to fetch something and notices our bins have suddenly disappeared and the wooden gate is smashed up from one side, most likely from being kicked in. He starts shouting his head off, and continues to curse all day. He's still going by the time we arrive home, and we see the thick black, burning smoke billowing in the distance. The pungent smell of the transient smog clings to everything around it. There have been earlier reports of arson in the area, but we couldn't do anything about it and no one else did anything about it because we didn't have proof, only missing bins.

When the weekend rolls around, business is booming again but we've run out of packaging for everything. I nip out back to restock the kitchen, searching for more poly lids and silver containers from the garage. I freeze. I see the same teenager who'd tried to wangle free food out of us and (we suspect) set our bins on fire earlier in the week, only this time he's trespassing in our back garden. I instantly recognise his spiky frosted tips and braces. He's wearing the same bright red puffer coat as he had on Monday and he's been causing havoc all week. There's no sign of his mates, it looks like he's on his own. I think he's trying to pinch another one of Mum's shark fin melons. Without saying a word, I sprint back inside through the lean-to and back into the kitchen. Alerting everyone that there's an intruder, my voice cracks and warbles from genuine fear. Dad immediately stops what he's doing and drops his wok mid-rock back into the wok burner hole, with the flame still left roaring high. Mum scoots out the way to make room for Dad to pass and, as he goes, he picks up a meat cleaver from a chopping board resting on the side. He goes out into the garden and finds the teenager loitering. The teenager spots Dad coming his way with a meat cleaver and freezes. My brothers and I rush out to the garden to watch on the sidelines – Dad seems so angry we fear for this teenager's life.

Everything in that moment happens in slow motion and we hold our breath from the suspense. Dad walks up to the boy and pulls his ear, dragging him towards the broken wooden gate he'd climbed over to get in. Grabbing him by the shirt with one hand, yelling and pressing him up against the corner with his back against the brick wall and gate, he raises his meat cleaver at him, shaking the heavy metal knife in the air. The boy is weeping and desperately wriggling, trying to break free.

'Dad! Stop!' Keen yells at a distance from the lean-to, not wanting to get too close in case he accidentally gets caught up in the incident.

'That's enough! You're hurting him!' Jacky shouts, rushing over to break them up, but before he can reach them, Dad loosens his grip and lets the boy drop to the floor. The boy frantically pats himself down to check if all his limbs are still intact and cowers.

'Go!' Dad flails his knife in the air, gesturing to the boy to scram. 'Don't come back!'

The boy whimpers and scampers away with his tail between his legs, stumbling while trying to make a break for it.

Dad quietly walks back inside, holding his knife beside him. We jump out the way like the Red Sea parting for Moses. He doesn't shout or lecture, he just carries on with the rest of the service as normal. All those years of putting up with bad customers and kwaai jais causing trouble has caught up to him. He's had enough of staying silent and had to take matters into his own hands. He fearlessly fought back to stick up for us.

As we're gearing up for the Saturday service the next day, just before we're due to open, we hear a loud knock on our window. It's the same teenager who'd broken into our garden, but this time he is with his mother. The boy sits on our bench apologising and crying. His mother gives him a bollocking in front of Mum and Dad to apologise, but she also gives my parents her two cents, too.

'I know he did wrong, but you should never hit or scold children with physical discipline like that,' the boy's mum protests. 'How *dare* you touch my child like that?!'

My parents' broken English means they can't really understand what's happening or communicate properly. They call Keen down from upstairs to translate and mediate. Dad argues that he was never going to cause any harm, only scare some sense into him. Their views may be old-fashioned, but using violence to discipline kids is a long tradition in China and my parents believe that corporal punishment for children is effective.

'I don't care! It's my job to punish him. What you did potentially could have long-lasting negative effects on a child,' she shouts, gesturing to her crying son as proof.

Keen relays the message back to my parents. Dad angrily replies in Cantonese, 'Well, you're not doing a very good job if he's running around wild stealing people's bins and putting insects in food!'

Keen falsely translates trying to diffuse the situation, 'We're really sorry. It won't happen again.'

Mum understands enough and catches bits of what Keen says. She intervenes in broken English. 'Sorry? Sorry?! We have nothing to be sorry about. Your child has been so naughty. Leaving a trail of destruction in his path this week. If anything, you should both be apologising to us.'

This conversation goes round and round in circles and nothing really ever gets resolved. Neither party

other fake notes. However, the teenagers aren't going to surrender and kick up a fuss.

'Oi! I want my money back,' one shouts over the counter and after my mum. 'I can't believe this ching-chong bitch won't serve me, this is ridiculous!'

The entire time, they talk about Mum to one another as if Cecilia or the three of us can't hear or understand from the back in the kitchen. They look right through us as if we don't exist, as if we're beneath them and are merely there to serve them. We manage to shake them off and get them out the door, but we know this isn't the last we've seen of them.

The next morning, we come downstairs and wake up to shards of broken glass strewn everywhere on the waiting-room floor. Thousands of glittering fragments have exploded everywhere and nestle in the floor's crevices. I'm gobsmacked and look on with a slack-jaw gaze taking it in. What *on earth* has happened? I turn to my right and see that there's a big gaping hole in the glass. One of the windows has been smashed in. Our lovely big shopfront window has fallen victim to an errant stone. I can feel my stomach sinking and my mind working in overdrive trying to piece together what has happened. Who could do such a thing? And why us? What have we done to deserve this?

My brothers immediately jump in to help and we start to carefully pick up any large broken shards with our bare hands.

'Don't!' Mum screeches. 'You'll cut yourself. I'll go

fetch the broom to clean up. You three get out of here.'

It was one of the many times I realised just how unsafe we were in our own home, and how unwanted we were by the village. No one saw the incident or knew much more about it because it happened late at night and we still didn't have a security camera or an alarm. Without hard evidence, we couldn't be too sure if it was actually the teenagers who had tried to use fake money. We had good reason to believe that our smashed house window was a purposeful act of vandalism, like how the kids setting fire to our wheelie bins was an arson attack. But my parents didn't flinch in the face of discrimination and targeted violent crimes. They just got on with it, didn't call the police and carried on as normal.

Mum sweeps up the sharp glass in no time and Dad finds a big sheet of wood from the garage somewhere to temporarily board up the window. One of Cecilia's friends knows a guy who fits windows and can double-glaze them for a discounted price. That's the way around here. Everyone 'has a guy' or knows someone for something, it's strictly local and word gets around. After all these incidents, we finally install a security camera for our safety and protection. It also enables us to gather evidence and prevent this from happening again to future-proof our little shop and home. Sadly, this is part and parcel of owning a Chinese takeaway.

Our bodies being perpetually in diaspora, I look ahead to a future in which we are no longer liminal, no longer subdued and silenced. A lot of people think we are easy targets and pushovers because my parents can't understand the language fully, or they feel that we can't defend ourselves. Having a Chinese face in a Chinese takeaway doesn't help either because it adds an extra level of alienation. We've always held our tongues and erred on the side of caution when confronted by racism. In reality, we're just cooking to survive. Trying to get through a night's service smoothly is just basic survival. Grinding, menial, demanding work puts food in our bellies, keeps the heating on and stops our eviction from rent arrears.

Shark Fin's Melon (Figleaf Gourd) and Pork Soup

For some much-needed quick-fix comfort for the bad days when everything goes wrong or the good days when you deserve a little TLC, tong (Cantonese soup) always has your back and it's there to provide a hug in food form. Despite this soup's name, it resembles more of a squash or a courgette than a melon. When cooked, the melon flesh will turn to strands resembling shark fins, similar to a spaghetti squash, which you can buy from most supermarkets, Asian supermarkets or greengrocers. If you want to make this veggie or vegan, use 100g of rinsed black eye beans and five soaked shiitake mushrooms and its soaking liquid in place of the pork and scallops to replicate the rich, savoury and umami flavour. This is a wet and cooling type of soup, which means it's good for healing sore throats, coughs or, when the lungs are too dry, this soup can help lubricate to get you feeling fit as a fiddle again.

Serves: 4–5 | **Prep time:** 10 mins | **Cook time:** 2 hours

Ingredients:
½ shark fin melon (if you can't find one, other hardy squashes work just as well, such as winter melon, spaghetti squash or pumpkin); reserve the other half for another time
1.2 litres cold water

2 pork bones

2 pork ribs

A handful of dried scallops

1 medium carrot, peeled and sliced

1 sweet corn, cut into chunks

2 honey red dates

6 red dates

1 tbsp wolfberries soaked in a bowl of water until puffy, drained

1 tsp bitter almonds (optional)

Method:

1. Cut the shark fin melon into big chunks. This way, you'll have longer 'noodle strands' when the soup is done. Leave the skin and seeds on, they'll help enhance the flavour of the soup. Once cooked they'll go soft and they're perfectly edible, too.

2. Add all the ingredients into a pot and use enough water to submerge everything you want with about 1–2cm of water above the ingredients. Bring the soup to a rolling simmer on high heat, then turn down to low heat and boil for two hours.

3. Sieve, serve and drink immediately, or it can be kept in an airtight container for 3–4 days or frozen for up to a month.

8

You Ring, We Bring!

Jacky passes his driving test with flying colours the first time when he's 17 (much to Keen's dismay – who didn't hear the end of it since he took four attempts to pass). To celebrate, my parents buy a second-hand aubergine-coloured Volkswagen Polo for them, and we name it Marco. Being able to drive in Wales is a must. Although you're constantly met with zigzagging, winding country lanes and it's not uncommon to be caught in a sheep traffic jam, it's still better than having to rely on the temperamental Welsh public transport system. Now that my brothers can drive, our world suddenly gets a bit bigger. While Dewi still helps deliver for us, he now only helps out on the weekends, and so my brothers become Lucky Star's delivery drivers as well as my personal taxi.

For our first road trip we drive around the neighbourhood, posting menus through people's letterboxes. Not only did we have to give up our Sundays for Chinese school, once a month we had to sacrifice Saturday mornings, too. We are prep cooks, line cooks, kitchen porters, dishwashers, food runners, waiters, and we did our own marketing too. My parents are in the car helping out delivering menus and my brothers and I are bundled in another. Mum's logic was that we'd be able to cover more ground, get through our boxes of menus quicker, and it did us good to get out of the house to exercise rather than being stuck inside playing video games all day. We'd drive Marco around the nearby areas in Tyn-y-Cefyn, Glendale, Mansion Chase and Gyriant Gwyrdd while my parents took on the other areas further afield in Llwyn Celyn, Pentref Capel, Efail y Clwyd and Ystrad. Wherever you went you found a cul-de-sac network of grey pebbledash suburban terraced and semi-detached homes that used to house coal miners. We often lost track of where we'd posted the menus and accidentally doubled up.

'Make sure you leave the menu half hanging out so you can see a peep of green in the letterbox, so that you know which houses and streets you've already done,' Mum instructs us on the phone, reporting from Dad's car. 'We've got about a box and a half left. Let's keep going and hopefully we'll be done by lunchtime.'

I moan and hang up. Sulkily trudging around the streets holding stacks of menus, I look up at the angry woollen-grey sky. It seems like the heavens might be about to open up any minute. Better get this over and done with pronto. I wish there was an easier and faster way to do this. I waste so much time trying to figure out how to open people's gates, and figure my way around people's gardens to find the front door. As I post one of the menus through the letterbox, suddenly the door flings open.

'No, no, no! I don't want any junk mail.' An old bald man wearing gold wire-frame glasses angrily scolds me, shaking his cane while telling me to get lost. 'Go! I don't want your kind around here. Shoo. Shoo.'

I furrow my brow and stamp off. What does he mean by *my kind*? Surely he didn't mean what I think he meant? The thought looms over my head. I'm sure he didn't mean anything by it. I let myself out and open his neighbour's metal gate to gain access into next-door's garden to post a menu through their letterbox. No problems there. I do the same thing over and over again, distributing menus door-to-door until my stack dwindles. Most people wouldn't think twice about a paper menu from a Chinese takeaway being pushed through their letterboxes. I think about the printing costs, the manpower to fold each menu by hand and the hours spent to deliver each one individually, only for our hard work to be destined for the landfill.

That night, the phone lines are ringing off the hook and it's family only on staff. Keen can't keep up with answering the phone, as soon as one hangs up another calls. Our direct letterbox advertising has worked but almost every order is for delivery. Tonight the weather is miserable. A rainy, windy Wednesday in May, it's the type of hard rain that won't let up and frightening howling winds sweep across the land. No wonder everyone wants food delivered, no one wants to leave the house in this abysmal weather.

'Okay, one . . . two . . . three . . . four deliveries,' Jacky counts while sellotaping tickets to each order. 'Three are quite far away in Pentref Capel, Efail y Clwyd and Ystrad, the other is nearby in Beddau. We'll probably be out for about forty minutes. Get the next lot of delivery orders ready for when we come back. Come on, mui, let's go.'

Jacky carefully carries a big cardboard vegetable box that Mum has specially made for multiple big delivery orders. Food orders sit in sectioned compartments, divided by cardboard and duct tape. While the nylon in-sulated bags that Dewi uses are good, they only manage to accommodate one or two orders at a time. I put on my raincoat and don a handmade messenger bag filled with coins and notes to give customers change, which Mum has made from offcut scraps of denim from old pairs of jeans. Reduce, reuse, recycle? Mum practically invented sustainability. She's always diligent and thrifty. She be-lieves that being frugal is a good approach to life and it's a core Chinese value. Mum's strict savings habit means she always manages to fashion something out of nothing in a bid to save money for future use, like buying a house or putting us through university.

I love doing delivery orders. Mainly because they're a much-needed welcome break from the hectic kitchen and counter. Leaving behind the madness of the service rush for a few minutes feels like a mini road trip around the village and to new places I haven't been before; a taste of freedom, seeing what else is out there beyond the four walls of our takeaway. Marco always has a faint smell of fried chips and curry sauce about him. My brother tries to eliminate it by hanging a little green tree air-freshener on the rear-view mirror, but it does little to dispel the scent of the takeaway, which has now seeped into the car seat fabric. I sit shotgun, trying to find the directions in our battered AA pocket atlas 1999 edition (six years out of date and this was a time before Google Maps and smartphones), and scroll through Jacky's iPod to find the perfect driving song while he's in charge of driving. I land on a carefully curated pop-punk playlist featuring the likes of Alkaline Trio, Blink-182, Green Day and Jimmy Eat World on full blast that can be heard outside the car. We belt out choruses whizzing through the meandering lanes and dead-ends as we get through all our orders.

'Ohh, you're getting soaked to the bone. Come in from the 'orrid rain, dear,' an old woman says, welcoming me into her hallway while she goes to grab her purse to pay me. I peer at the inside of her home while I wait and she isn't looking. Terracotta carpeted stairs go up to the bedrooms, ornate family pictures decorate the red and white wallpapered hallway and there's an enormous magnolia living room with a gigantic TV set that takes up most of the room. It seems like a palace compared to our compact living quarters and it's like stepping into another world. I dream of the day when we'll live in a home where there's no constant hum of the extractor fan and wok roaring in the background. I wish I could have what this lady has, but I also know we could never afford it.

'Here you are, my love, twenty quid. Keep the change.' She hands me a note and in exchange I hand over her bags of hot Chinese food.

'Thank you and enjoy!' I stuff the money in my messenger bag. I wave and let myself out back into the rain, a steady serenade drumming on the windows and garden pathway.

We often get tips. Dad lets us keep them and split them between ourselves. We pool all our earnings together to buy new video games (although our frugal, money-saving mother always thinks games are a complete waste of money and that we should be studying at all times instead).

'Okay, where next, mui?' Jacky asks.

I climb over the front seat to look into the back with its box full of orders. I pull a ticket off a bag that reads:

39 Fford Cae'r Mynach
Pentref Capel
CF76 9JD

'Where the hell is that?' Jacky questions.

I flick through the pages of the map on my lap, squinting as I try to read in the dark. I switch the car interior light on and still can't see anything. The torrential rainfall hitting the car roof and windscreen makes it sound like we're stuck in a carwash spraying rotating water jets at us relentlessly.

'Uhhh . . . It's not on the map!' I panic. 'We must have an old edition, and this must be a new build.'

'Let's just drive around in that area and hope for the best. We might stumble upon it.' Jacky says.

He puts the keys in the ignition and starts the car. It was only supposed to be a ten-minute round trip to the nice part of town, but we drove for what seems like hours up and down the same cluster of residential roads with family cars on drives and neatly trimmed hedges barricading flower beds on gigantic front gardens. Big red-brick detached houses roll behind us and melt into one. It's a nightmare; they all look the same. The pitch-black darkness and heavy downpour only make things worse, as trying to spot street-sign names and house numbers was impossible.

'No! We've been down this street before! I recognise the yellow grit bin,' I argue, and point out the box next to the streetlight that highlights the sheets of rain sweeping sideways in the wind.

'Ah, okay. Let me turn around again,' Jacky sighs while turning his head round to look in the back window, vigorously turning the steering wheel with the palm of his hand.

'Wait! I see it down at the bottom of the hill, there's a street sign there. It's partially covered by the giant bush,' I say, and point forward.

Jacky loops around and coasts down the hill. He

turns down the volume of the stereo so he can see better and tries to concentrate on navigating where we're going fully.

'See anything, mui?' Jacky asks, driving slowly and darting his head around trying to look for the house. 'I don't see anything. I got even numbers on my side.'

'Number thirty-five . . . number thirty-seven . . . thirty-nine! There! The one with the red garage door.' I tap the window on my side urgently to signal him to stop. I take my seatbelt off and climb over the seat again to take the bags of food out of the box behind us, put them down by my feet carefully and flick my hood up. I rush through the front garden, trying to minimise my time outside, and ring the doorbell. I wait with the bags in my hand as I struggle to see anything through the huge globs of water smacking me in the face. The lights flick on inside and I see some shuffling around before the door opens to a middle-aged man with glasses in a grey dressing gown who looks confused and surprised to be greeted by a small teenage Chinese girl.

'Hiya, your Chinese delivery is here,' I say, lifting the bags into view to show him.

'What time do you call this? You're thirty minutes late!' He shrieks.

'I'm sorry, we're extremely busy tonight and we got a bit lost trying to find your address,' I explain.

'Hmph, whatever. The other Chinese I usually go to are always on time. What's the damage?'

'Seventeen pounds fifty, please,' I ask politely.

'Here, seventeen-fifty,' he grunts, and hands me the exact money, which I stuff into my messenger bag. I pass his food over to him.

'Thank you and enjoy!' I say with a smile, trying to show some common courtesy.

'Yeah, yeah. Thanks for nothing. My food better be warm, definitely won't be ordering from you again,' he says scornfully, and slams the door in my face.

If we were at fault, we'd always admit to it, but sometimes there are things you can't control, like busy delivery times or getting lost. We do make mistakes sometimes – we're only human – but we'll always try to rectify or compensate the customer, even if they are unnecessarily rude.

I stomp back to the car through a puddle and pull my hood down when I get back in the passenger seat.

'All good?' Jacky asks, wiggling the gear stick to set to neutral and putting his other hand on the steering wheel, raring to go. 'I think Efail y Clwyd is next. This one's a regular, I know where it is.'

I nod in silence. I'm still thinking about how much of a jerk that customer was. It makes me sad, and I wish people appreciated what we do more. I try to forget about him and start to wring the wetness out of my hair. Water droplets drip down on my lap and onto the car floor. Jacky unclicks the handbrake and pulls away. He speeds off to our next destination on our delivery hit list, curving around the sharp blind bends far too quickly and chugging up the steep lanes.

I climb over the car seat to fetch the last order from the box and disaster strikes. I lift the bag and notice sweet-and-sour sauce has spilled out of the sides of the silver container. The bottom of the bag has been collecting a pool of scarlet liquid.

'Oh no! It's gone everywhere!' I panic and look at the bag and box, trying to assess the damage. 'You were going way too fast! Your mad, reckless driving did this!'

'Well, we're here ahead of schedule and in one piece, aren't we?' Jacky protests. 'I'm sure it can be easily cleaned up.'

Ugh. I climb over from the front and slide into the backseat. I grab fistfuls of tissues from the tissue box on the parcel shelf behind the headrest, then start pulling out silver containers, wiping the wet bags to dab and mop up the spilled sauce, trying to salvage the dishes and make them look presentable before handing the bag over to the customer. I nervously ring the doorbell and look down at the bag of food to double-check nothing else has been leaking and there aren't any more spillages. I can feel my stomach clenching with worry, hoping that we won't be found out. I hope it's still okay and passable.

A young, short brunette woman greets me. She already has her money ready and waiting by the shelf in her cream-coloured hallway with a hanging wooden-heart wall art that says 'home sweet home'.

'Hiya, your Chinese delivery is here.' I gesture towards the bag.

'Hiya, love. Aw, that smells lush. I can't wait. It's

£16.25 innit?' she says with a smile, and hands over a £20 note. I give her her food in exchange and put the money in my messenger bag, rummaging around for change.

'Aw, don't worry about the change, love. Keep it. Cheers! Ta-ra!' She raises the bag at me and gently closes the door.

Phew, she didn't notice. What a relief. Time to head back to the shop for the next batch of deliveries.

'Thanks so much! See you next week!' I wave back and wipe my brow from the sweat and rain.

I don't think people realise how much effort and care goes into couriering food. The logistics behind getting food from A to B can be a real nightmare. Now more than ever, we're reliant on home deliveries for everything. Couriers and delivery drivers have become the new emergency services and have played a critical role in keeping people fed. Sure, a Chinese takeaway isn't deemed an essential, but it's food for the body and stimulation for the soul. Delivery drivers are always perceived as low-paid, precarious workers, but they're also lone workers, out of sight and earshot, working in the background to keep the cogs moving in a bigger society. Restaurants and customers need to see the delivery driver as an integral part of what they do, rather than a nuisance or a pest – they deserve respect.

The rest of the week seems like a downpour blur. I can't believe it's Friday already. The phone rings and Mum answers.

'Haiya! Stupid Dewi!' she shouts from downstairs.

My brothers and I are upstairs holed up in our room, still in our school uniforms. Unbuttoned light-blue shirts and undone ties. A quick gaming session before service. I'm watching them search for clues and getting scared senseless by zombie attacks on Resident Evil on the GameCube.

'What's wrong with Mum?' Keen asks without breaking concentration.

'Go down and check, we're busy in the middle of a mission.' Jacky nudges me.

'*Tsk*, why do *I* have to?' I complain.

'Because you're the youngest,' they both chorus.

I roll my eyes and make my way downstairs. I stand on the stairs by the counter and poke my head round to peer into the kitchen. I can see her throwing her hands up in the air and angrily slamming the phone down.

'Everything okay, Mum?' I call out.

'Who calls an hour before they're supposed to start their shift?' Mum yells, totally ignoring me.

I can see her frantically flicking through her little floral-pink contact book hanging on the wall with a string by the phone and punching some numbers in on the white-corded landline phone. She's desperately trying to find a replacement delivery driver at such short notice.

'Hello, Stephen? Yeah, it's Jin from Lucky Star. You free tonight to work?' she asks. 'No? Okay then. Thank you, bye-bye.'

'Grr . . . Let's see . . . Mark?' Mum mumbles to herself while flicking through pages. She button-bashes the phone again and tries another number.

'Hello, Mark? It's Jin from Lucky Star. Can you help me tonight? No? Okay, no worry,' she says and hangs up. 'Gah! Is everyone busy on a Friday night?! Guess it'll have to be family and Cecilia.'

Mum has finally spotted me spying on her.

'Ah mui! Hurry up and get dressed for work. We're going to have family meal earlier, as we have a lot to prepare for tonight. Go tell your brothers too!' she yells from the kitchen.

It's so typical, the nights when we're short-staffed we're the busiest. The counter isn't as busy as normal because, again, no one wants to come in and brave the miserable weather to collect, and so every order is a delivery. The weather has been raining cats and dogs all week and tonight is no different. There's an overwhelming number of deliveries and no delivery driver. Me, Jacky and Dad do two separate delivery routes to try to handle the surplus.

'Where the hell is your father?! He's been gone for ages,' Mum shouts out while manning all the woks and deep-fryer stations in Dad's absence. 'I can't handle everything in the kitchen!'

Jacky and I have been blitzing through the deliveries all night, we've made good time and come back for the next round of deliveries that's due to be out by 8pm. But in terms of getting the food out, we are seriously lagging behind. With only Mum and Keen in the kitchen and Cecilia on the front, there's not enough manpower and there's a massive backlog of orders. The counter has suddenly packed out with people and phone calls are pouring in all at once. But there's still no sign of Dad and no answer on his mobile phone, he's probably driving. Something must've happened on his delivery route.

After what seems like an eternity, Dad finally comes back, all guns blazing, shouting his head off and flinging the undelivered insulated delivery bag on the silver island, spilling its contents everywhere, before making his way into the kitchen.

'I can't find this address! I've been wandering around for hours looking for this damn place!' he howls. 'Circling around in the same area for ages and I still can't see shit. Where the hell is it?! What a waste of time.'

'Haiya, stop stressing and calm down. I'm sure the kids can help show you where it is on the map,' Mum explains with an annoyed tone. She stops cooking and walks towards Dad. She rummages around and lifts things, trying to help find the map in the storage rack underneath the security camera and TV.

Customers keep coming in, phone calls come through from people at home asking where their food is. We're getting busier by the second. Suddenly Dad snaps. He starts screaming obscenities in Mum's face. The shouting intensifies and gets louder. Mum tries to get away from Dad and runs over towards the lean-to. Dad grabs the meat cleaver and, wielding it in the air, threatens Mum in front of us. As she tries to run away, he chases after her and attempts to lunge at her. I know nothing will calm Dad down in this situation and so I do the only logical thing I can think of: I physically stand between them to try to defuse the situation and split them up. I stand there like a starfish pillar, puffing my chest out, a 15-year-old, unafraid, with my arms and legs wide apart. I block Dad and create a protective barrier to keep Mum out of harm's way. Dad tries to shout and get to her over my shoulder, screaming in my ear, and his hurtful words pierce all of us. I know the most important thing in this situation is to protect Mum at all costs, even if it means throwing my own body in front of something dangerous to save her. It's as if I have tunnel vision – nothing else matters. My heart is beating so fast that I can feel it in my throat and my legs are quivering. But I don't cry.

I glare back at Dad and sternly keep repeating, 'Stop!' and 'Don't you dare!' in the hope of getting through to him, wishing that he'll actually listen and heed my words.

My brothers scream on the sidelines, begging our parents to stop arguing. Keen tries to pull Dad away and is crying – heavy, heaving sobs. Cecilia comes to the kitchen to bring more ticket orders in and to check if everything's okay after hearing all the screaming. She wants to see what the hold-up is. Jacky collects the ticket in the hallway and ushers her away to prevent her from seeing the commotion that's happening in the kitchen.

'Would you be able to tell the customers we're on it

and apologise for the wait, we're slammed and short-staffed? Thanks,' Jacky orders calmly, as if on crowd control.

The look in Dad's eyes is crazed and feral. His brows are furrowed, his face purple and there's a pulsing vein in his neck. I've never seen him like this, as if the anger's taken over and he has no control. Hong Kong Dad is nowhere to be seen.

'Don't you dare speak back to me like that! You think you're so clever, don't you!' he yells, pointing his cleaver past my shoulder and at Mum. His voice is getting hoarse and cracks. 'If you're so good, why don't you do deliveries, then!'

After several more attempts trying to get past me, Dad finally calms down and gives up, like he's running low on batteries.

He silently puts the knife down and walks out of the kitchen. He grabs his car keys from a repurposed silver pineapple tin where we store loose change, storms out the house and slams the door behind him so hard that I think the door might break and the windows shatter. Confused customers look at the door, then at Cecilia in disbelief. Cecilia pokes her head down the hallway with a look that says, 'What the hell is going on?' No one knows where Dad has gone, but no one questions it. Everything in the kitchen is still ticking over in the background: chips sizzling in the deep-fat fryer turning a touch too dark, burnt fried rice sticking to the woks and sauces starting to bubble over.

Mum dusts herself off, composes herself and manages to take charge to set the kitchen straight again. None of us say a single word. She tightens her blue apron, walks back over to the wok station and turns the cooker hob with the sauces down.

'Keen, take the chips out of the fryer and put a new basket of chips in. Jacky, tell Cecilia not to take any more delivery orders for the time being. Apologise to the customers at the counter for the wait. There'll be a ten- or fifteen-minute delay, but we'll be on it as soon as we can and it won't be long. Mui, take the wok with the burnt rice, scrape the rice in the bin, wash it and bring it back to me,' she commands.

We all disperse and spring into action to get back on track with service. There was no time to be upset. Mum grabs a ladle and spoons some vegetable oil to coat the other free wok. She gets started on cooking a new batch of egg fried rice. We work in silence, stick our heads down and go into overdrive to work our way through the pile-up of orders, trying to get them out the door as quickly as possible with another team member down. Despite the kitchen sounding like we're in the midst of a chaotic typhoon with its crashing spatulas, whirring fan sounds and crackling deep-frying bubbling noises, all of that dissolves into the background. Suddenly, everything seems harmonious and calm. A complete one-eighty from moments ago, it's as if we're in the eye of the storm, preparing ourselves to battle our way through to get to the other side of this hectic wave. Before long, the outstanding orders are fulfilled, the restless crowd of customers waiting by the counter subsides, and the phone calls are less frequent; we have made it out alive without the help of Dad.

'Any more orders, Cecilia?' Keen calls out to the front.

'Nothing at the moment!' she calls back.

Soon, it's closing time and there's still no sign of Dad. We lock the front door to stop more customers coming in, flip the sign and turn the front signage lights off.

'Is everything okay, Jin?' Cecilia asks with caution. The concern on her face is obvious but she knows not to delve into things too much. She hovers around the till waiting to be paid.

'Yeah, okay, no problem. See you tomorrow?' Mum quickly replies, trying to change the subject, and tallies up tonight's earnings. She gives Cecilia £30 for her shift, with an extra £10 bonus for tonight's troubles.

'Thanks, Jin. No, I can't work tomorrow, remember? But my daughter Delyth is covering for me,' Cecilia says. 'Take care. I'll see you in two weeks.'

Cecilia grabs her crutch and limps to the front door. Mum unlocks the door to let her out. 'Okay, no problem. Get home safe,' she calls out to her, as Cecilia hobbles into the dark tranquil street. The pure black of night is thick, the row of houses opposite barely visible. On the floor the black tarmac glistens from the rain, picking up and reflecting the smallest amount of light back into the night sky.

Remarkably, we never mention this incident again.

It's brushed under the rug and forgotten about. A stain on our takeaway experience Tippexed out. No one knew where Dad disappeared to that night. He didn't come back until the early hours of the next morning. I look back on this moment and don't think of Dad abandoning his family in a time of need when we needed him the most, nor Keen's cries of genuine worry, nor the silent fear in Mum's eyes. Instead, I remember the rush of adrenaline and clarity, knowing exactly what to do in a crucial moment. In the face of Dad's wrath, I was no longer a child and I refused to be the cry-baby I once was. This gave me absolute certainty that I knew I wanted to move as far away as possible from Beddau and I wanted nothing more to do with the takeaway.

My brothers and I help Mum with the deep-cleaning process. Jacky starts putting lids on containers and stores leftover stock back in the fridge. I grab a broom and start sweeping the kitchen floor to loosen the trodden chips and grains of fried rice stuck in between the gaps of the tiles. Keen fills a soapy bucket of water to wipe down surfaces. The house falls silent. A dark cloud of depression hangs over us, a heavy-laden feeling in my chest, as if someone I love dearly has died; nothing is dead – except, perhaps, my relationship with my father.

The following day, I see Dad with his back turned to me hovering around the kitchen. I can see his arms moving up and down, really going at it whisking eggs with chopsticks in a bowl. There's no sign of Mum anywhere, yet. She must have gone out to avoid another potential face-off. I don't blame her. Dad is making steamed eggs for family meal, my favourite. He must be really, really sorry.

'Hi, wong dai lui.* Have you eaten yet? Are you hungry?' Dad says softly, and his face lights up. I can see steam billowing from the metal steamer tower behind him. He's acting like normal, as if he has no recollection of what happened the night before. How do you find the right words to say to a man who's meant to protect you, but is the one who has endangered you and your family less than 24 hours ago?

I feel confused and conflicted. I know I'm supposed to love my father, but how can I after what he's done? How can I love him the same way as I did before? After the way he's treated Mum and all of us over the years? Of course, I love my dad, I always will, he's my father, but what he did last night was unforgivable. My parents believe in staying together for the kids and it's no secret that they married out of necessity – the chance at a new life in a place more suitable to raising kids than Hong Kong – not for love. If Mum were to leave Dad, she fears she would disrupt the social harmony of the family and provoke the disdain of the Chinese community. My extended family turns a blind eye to what's going on. As the saying goes, 'Don't wash your dirty linen in public.'

---

* Wong dai lui – princess in Cantonese. Dad would often call me princess to butter me up and try to get back in my good books after his wrongdoings. Being the only daughter in the family, he'd treat me differently compared to my brothers and would often try to spoil me.

Violence against a woman by her husband is concealed within the sphere of private life and, as such, is largely overlooked. The home is often the most violent space for women. Abuse can happen behind closed doors, but what if home is where you live and work? How do you escape then? In Chinese culture, beating shows intimacy and scolding shows love. Indoctrinated with ideas of female subordination and that being beaten by their significant others is normál, women rarely stand up against their partners even if they are abused. These two facts exist at the same time, although they seem to contradict each other. Why? Because of forgiveness. Although, I'm not sure I'll ever be able to forgive my father for what he's done and all those times he's done similar things in the past. Maybe one day, I'll be able to find a way to live in a state of resolution with it.

The atmosphere in the house is charged and electric, as if we're on the cusp of another T8 typhoon. I can see Dad still looking at me, trying to fish an answer out of me. I can see he's begging for forgiveness in food.

'I've added stock for a more luxurious steamed egg, and I bet you it's going to be waat waat leng leng (beautifully silky) by the time it comes out of the steamer,' he explains excitedly.

I don't say anything. I stare at him blankly, unsure how I should react and respond. It is my favourite, after all. The subtle egg-custard flavour. The smooth and soft texture that glides down your gullet. Gently hugging you from within, a soothing and comforting ploy, tricking you into thinking that everything is going to be okay. But I have no appetite, I feel empty and I have forgotten how to enjoy the simple pleasures of food. How can I feel hungry when I'm full of trauma? I half-smile weakly and give him a thumbs up, even though I don't want to.

'That's my wong dai lui,' he says, chuckling.

Chinese Steamed Egg

Steaming foods is one of the most popular methods of cooking in East and Southeast Asian culture and what I love about this dish is its simplicity and clean taste. Chinese steamed egg, sometimes better known as water egg or custard egg, is smooth and soft. It's wobbly in appearance and delicate in flavour, which reminds me a lot of the relationship between me and my father. A fine balance to get it spot on and right. The ideal egg–water ratio should be around 1:2 in volume. Too much egg will result in a hard curd (just as too much conflict means endless fights), whereas overdo it on the water and the mixture will never set into a solid form (and overdoing it on the bickering usually ends in tears). Sometimes it's hard to get the balance right, but you learn by experience.

The creamy, velvety texture of the egg over plain boiled rice with a drizzle of soy sauce is super-comforting and will lift even the lowest of spirits. Use this steamed egg recipe as a blank canvas. Don't be afraid to get creative. Try using different toppings such as shiitake mushrooms, stir-fried pork mince, prawns or char siu.

Serves: 2 | **Prep time:** 5 mins |
Cook time: 10–14 mins

Ingredients:
4 eggs
300ml water or chicken/vegetable stock
Pinch of salt and pepper

For the toppings:
Drizzle of light soy sauce
Drizzle of sesame oil
1 spring onion, finely chopped
Drizzle of chilli oil, to taste (optional)

Method:
1. Crack eggs into a steam-proof dish. Add water/ stock and mix together with the eggs until combined and smooth. Season with salt and pepper.
2. Using a small teaspoon, scoop away any bubbles or foam on the surface that may have formed.
3. Cover the eggs with aluminium foil. This is to prevent any water droplets from the steamer from falling directly onto the eggs, making the surface of the steamed eggs rough.
4. Gently place the bowl onto a prepared steamer. Steam over low heat until the eggs are set, about 10–14 minutes, depending on the shape and depth of your bowl. The eggs should be steamed until just firm, so that the texture of the eggs is still smooth and silky.

5. Carefully remove from the steamer and garnish with desired toppings. Serve warm.

9

Drunk and Disorderly

Months have gone by and my parents still haven't spoken to each other properly. Besides saying the odd request to fetch the soy sauce or pass the white pepper to each other during service, they've barely said a word. The ambience in the house is still sour and I can imagine that they'll simply carry on not saying anything or even acknowledging the incident. They'll bury the hatchet, admittedly, but the hatchet will still be there, just under a bunch of dirt, or a bunch of denial. Buried or not, I don't think the two of them will ever find peace with what's happened.

We make our way into Cardiff for our weekly shopping, dim sum and Chinese school ritual. The car journey that's usually filled with Dad's cheerful Canto-pop bangers is now replaced with silence, unavoidable nothingness. Everything seems like a drag today. The half-hour journey on the motorway feels like hours, the sound of the tyres roaring as they roll on the roads underneath and cars whooshing past us. I don't recall the scenery from the drive. My eyes barely register the patch-work of new housing developments and hay crop bales wrapped in black plastic bags on farms in the distance. Instead, I focus on my father's stern face in the rear-view mirror, concentrating on driving. He has always tried to cope in difficult situations with the same stoic attitude. Shaking off the past and ignoring the problem at hand. It's unnatural for Chinese parents to be open with their feelings and emotions, but I wish at this moment that someone would just address the elephant in the room so we can get over the ugly darkness that looms over us and move on with our lives.

The five of us sit around a table in the restaurant. It's awkward knowing that we're playing happy families, when we couldn't be further from that. I can tell from the disdainful faces and outward body language that my parents don't want to be here together, or have anything to do with each other for that matter. My brothers and I sit between them, so that they aren't sitting next to each other – we're acting as buffers. The usual happy yum cha affair feels drawn out and long, as we pick at har gao and siu mai dishes from steaming bamboo stacks. Mum keeps getting up to wander over to other tables to chat with friends and Dad does the same on the other side of the room, talking to family members, trying to avoid each other. The three of us are left to pick at the remaining dishes, guard our belongings and entertain ourselves. My brothers and I don't say anything to each other and eat the rest of the meal in silence, while the rest of the banquet hall around us is its usual buzzy, loud self. I can feel the gloominess radiating off us, a physical sad blue aura sucking out all the fun from whoever comes within a two-mile radius of our table.

Soon enough it doesn't matter to my brothers any more because, while I'm only 15 years old and still in school, they're off to university at the end of the month and won't have to deal with this drama on a daily basis. Jacky got into Cardiff University to study civil engineering and Keen, who'd previously done an art foundation diploma at University of Glamorgan in Treforest, is going to the Cardiff campus to study computer games design. They are the first in our immediate family to go on to higher education and it makes my parents immensely proud to be able to give them the education they never had. Jacky will stay in university halls in the city, while Keen will still live at home, but he'll be in-between the takeaway and the new empty house my parents have just bought. He often stays at the new place on his own for his break of freedom. Both Jacky and Keen come back on weekends to help out, but they are beginning to transition out of their roles.

Despite my parents' rocky relationship, they have decided to buy a home together in addition to the takeaway, a place ready for when they eventually retire from the takeaway business. They've been planning on getting on the property ladder for years to future-proof themselves once they are too old and frail to carry on with the demands of the kitchen. They are building a space for our family just as we are starting to fly the nest. Everyone is preparing to move on with the next stage of their lives, while I still feel like a spare part, unsure where I fit in all of this. Admittedly, my brothers are both still local and only down the road, no more than half an hour's drive, but it feels like they are going far, far away. Our five-strong family unit is starting to crumble. My parents start sleeping in separate beds. Dad takes over our room and I have to share a room with Mum. She insists this is due to Dad's late-night casino trips, coming back in the early hours of the morning and waking her up, but I can work out other reasons why they don't want to be in the same room, so I oblige and have to endure Mum's incessant snoring in the same room.

I take on the brunt of takeaway work while starting to prepare and study for my GCSEs. Teachers have split me and Lauren up because we were talking too much and it was affecting our grades, so we are never in the same classes any more. We hang out less often, then not at all. We never argued, we simply drifted apart. I feel lonely, lost and stagnant, while everything around me changes – and change scares me.

After unloading the weekly shop from the boot to the garage, as soon as we get home the five of us disperse, as if none of us want anything to do with each other. Mum goes to lie down on the sofa, catching her

TVB dramas and variety shows.* Dad shoots upstairs to shower off the mud from football and squeeze a nap in before service. My brothers hibernate in our room to shoot each other on Call of Duty on the new Xbox 360 Jacky has gotten for his 18th birthday. I'm still holding a white plastic doggy bag of unfinished dim sum. I rub my stomach, still too full from yum cha. I guess we'll most likely skip the family meal tonight, and put the leftovers away in the fridge.

Service at the end of the week is usually pretty chilled. Busy, but not to the point where you're swept off your feet. A chance to take a breather and recuperate, with regular breaks in between. I sit on the counter and spread my coursework out, cramming in a quick algebra study session that I don't understand before we open up shop. I look up at the wall clock. Quarter past five, 15 minutes left. I can see the first wash of autumn from the counter looking out. Wind moves the terraced houses like a shallow wave, people wearing hats and scarves. Everything slows down to a quieter pace, even the world outside the takeaway is changing. I can see two figures hovering outside: it's the cute old couple who always arrive together a few minutes before we open. As with many of our regulars, we don't know a lot of

---

* Mum was always glued to the screen watching her Cantonese TVB dramas and comedy shows in her down time. They always had over-the-top love triangles and far-fetched storylines. She carefully recorded on our clunky old VHS titles like *A Kindred Spirit*, *Journey to the West*, *A Step into the Past* and *The Super Trio* series.

our customers' names, but we know them by their order. Mum's named this lady bak fan por (boiled rice granny) because, no matter what, she always orders boiled rice with her order. They're wearing hats and gloves and wave at me from the window like an old family friend, waiting patiently and loitering around.

'We're not quite ready to open yet, but if you'd like to wait inside on the bench rather than standing outside in the cold you're welcome to,' I say, as I open the door and gesture for them to sit.

I don't even need to write a ticket because I know exactly what they are going to order: two small boiled rice and one large beef curry to share. I walk down the hallway and to the kitchen where my parents are already busy setting up shop. I can hear the extractor fans humming on low, Dad at his station reducing down a giant pot of bubbling curry sauce, an amber gloop that gives off the most wonderful blend of aromatic roasted spices, onions and coconut cream. Mum's opening and closing the fridge, taking the prepped items out.

'Bak fan por is here!' I say, alerting both of them.

'Eeeh! That's quick! I don't think the rice is ready. Quick, go check, mui,' Mum orders.

I walk over to the wonky tiled shelf that separates the kitchen and lean-to to check on the industrial-sized silver rice cooker. Steam is billowing out, giving me a rice-cooker facial as I move in closer. Fragrant popcorn-like jasmine rice fills the air; the flip switch is still down in cook mode. I walk to the counter to tell the old husband and wife.

'The rice isn't ready yet. It'll be about another five- to ten-minute wait, if that's okay?' I say.

'Yeah, that's fine. How are you and your family doing?' she asks, slowly shuffling towards the counter to chat. She's so tiny she barely reaches the counter.

'Oh! We're fine, good. Same old. Nothing new,' I lie, and laugh nervously. I'm not a great conversationalist. I cannot do small talk. I often come across as cold because I don't know how to start a conversation, and people think I'm mean because I don't really talk, when in reality I'm too nervous. I'll often attempt to try to connect with customers, asking 'how are you doing today?' or try the 'what lovely weather we're having' pleasantries, but once conversation dries up or comes to an abrupt end, I panic. I smile and keep it to the point as I try to hobble over the finish line with our transaction.

Mum comes out to the counter with their order and recognises the old couple instantly. She beams and asks, 'Hello, boiled rice granny! How are you? How's the family doing?'

She has such a way with people that I do not. Mum is good at turning on the charm. Customers and staff adore her, even with her broken English, she really makes an effort to listen, learn and get to know the people that come through the door. No one in Beddau has a bad word to say about my mother. Customers are the backbone to our business, they are inevitably the best and worst parts about working in hospitality. Everything we do is down to them and their loyal custom; without them we wouldn't have a roof over our heads. But still, I wish some customers were more like this couple, treating us with a little more respect and being kinder to us.

Shortly after they leave, Delyth comes through the door just as the shop officially opens at half past five. Delyth is Cecilia's daughter and is covering for her shift tonight. Whenever Cecilia is unavailable, Delyth usually steps in. She's lanky, brunette and has the same headstrong temperament as her mother. I imagine this is what Cecilia would look like if she was 30 years younger, as well as doing less smoking and limping.

Despite the drop in temperature, a lot of Beddau's locals still walk around in shorts – it's the Welsh uniform no matter the weather – and customers keep coming in and out like a revolving door. It isn't a match day or anything in particular, but we are unusually busy. A grey-haired man in his late fifties with a bright-red bulbous nose wearing a brown parka coat and navy Adidas shorts fumbles with the door and stumbles in.

Noooo. Not the steak man. Anything but the steak man. He's been here a million times and always asks for the same thing. Me and Delyth exchange worried glances, bracing ourselves for what we know is coming. Coincidentally, the phone rings at the same time as he enters and Delyth quickly tends to it. Damn, saved by the phone. Guess I'll have to get this over and done with.

'Sssswhmae! Ni Hao!' he slurs and bows. 'Rydw i eisiau stêc a sglodion.' (Hello, I want steak and chips.)

'Dim problem,' (no problem) I reply, trying to be polite, speaking back in Welsh.

'Eh! YOU speak Welsh? Where are you from? But you're Chinese?! How can a Chinese person speak Welsh!' he says, looking aghast.

'I was born here,' I answer in a civil manner, not wanting to cause any drama.

'Nooo, I don't believe you. Where are you really from?' he mumbles, confused.

'My parents are from Hong Kong and China, if that's what you're asking,' I reply curtly, itching to get away from this man.

I know this is harmless and he's probably just a bit naive, but I get asked this question a *lot* from customers, strangers and classmates, and I'm feeling pretty sick of it.

'But if you're from Hong Kong, why is your English and Welsh so good?' he says.

I stick my head down to write out his order on the ticket and pretend I didn't hear his question. He takes this as an opportunity to continue chatting, winking as he goes for the kill. 'You know, you're pretty for an Asian woman.'

'Um . . . I'll go check . . . and ask the kitchen if we have steak on the menu. Hang on a second,' I say, excusing myself. By this point, I'm so done with the conversation and am already walking off to the kitchen.

'You berra have my sssteaks!' He pauses to hiccup. 'You never seem to have them in!' he shouts over the counter after me.

His words circle around my head as I walk down the hallway. *For an Asian woman, for an Asian woman, for an Asian woman.* I feel angry and frustrated at myself that I didn't say anything to him right there and then. He made me feel like I was an object; like I was some exotic animal. Degrading and hypersexualising me. My body is changing. My chest is growing bigger than the other girls and my hips are getting wider. I hate the attention that they draw. Instead of being proud of my body, I always want to hide and cover up.

'Do we have any steaks in?' I shout to the kitchen, angrily. I'm clearly annoyed.

'*Tsk.* No steaks!' Dad replies. 'They're just too expensive to buy these days. Offer the customer something else.'

I run back out to the front. My heart starts to beat faster, knowing that I have to confront him again. I can see the steak man swaying and struggling to stand up straight. He holds the counter for support.

'I'm sorry, sir, I'm afraid we've run out of steaks,' I tell him.

'No steaks? No steaaaaaks?! Nooooo!' He throws his arms in the air and garbles incoherently. 'I'll have a . . . [*sniff*] Chicken Maryland and chipsss,' he says. His nose is running so much, it actually makes me gag a little.

I take down his order and money, and quickly run

back into the kitchen, trying to get as far away from this man as possible and to minimise our interaction.

'One ma lun fan (fucking annoying)*!' I bark the order back at Dad.

'Tsk. Cher!† One ma lun fan coming up!' Dad replies, without looking at me, focusing on getting the wok hei‡ right on the chicken chop suey he's working on.

'I really wish you'd stop swearing and calling that dish that,' Mum complains while getting a basket of chips ready for the fryer. She shouts to the room without turning around, 'Someone get a small sausage and bacon out of the fridge for the Chicken Maryland dish.'

I jump at the chance and open the fridge. My brothers move out the way to allow the door to open fully and I grab what Mum needs from the bottom shelf. I want to loiter around the kitchen to avoid talking to the steak man.

Delyth comes into the kitchen with a phone-order ticket from earlier. 'Can one of you come to the front to

---

* Ma lun fan – Dad nicknamed certain dishes, which stuck and we all started calling them that for easier understanding. Number 73, Chicken Maryland and chips, was dubbed as 'fucking annoying' due to the multiple component nature of the dish: deep-fried breaded chicken breast with a small sausage, onion rings, fried bacon, peas and a bag of chips. It was one of our popular dishes because it contained a bit of everything.
† Cher – there's no literal translation for this. In Cantonese, we use 'cher' phonetically when things aren't as good as they seem or a general annoyance.
‡ Wok hei directly translates to 'breath of the wok' and is a Cantonese term for imparting a smoky char flavour and taste in stir fries.

help out? I'm slammed out there and there's a big group of men that's just walked in.'

'Mui, go,' Jacky instructs, while he presses the lid on a chicken chop suey that Dad has just placed into the silver tray.

'I don't want to. Keen, you go,' I plead. 'I'm busy working on wrapping chips.'

'Nuh, Ange, you go. You were already out there,' Keen argues, and gets a brown bag to wrap the polystyrene pots of sauces.

'One of you just go!' Mum scolds, as she gently lowers a breaded piece of chicken breast into the hot oil with her hands. I refuse to budge and carry on doing the chips.

'Ugh! Fine!' Keen moans and quickly stamps to the front to lend a helping hand.

Thank God I don't have to deal with steak man any more, I think. But we have bigger fish to fry because everything is starting to sell out like hot cakes and we've only been open for two hours. Mum is quickly dicing more chicken to replenish stocks. I keep going back and forth to the garage to fetch more peas and pre-prepped shredded crispy beef strips from the freezer. Keen returns to his post in the kitchen to help peel spring roll wrappers. Jacky gets a new tray of eggs from the pantry and starts whisking a new jug of beaten eggs. It's one of those nights where we run out of everything early on and underestimate how busy we'll be. So much for a chilled-out Sunday.

Paper tickets continue to stack up on the nail stumps

and the phone lines are going crazy. The drunken chants coming from the crowds gathering by the counter are getting louder and louder, competing with the sounds of the kitchen, as if two cymbals are crashing from either side trying to outdo each other.

'Delyth, please!' Jacky calls.

She walks down the hallway to fetch an order and we hear worrying shouts of 'Hahaha, yes, mate!' and 'Go on, Steve, butt!' coming from the front. We can see on the security camera that one of the guys from the group is trying to climb over the unattended counter. The group of men hoist him over the edge to try and steal the soft-drink cans on display on the shelves behind the counter. Before we have the chance to rush back out front to stop them, we hear a massive crash and things smashing.

'Woaaaaah! Oh my God!' they all holler.

We run out to the front to see the damage. Delyth carries on working, bringing an order out with her pretending nothing's happening and I cower by the till, peering behind Jacky's shoulder to see a man lying on the floor by the mini-fridge covered in soil, smashed ceramic plant pots, cans rolling around and broken pieces of wood from the shelf. He's rolling around laughing, drunk.

'Oh boys, did you see that?' he shrills. 'Almost got it!'

The room erupts into laughter, but none of us from the takeaway can see the funny side. This is our home that they have just invaded and vandalised. Our private space. There's something about working in the service industry that makes people think it's okay to treat you poorly. Being in a superior position tends to bring out the worst in people – I certainly wouldn't go into your home to start smashing stuff off the shelves.

'My plants!' Mum yelps. 'Up! Up! Up! Out! Out! Out!'

She helps the man up and escorts him out the door, leaving a trail of soil behind him with every step.

'Please wait outside, sir. You can't sit inside any more, we'll bring the food to you,' she says sternly, treating this grown man like a child. Mum continues to stand there with the door open, gesturing for the rest of them to join him without saying anything. Miraculously, they do as they're told and form a single file. She manages to command a room in her foreign tongue and closes the door on them. The group loiter outside, confused at what has just happened, but not daring to question or talk back. I don't know how she does it.

'Hurry, go get their orders done first so they won't cause any more trouble. Jacky, you're the strongest, stay out front with Delyth to keep an eye on them in case anything happens. Keen and mui, back to the kitchen with me,' she instructs.

When this incident happened, I tried to move on from it quickly and had largely forgotten about it. I remember it being so intense that I blocked it out completely because I was petrified for our lives and safety. My mind went into overdrive. If this man could easily climb over the counter, what else could he have been capable of? Stealing the till? Smashing the TV? Holding us hostage? I dreaded to think. Sadly, immigrant businesses are frequently the target of harassment and antisocial behaviour. Each time it happens, it's terrifying for my family and our staff.

After they've dispersed into the night, we breathe a sigh of relief, as if the shop itself has unbuckled its belt. Finally, some peace. Mum hands me a broom to sweep up the whirlwind of mess they've left for us clean. Delyth helps pick cans and pieces of broken wood off the floor. Trying our best to soldier on as normal and recuperate, as we tidy up the place to make it look presentable again before the next wave of customers.

I quickly glance at the wall clock. It's nearly 11pm, closing time, but there's no sign of pub revellers dying down; they keep trickling in. Just one more customer turns into a few more and soon it seems like the whole of the nearby welfare social club is crammed into our waiting room. It's all hands on deck, and my body is screaming out at this point. Everything aches and hurts. We're going flat out to get through the crowds for one final push before we can call it a day.

'Closed? Nooo! C'mon, please serve me! I only want a battered sausage, barbecue sauce and chips in a tray,' the last straggler outside the shop begs, banging on the window.

'There's one more customer. Should we let him in to serve him?' Delyth asks. She's already switching off the lights of the counter and packing her things, getting ready to leave.

'Fine, fine. Let him in,' Dad calls from the kitchen, gesturing to her to let the customer in.

Delyth welcomes him in and takes his order and money. She comes back out almost immediately with his tray of chips and discovers that the man is now lying down on the bench.

'Sir, your food!' Delyth shouts.

There's no answer and he doesn't move.

'Sir?' Delyth repeats, worried. She opens the counter door to get a closer look at the man in the waiting room to check to see if he is breathing, because he looks like he's dead.

'Oof, yeah. He's definitely breathing, alright. Absolutely reeking of booze,' Delyth says, as she leans in closer to investigate, waving her hand left and right over her nose.

Mum comes out to see what the hold-up is. She tries to clap in the customer's face really loudly to get him to wake up, so we can kick him out and close the shop, but no dice.

'I don't have time for this. Call the police,' Mum commands.

In all the years we've been open, we've never ever called the police – not even when our windows were smashed in, or our bins were on fire. My parents believe that calling the police is pointless because calling for someone else to help is a sign of weakness that you're not able to handle the situation yourself. Normally, we're pretty hardened to dealing with resistant customers, but with this man we have no other option. We're desperate, even though we don't have confidence in the police taking our pleas seriously or them doing their job properly. This man won't budge and we don't want to touch him in case we're liable. Keen punches '999' on the phone and asks for the police to come and visit the premises urgently. He reports a drunken disturbance.

'At least half an hour?! Ugh. Fine. We'll wait.' Keen raises his voice and hangs up.

'When are they coming? I need to close,' Dad asks, and locks the front door so no more customers can get in.

We carry on with our deep-cleaning process and shut up shop while the man lies on the bench, snoring away. After what seems like an eternity (the police sure took their sweet time to arrive at the scene of the crime), they take one look at the man lying on our bench and laugh.

'*This* is the urgent disturbance?' they chuckle. Their tone implies that we're a nuisance to them and we shouldn't have bothered them over such a small, trivial thing.

'Right, come on then, mister. Up you get.' One of the policemen nudges the drunken man and lifts him into an upright position.

'You get his arms and I'll get his legs,' the other policeman tells him. Eventually, they have to carry him out and only then does the drunken man come round.

'Wha . . . What's happenin'? Where am I?' the man slurs. 'My chips! I want my chips!'

'I'm sorry, sir. You must vacate the premises now,' the police instruct, and take the drunken man home. The bobbies on the beat wave in the window to silently acknowledge that this is all just a misunderstanding. No harm done. This is the first time I've ever seen a police officer up close. I eye up their traditional white shirt and tie uniform, which looks smart, but feels intimidating. I have a weird sense of guilt and paranoia when I'm around them, even though I know we haven't done anything wrong and we did the right thing by calling them. However, I can't help but feel on edge the entire time they're here, and my palms are sweating buckets.

That night was a roller coaster. We didn't manage to finish until midnight because of the late-night drunken antics and our brush with the police. By the time we have deep-cleaned everything it's half past midnight and I have school the next morning. I can hear a rumbling sound of distant thunder – it's coming from my stomach.

'Sik siu yeh?'* Dad asks, sensing my hunger. He's surprisingly cheery after such a manic day. Even with the drunken customers causing chaos, there has been no frenzied outburst from him today. When Dad doesn't raise his voice and manages his emotions, everything ticks along smoothly, working alongside him and

---

* Siu yeh – Hong Kong's secret late-night meal, aka the best meal. It comes after dinner, and is similar to supper. Mealtime may start from about 9pm onwards until 4am. More comfort-based, less fussy Cantonese dishes.

service can actually be enjoyable. My brothers and I nod enthusiastically simultaneously. We're starving. At this point we haven't eaten for almost 12 hours. When you're busy working such a high-pressure job feeding others, you often forget to feed yourself. Your priorities shift, your wellbeing takes a backseat in place of serving others, and by the time you're finished working, it's at an ungodly hour and everything nearby is closed.

'Is everyone hungry?' Mum asks. 'I've pre-made a load of emergency wontons in the freezer that won't take long to cook. I'll go fish them out of the garage.' Without waiting for a reply, she's already walking off.

Dad puts his mop away by the lean-to and walks over to his usual spot by the wok station. Turning up the gas, a bright blue-orange flame shoots up, as if a rocket launch is about to go off in the kitchen. He scoops a couple of ladles of the master chicken stock from the vat and tops it up with water from the pot filler by the silver shelves. He ladles soy sauce and sesame oil, then turns around to grab the oyster sauce, smacking the base of the glass bottle to shake out the dark-brown viscous sauce. A delicate aroma of chicken, soy sauce, oyster sauce, sesame oil and white pepper swirls around the kitchen. Mum comes back with the frozen wontons and prepped pak choi, plopping them together in the simmering broth below. Dad bulks up wontons and adds five packets of chicken-flavoured Nissin Demae instant ramen from the cardboard box above where we store the polystyrene pots.

Within ten minutes, we're all sitting on plastic stools in the kitchen around the silver island kitchen table. A speedy quick fix for late-night supper. We slurp on bowls of plump wontons and inhale strings of noodles with the lights half-on. The frankenstein-like jumbo pork and prawn meat filling is generous, giving a bouncy, chewy mouthfeel with chunky bits of sweet prawn. The chicken soup is precise and clear, fizzing with a light sprinkling of MSG, topped with crunchy-soft blanched pak choi for health. We eat in silence apart from slurping noises, a sign of a good meal. Too focused on eating mindfully, absorbing the taste and inhaling the nourishing, hearty bowl in front of us.

'Ah!' We all sigh out happily in unison. Dad pats his stomach, satisfied, and Mum reaches for the green plastic toothpick holder on the table. She covers her mouth with one hand while trying to unlodge fragments of wonton with a wooden toothpick with the other. Eating these little wrinkly cerebral balls of joy reminds me that whatever happens in our lives or however things change around us, some things will always be the same. No matter the hour, there will always be time for food together as a family. Unwavering loyalty, and a lot of food. Our family love differently – not better, not worse, but definitely different.

Emergency Freezer Wontons

Find a day to batch-make a load of wontons to eat fresh or store in the freezer. Whenever we had some downtime, I loved spending rare quality time with my mother chatting and making wontons together. There's something about folding dumplings that requires your undivided attention and keeps your hands busy so that you're completely immersed in the task at hand – for me it's therapy. Having emergency freezer wontons for whenever the feeling hits, or for the days you simply cannot be bothered to cook properly, is always, always a good idea. I can guarantee your past self will thank your future self for batch-making a bunch. These plump boys are best served on their own as a soup starter or bulked up with egg noodles, choi and almost always doused in chilli oil. There's something so soothing and satisfying about biting into the dumplings. The silky wrapper that breaks apart and coats the roof of your mouth to reveal the bouncy, juicy filling inside. Heaven is a steaming bowl of wontons.

Makes: 30–32 wontons | **Prep time:** 30 mins | **Cook time:** 5–8 mins (until they float)

Ingredients:
For the wonton skin:
1 pack of fresh wonton wrappers (if frozen ensure it's defrosted completely before use)

For the filling:

300g pork shoulder, cut into mince (mouthfeel is
    better and more bouncy) or you can use minced
    pork

200g/20 king prawns, deveined and shelled. Save
    five prawns to be diced and the rest minced for
    texture

1 tsp white pepper

1 tsp salt

½ tsp sugar

½ tbsp cornflour

1 tbsp oyster sauce

1 tbsp sesame oil

1 tbsp Shaoxing wine

For the soup stock:

400ml chicken, vegetable or shrimp stock (or, use
    a stock cube or chicken bouillon powder mixed
    with water)

1 tsp chicken bouillon powder or MSG

2 slices of ginger

A dash of soy sauce

salt and white pepper

1 packet of instant ramen (optional)

2 stalks of pak choi or choi sum (optional)

1 spring onion (optional)

1 tsp chilli oil (optional)

Method:

1. Add all the filling ingredients together in a bowl and place a tea towel underneath the bowl to prevent the mixing bowl from moving.

2. Wet your hand first before handling the filling to prevent it from sticking to your hand as much. Mix by hand in a clockwise motion (it'll make for a bouncier wonton) or alternatively you can use a dough hook to mix on low speed. Gradually add a little splash of water at a time to emulsify to make it more 'dan gnar' (bouncy). Add a bit of water at a time until the texture is sticky and cohesive. Pick the filling up and throw it back into the mixing bowl to add air into the mixture. Repeat 4 or 5 times.

3. Use your finger to wet wonton skins on each corner. Add ½ tbsp of filling to the centre of the skin, to meet the opposite corner to create a triangle shape and press down around filling. Ensure all air is pressed out, gather the corners to the centre and press the skins together to seal, creating a money-bag shape. There are plenty of fancy ways to fold wontons, but this is the easiest, short-on-time, lazy version. There are no right or wrong ways to fold wontons.

4. If freezing, lay them on a tray without the wontons touching each other. Freeze for 3–4 hours, then, once half-frozen, transfer the wontons into a freezer bag or container. They keep for up to a month and you can cook them from frozen in 8–10 minutes.

5. If cooking fresh, cook the wontons in hot water on

a rolling simmer. Add a few wontons in at a time and cook for about 5–8 minutes or until the wontons float. Sieve and set aside.

6. For the soup base, cook your chosen stock. Add the chicken bouillon powder, or MSG, ginger, a dash of light soy sauce, a pinch of salt and white pepper. Add the wontons into the soup. Eat on its own or optionally serve with noodles, choi, sliced spring onions or chilli oil.

10

The Customer Is Wrong

I spend all my spare time online on the clunky family computer, practically running home from school to crank up the dodgy, screeching dial-up connection. I only have a small window to go online and chat to my classmates from the moment I walk through the door to when service starts at 5pm, and even then it's always interrupted by Mum accidentally kicking me off by using the landline. I'm in the full swing of my teenage years, my personality evolving and shedding the person I once was. At 16, I'm no longer the shy wallflower or the people-pleaser who seeks popularity. I ditch the dodgy brassy blonde highlights in my hair, the Kookaï bags and the big hoops, and become angry, bold and rebellious. I'm discovering the thriving Welsh alternative music scene, begging my parents to let me out to meet mates at gigs on weekends or end up sneaking out to go anyway. My taste in music has changed from happy pop-chart music to thrashy angst rock and pop punk bands like Alexisonfire, Fall Out Boy, Funeral For A

Friend, Glassjaw, Taking Back Sunday, My Chemical Romance, Panic! At the Disco and The Used. I have also started to come out of my shell and feel more myself. I dye my hair every colour of the rainbow, drink, smoke and shoplift for the thrill. I make every effort to be the opposite of gwaai. In Chinese culture, the word gwaai is the highest praise an adult can give to a child and it represents traditional Confucian family values. Filial piety is the central pillar in society and encompasses personal duties and family unity. Arguably, it's one of China's most important moral tenets and a social obligation for children to respect, honour and pay virtue to their parents, grandparents and elderly relatives. In addition to being a good, trustworthy individual who is loyal to her parents, a gwaai girl has to look and dress the part. She covers up with a conservative wardrobe, keeps her natural hair colour, and wears little makeup. I don't want to be the perfect model-minority Chinese girl wrapped in a traditional parent-pleasing package, whose purpose is to serve men and marry.

My wild dyed hair and over-the-top makeup is then a natural extension of that. I want to be fearless, reckless and tough, but most importantly independent. It's my way of pushing back, breaking free and carving my identity on my own terms. But, in doing so, I develop a hatred towards the older generation and I'm viewed by older family members and friends as a shameful and bad character. Mum and I constantly bicker, she calls me a kwaai mui and complains that I wear too-short skirts, too much makeup, and she compares my new look to a cheap prostitute. My extended family always police the way I dress and act too, gossiping about me that my parents haven't raised me right.

My social circle shifts as well. I've managed to make a new group of friends at school who actually want to stick around. My best friends, Tommy and Jamie, are twins and no one can tell them apart except me. There's also effortlessly cool Gelsei, who has the best fashion sense (even in school uniform); hilariously lanky Claire, who can make anyone laugh; little Gabby, who looks like a stunning pixie; smiley Annie, the eternal ray of sunshine; and virtuoso Tyla, who's in a band. We're all outcasts who don't fit into cliques, bonded over emo, indie and rock bands, and we all get on like a house on fire.

One day, a guy called Steffan asks to be my friend on Myspace. He goes to college in the next village over and is a few years older than me. We have mutual friends, but then again, in the Valleys it's not hard to have mutuals because everyone knows each other. He has shaggy blonde hair, wears shells around his neck, has a cute lopsided smile and I think he is the coolest thing on screen. We talk to each other every night for weeks about travelling the world, escaping Wales. We become each other's number one on our carefully curated top-eight friends and have each other's name in our screennames. He asks if I'd like to meet him and see a film on Saturday. The film he suggests is a superhero action-packed blockbuster, which isn't my cup of tea, but my parents have said yes and it's rare for me to be granted an evening outing when the shop is open, so I say I'd love to.

After that, we grow to become inseparable. We watch rock bands at local gigs and kiss each other at Starbucks until we get kicked out. We hang out in his room at his house playing Call of Duty. His family are, let's say, comfortable. He has an en-suite in his bedroom, the cutest Labrador called Sid, a conservatory, and we talk about their family holiday to Cuba over dinner in a proper dining room on an actual table and not on an old door or mahjong table. His world is everything mine is not and I can't relate, so I separate them because I'm so awkward and embarrassed about how we live at home. I never, ever invite him back to mine to meet my parents at the takeaway and I keep him at arm's length. In fact, I don't even tell my parents I'm dating someone, I can't. I know they'd go ballistic that their youngest is out there fooling around, and I'm not ready to have that conversation. It would also inevitably lead to having the whole extended Hui family and the South Wales Chinese community judge me for my choices. I can't handle the wrath of the disapproving aunties and uncles. It's a horrible game of Chinese whispers and I want no part of it.

It feels wrong and forbidden for me to date a boy, let alone a white guy. Being in a predominantly white town is one reason that I don't date many Asian men. Simply, there aren't many around to begin with, but I also don't want to be associated or paired with anyone who reminds me of my non-whiteness – not friends, and definitely not boyfriends. For two years I keep Steffan hidden from my family and, despite the relationship being one-sided, all I remember of that first year is belly-laughing and that feeling of complete happiness that only your first love gives you; soft and mushy like congee.

Steffan texts:

Ur always wrkin when am I seeing u next? I miss u? :(x

I stare at my Samsung mobile flip phone under the counter, struggling to find the words to reply to tell Steffan that I'm not sure when I'll be allowed to see him next. Trying to juggle both lives is exhausting, as is trying to escape the dysfunction at home instead of confronting it. As much as I try to deny it, I carry the weight of not having a good relationship with Mum and Dad, or my parents having a good relationship with each other, everywhere I go. I want to please my parents by continuing to help out in the shop because I feel obligated and I know I owe them that much. But I'm also worried about what Dad might do if left un-attended. On the flip side, I also want a chance to enjoy my youth and enjoy normal teenage things beyond these four walls. My overbearing and overprotective parents keep a tight leash on me, but let my brothers have free rein because they're boys. With every passing day, then, we butt heads over what I can and can't do, curfews, who I'm going out with and where. They have the idea that girls shouldn't stay out because it 'gives the wrong idea', or I'll get abducted as soon as I step foot outside the takeaway door.

I start texting Steffan back, but before I can finish and hit send, the short, stubby bald man who lives on our street and who I have just served walks back through the door. He comes bursting in holding an open container of yeung chow fried rice.

"Appenin? Is your Mum around? There's a nail in my food. Look at it, it's absolutely 'anging,' he says with a silent h, in an almost incomprehensibly thick Welsh accent.

He points to what he thinks is Mum's nail in his food with a look of pure disgust. Panic washes over me and my muscles tense. I have a sinking feeling that something bad is about to go down. I call Mum to the front and the first thing she notices is that the tray of rice is almost finished.

'Tsk. He's already eaten most of the rice and he's being cheeky by pushing his luck, trying to get a free meal out of us,' she tells me in Chinese.

'Hi, sir. What's the problem?' she asks in English.

'Look! Your fingernail is in my food!' He points angrily at the rice.

Mum picks it out to inspect it and holds it up to the light to get a better look.

'Pssht. As if it's my nail. I can tell from a mile off it's a prawn shell. The cheek of this joker,' she protests in Chinese to me.

'Sir, this is a prawn shell. It's definitely not my nail. I don't have long nails because I work in the kitchen.' She places her hands on the counter, showing off her hands as evidence. There are a few customers waiting by the counter and Mum gets everyone in the room involved to come together to review and weigh in.

'Nah, that's definitely a prawn shell. Look, it's pink,' a woman explains.

'Yeah, the way it's see-through and curves around, that's not a nail,' another male customer chimes in.

'No way, I ain't having that. That's a fucking nail and I want a refund,' he says, angrily.

'I can't give you a refund. You've eaten almost all of your food!' Mum argues back, refusing to back down, defending herself and our business.

The room falls silent. They're locked in an intense staring contest for what seems like an eternity and the clock on the wall ticks, slower than ever. Suddenly, without warning, the man smashes his rice on the floor and it explodes everywhere like confetti. Everyone jumps back, shocked, the other customers gasp and let out a small yelp, not expecting what just happened.

The bald man walks off shouting, 'Fuck you! You lying chinks. Go back home to China!'

He slams the door and everyone exchanges nervous glances, but no one says anything to check if we're okay or steps in to help de-escalate the situation. For the next couple of weeks we see the same man wandering around in the street, giving us dirty looks every time he walks past, and we keep finding specks of rice appearing out of nowhere in crevices despite multiple deep cleans. Some customers, no matter what happens, are determined to have a miserable time. Whether the food or service is great or not, they will always have something to complain about.

When my parents came to the UK it was a big milestone for them, but in reality, it was survival of the most adapted. Whoever does not assimilate in a different land is destined to be secluded and annihilated. Socially integrated and upwardly mobile, compliant workers are valued for their economic usefulness. Despite my mum's attempt to learn English and my parents obtaining driving licences and applying for British passports, the anxieties remained; we would always be perceived as outsiders and never be considered 'one of us'. When tricky customers walk through our door, into our home, telling us to go back 'home' or throwing the food we've served back in our faces, it's a reminder that we aren't welcome and shows how easily our voices, even at their most unified, can be ignored. We're on little more than probation.

That's not to say that all our customers are difficult. It's always a small percentage that kicks up a fuss or causes trouble; the majority of customers who walk through our door are wonderful and loyal. There's Melissa, a lanky blonde lady who always orders chicken fried rice with a barbecue sauce. (She even did a couple of shifts behind the counter to help out in the early days and taught me how to sing the Welsh national anthem properly.)

There's also single dad Steve, who comes in every day with his seven-year-old daughter. A large chicken curry for himself and chicken balls with sweet-and-sour sauce for her. She's always fascinated by how chicken balls are made, so we invited them into the kitchen once when it wasn't busy, so she could see the cooking process. Some regulars have been coming to us for years and those who have moved further afield to neighbouring villages miles away still come back to visit to order from us once or twice a week. People give us Christmas cards, buy us gifts, involve us in charity events and even throw us the odd street-party invite. While it has its flaws, Beddau is a close-knit, mostly friendly community and we've come a long way since my parents first opened in the 1980s, when they were met by harsh social conditions and an eat-or-be-eaten world. They were thought of as heathens, foreign and dangerous, but over the years customers have softened their stance on us and now welcome us into their circles.

I'm flying solo to help Mum with the prep work making prawn toast on Saturday. I want to get all the work out the way early so I can see Steffan later. My brothers are busy this weekend with university work and can't come back to help. Way to dodge a bullet. Working with prawns is the worst, I think. Despite the gross nature of handling prawns, I always find it mesmerising to watch Mum chop prawns with two meat cleavers, one in each hand, mincing them like a pro, as if she was going all out on a drum solo. She's breaking down prawns from chunks to a smooth pinky paste. Mum transfers the paste into a large metal mixing bowl, adds egg white and cornflour to bind, along with a variety of spices and various glass-bottle concoctions. She holds the bowl with her left hand and picks up the paste with the other hand to throw it back into the bowl with such force that the silver worktop island vibrates. She is throwing her anger, throwing her frustrations and throwing her love into the bowl. She's breathing daan ngaa* bounceability into the paste and that's what gives our prawn toast a signature bite. I slather the minced-prawn mixture on the thick white bread with a knife and press the bread firmly into a massive tray of white sesame seeds. The dunking is the fun part because it feels like an art project, stamping things and making a masterpiece. I lift and check the toast to ensure the entire surface is covered in seeds, then carefully put the pieces of prawn toasts back in the bread bag they came in. One down, fifty more to go.

As he gets older, Dad is losing his appetite for the business. He starts waking up later and later, and he's becoming increasingly more agitated than before. The littlest things trigger his temper, as if he's looking to scold and fight anyone who gets on the wrong side of him. When he finally emerges downstairs to help with the prep work around midday, Mum bites her tongue

---

* Daan ngaa – al dente, bouncy and firm when bitten. The literal Cantonese translation means 'it's so springy it bounces off teeth'.

and doesn't say anything about his tardiness or ask how much money he gambled away last night. She knows it would ignite an explosion of arguments and it just isn't worth it before service, because it would throw the rest of the day and evening off balance.

I lie to Mum about where I'm going and say I'm heading to Lauren's house (even though it's been years since we last hung out together) because she's one of the few friends of mine who Mum actually knows. I'm now hanging out in Steffan's room instead and I check my mobile to ensure I'm back for work in time. The screen reads: SAT 29 AUG 4:32pm.

'Put your phone away. You've been checking your phone every five minutes. I want to spend time with you,' he says.

'Sorry. It's bank holiday weekend and I know it's going to be busy. I don't want to be late,' I say, folding my phone down.

'Can't you get someone to cover you tonight, pleaaase? We've barely spent any time together.' He pleads with me and pulls me closer to him, trying to persuade me.

'I'm sorry, I wish I could. My parents need me tonight,' I say.

'*I* need you. I never see you, you're always working,' he says sadly, like a puppy dog.

'Well, if you passed your test and could drive, maybe I'd be able to see you for more than two measly hours instead of spending most of my time on the stupid bus,' I snap, instantly regretting my words as soon as they leave my mouth.

'Well, why can't *you* learn to drive, you're old enough now!' he argues, looking taken aback.

Technically, he's right. I've finally turned 17. I've got my provisional licence and I'm learning to drive, I just haven't gotten round to passing yet. Neither of us have a car or a licence, so we're limited when it comes to going to see each other. We have to rely on the useless public transport system, his parents, or my brothers to drive us around. I cross my arms and sulk. I flip open my phone: SAT 29 AUG 4:43pm.

'I have to go. Can your Dad drop me off? I'm going to be late for work,' I say miserably.

Steffan is right. I barely see him. I make promises that I will see him, but I break those promises because I can't get the time off or some emergency has come up at the takeaway that requires me. I become erratic, demanding and hostile. Eventually he learns that no matter what I want, I'll never be able to keep those promises as long as my situation at the takeaway remains the same. So I stop making promises, feeling frustrated by my situation of having to work endlessly, being the parent to my parents, and dealing with the pressure of doing well at school to get good grades in order to go to university like both my brothers have done. I vent all my anger, every fearful frustration and raging resentment I've ever felt, towards Dad, Mum or Steffan, a loving boyfriend who only ever wants to help me.

The last remnants of summer cling on. The hot and sticky weather makes everyone moody and unproductive. Work is an absolute car crash. It's one of those nights where everything is going horribly. There are so many no-shows tonight. Customers phoned in beforehand but didn't bother to turn up. Dewi tries to deliver food but there's no answer. Everything that we've cooked ready for collection is growing cold on the shelves and we're desperately trying to keep them warm for people who will never arrive. The prawn toast someone's ordered is left on the sidelines soaking up the oil, getting saturated and heavy with every minute it goes uncollected.

'You might as well eat it, mui. It's only going to go to waste,' Mum suggests.

I can see that the oil has already seeped through, which makes the thick white bread greasy, but I don't mind because I'm starving. The prawn toast is still crispy, a golden-brown block with a glossy oil-sheen coating. I crunch down and from the first bite I can taste the wonderful nuttiness from the sesame seeds, followed by a punch of succulent prawns. The fishy smell is gone and replaced with delicate, sweet, tender meat. People always have the misconception that because we own a takeaway we eat well but, in reality, we often eat whatever leftover scraps no one wants or find ways to use the unused ingredients to prevent food waste.

'Cecilia, please!' Mum shouts from the kitchen.

I emerge from the counter to fetch the order in the kitchen to give Cecilia a helping hand.

'Where is Cecilia? She's so lazy! Why are you doing most of the leg work for her? What am I paying her for!' Dad shouts in Chinese at me.

'What was that?' Cecilia asks, as she hobbles behind me down the hallway without us realising.

Dad grumbles, swears under his breath and gives her a stinking side-eye. I pass the order to Cecilia and she disappears to the front.

'Don't talk to Cecilia like that,' Mum says, her voice raised.

Soon they're both shouting. Dad tries to berate her for sticking up for Cecilia over him, to subdue her with a show of anger, the way he always has, but this only makes her more stubborn. Cecilia walks back into the kitchen; she can hear the shouting rising from the back.

'I don't understand what you're saying, but I can tell it's something not very nice about me,' Cecilia says, angrily.

Dad has an initial look of confusion because he doesn't understand what she's saying to him, but this only sets him off even more. I've never seen him shout like this to someone who isn't Mum, Keen, Jacky or me. He waves his arms at her, shooing her away.

Cecilia apologises to me before she starts to gather her things and walks out mid-service in a huff, leaving me to man the counter on my own and trying to keep a lid on what is about to explode in the kitchen. Dad keeps ranting and raving about Cecilia all night, even after she's long gone, until his voice dies down to a low, constant grumble at the end of service. No one says a word, we just carry on ploughing through the rest of the hectic evening with one man down.

The next day Mum calls Cecilia to apologise on Dad's behalf, begging her to not quit because it's impossible to find good staff these days and return to work because we can't handle service on our own without her.

'Please, Cecilia. We need you. Gary says he's sorry,' Mum pleads on the phone.

'Fine, but I'm only doing it for you, Jin. I'll see you tonight,' Cecilia replies, and hangs up.

The air is bitter and confrontational. Daggers and worried glances are exchanged as everyone nervously looks across the room at each other, like a Mexican standoff. Tonight's service whizzes by, though, without any troubles. So far, so good. No shouting, no arguments. At the end of the night Dad tots up the night's earnings but they don't add up. Something is off. He counts again and they still don't match up. Once more to be triply sure. Forty quid is missing from the till.

'Are you sure?' Mum asks.

'Of course, I'm sure. I counted three times already,' Dad says, furrowing his brow, growing increasingly annoyed.

He has his reading glasses on and they're falling off his nose. Dad is deep in concentration, surrounded by small piles of money and ticket orders on the silver worktop island. He shuffles notes in his hands and complains.

'I'm sure you just counted wrong. Count again,' Mum says.

'I've already counted a million times, woman!' Dad says, shooting her a dirty look.

'Are you one hundred per cent sure it's her?' Mum questions.

'Well, who else could it be?! No one else was on the front counter,' Dad yells.

Cecilia is hanging around by the till, waiting to be paid for tonight's shift, oblivious that my parents are talking about her. The lights are half turned off and the front door is locked to prevent more customers from coming in.

Dad pays her for tonight's shift, but also confronts her and accuses her of stealing money from the tills. However, he can't articulate what he wants to say in English. What comes out instead is broken caveman-esque speak. 'You, no money till. Forty pounds. Gone. You take,' he shouts.

'You think I took money from the till?!' Cecilia raises her voice and looks bewildered.

Dad doesn't understand and roars obscenities back in Chinese. After a night of pleasantries and no arguments, the two of them explode and are at each other's throats. Neither refuses to apologise or back down.

'This is the last straw, Jin, I'm too old for this and I can't work when Gary's here. Thank you for everything over the years,' Cecilia huffs, walking out the door.

Mum tries to call the day after to apologise and

reconcile, asking her to please reconsider, but she isn't having any of it. No one knows what really happened, whether Cecilia did take the money or didn't take the money or if we miscounted, but our fractured friendship quietly falls to the wayside, trailing off into ambiguity. After 18 years of service Cecilia is gone. Her daughter Delyth carries on helping out over her notice period out of courtesy, but shortly after leaves too. It's weird not having them around. They have watched me and my brothers grow up behind the counter and been there for birthdays and Christmases. Things escalated so quickly to the point where there was no way of resolving everything, and suddenly not having them around felt disorientating and it hurt.

What was going on behind closed doors with my parents was this deep, dark secret that I hoped nobody would find out about, not my extended family members and especially not Steffan. I desperately wanted to hide the kind of person I was at home, at the takeaway – impatient, selfish, and a stick of dynamite waiting to go off – but it was starting to permeate into other parts of my life. I became paranoid that I was shouting all the time like my parents, trying to speak above the deafening sounds of the kitchen. I was anxious about whether I smelled like a deep-fat fryer no matter how much I showered. I heard tickets being stubbed in my sleep, the sounds of the fryer sizzling my brain and dreams haunted by images of a never-ending, horrendous service. Each scorching-hot curry sauce splatter scarring my skin, branding me to never forget that this is who I am, this is what made you and this is who you'll always be.

I put on nice clothes and makeup to meet Steffan in Cardiff, trying to hide who I am. I get the bus into town, leaving myself behind in Beddau and pretending to be someone else hanging out by the fountains in the park opposite the city's museum. We're lying on the grass, my head resting on his stomach as we stare up at the azure-blue skies together, trying to picture faces and objects in the fluffy white cotton-wool clouds. We're daydreaming and talking about travel. His parents have booked an upcoming holiday to Japan.

'Oh, cool, how long are they going for?' I ask.

'Two weeks. Yeah, they've been everywhere in Asia. Hong Kong. Cambodia. Thailand. Vietnam. They're more Asian than you!' He laughs.

I cackle loudly to overcompensate my awkwardness. Secretly those words sting and irk me. *How could they be more Asian than me when they are white?* It's like a game of Pokémon, who can collect all the countries? My culture feels like it's his family's playground and here I am afraid of being judged for my Asianness and failing to earn acceptance as a real Brit while others deem themselves as 'basically Asian' for being well travelled. I feel frustrated at the impossible process of pouring myself into another culture while holding on to a sense of self. I want this relationship to prove my Asian bona fides while seeking acceptance within white culture, but I don't think

I ever see that in Steffan. I don't fit into his world, and he doesn't fit in with mine. We're too different. For the most part, I feel unwanted by my country and unwanted by my family. No matter how hard I try to escape it, I can never outrun my exotic status and I don't think he can ever understand.

I'm too busy daydreaming and lose track of time. Shit, it's already 5:15pm and I'm still in Cardiff. I rush to the bus to try to make it for opening time like my life depends on it.

'It's five forty-five! You're late! The shop's already open. Where have you been?' Dad yells from the kitchen without turning around to see, as he hears the wooden counter door creak open.

'Um . . . Sorry, the bus was late!' I shout back, my voice echoing in the empty waiting room as I drop my bag by the counter.

Mum comes out to the front and immediately starts shouting her head off, bombarding me with questions. 'Where have you been? Who were you with? A boy? Why are you late? Have you been drinking?'

'NO!' I argue back.

'Well, where have you been? I tried calling you but no answer. There's been lots of phone orders already that I had to answer,' she presses.

'LEAVE ME ALONE!' I scream in her face, fed up with the interrogation as soon as I walked through the door.

'Haiya, I work so hard for you. How did I raise such

a troublesome and disobedient daughter? Are you serious? I'd rather give birth to a piece of char siu than you,' Mum bellows, matching my volume.

I hang my head in shame and feel a hot prick at the back of my eyes. I bite my words and surrender to her yelling because I'm fed up and don't want to butt heads any more. Something has to give. I can't keep sneaking around pretending that things are okay when they aren't. I've had enough. I know Steffan loves me and has served me with his whole heart, but I can't do the same for him. Only I can help myself. I have no choice. To break up, or to tell him everything that's going on in my life: the takeaway, my parents and all. To let him in, merge the two worlds together so he can accept me for who I am. So, I text him saying that we need to talk and meet up.

It's the last weekend before terms starts again and I'm about to start upper sixth form. The weather has turned in the last couple of weeks from a scorching-hot heatwave to a thick blanket of grey clouds. We've arranged to meet at Starbucks in our local shopping centre that's equal distance. We order coffee and sit there awkwardly in silence. I've barely seen him in the last month and he knows something is up, a dark looming cloud over us that something bad is about to happen. I stare at my coffee getting cold and people-watch all the couples and friends sinking back into the comfortable leather sofas that cocoon you. It's crazy to think that at the beginning of our relationship we were in the same spot, getting dirty looks for being madly in love with each other.

Now, I'm not even sure what we are because it all feels alien and foreign. I've practised what I would say to him at this moment for weeks, but I have stage fright. I look at my feet and can't say anything. He can see that I'm struggling and takes my hand.

'Just say it,' he says bluntly, breaking the silence.

'I . . . think . . . we should . . . break up. I'd still like to be . . . friends,' I say, in between sobs. Desperately gulping air. My face is soaked.

He immediately lets go of my hand. Without another word he gets up and leaves. I can still feel his hand slipping away from mine long after he's left. The touch of his skin on mine for the last time. I sit there, hugging my knees, rocking back and forth, crying. In hindsight, being the dumper should feel easier because I've had time to think and evaluate things prior to breaking up, but I still feel crushed. In my heart I know we just aren't right for each other. I have let our relationship wither and die like a neglected under-watered plant. Did I just make the most stupid mistake of my life? It hurts a lot to leave him, but I know that I'll end up hurting him if we stay together any longer. I love him, but I can never be enough for him, or be that person he wants me to be. Maybe I don't love myself enough to love another human being. Maybe I don't love him enough, or maybe love by itself is not enough in the first place. I'm ashamed that I never gave him a chance to understand my situation by explaining things to him. How the takeaway has a hold on me.

Perhaps Steffan was my stepping-stone to be a little reckless, to break free from the narrow definitions that frame Asianness in today's multicultural Britain. He made me feel older than 17, but now I feel like a childish, cold-hearted arsehole who's just ripped someone's heart out and stepped on it. I don't realise how long I've been sitting in the same position, but a barista comes by and hands me a serviette to wipe away the tears.

'Ma'am, are you okay? I'm sorry to ask, but if you're not going to order anything else you'll have to leave, we're short on chairs,' he says, gesturing to another couple who are waiting on the sidelines ready to swoop in to sit in my seat.

I wipe my tears on my sleeve, silently stand up, embarrassed at my public display, and walk away.

Prawn Toast

I'm going to be honest. I hate deep-frying in a home kitchen because it is a massive pain in the arse, what with the smoke that accidentally sets off the fire alarm and the dilemma of what to do with the leftover oil after frying. I recommend cooking in a small sauté pan or a deep frying pan to ensure the toast has room to move but is also able to be submerged and doesn't use too much oil. Or, for a healthier alternative you can pan-fry prawn toast or cook them in an air-fryer. One thing Dad taught me is that when it comes to deep-frying, never fear it, because the scalding-hot oil smells fear; you have to be confident, work quickly and own it. Fried foods like prawn toast were often forbidden in my household due to its unhealthy yeet hay nature, but we always found sneaky ways to eat fried things when my parents weren't looking. Crispy, light and addictive, sesame prawn toast is a Chinese takeaway classic and every place has their own variations. Ours? A slab of white bread that's as thick as a brick with the same ratio of generous prawn filling.

Makes: 3 prawn toasts (12 triangles) |
Prep time: 5–10 mins | **Cook time:** 2–3 mins (or until golden brown)

Ingredients:
For the prawn spread:

8 king prawns, deshelled and deveined
¼ tsp salt
¼ tsp white sugar
¼ tsp white pepper
1 tsp sesame oil
½ tsp corn flour
A splash of water for consistency (keep adding
    slowly until right consistency)

For the topping/toast:
1 egg, beaten
3 slices of thick white bread (I like to use Braces
    XX thick or Doorstep)
White sesame seeds
Vegetable oil, for frying

Method:
1. Beat the egg in a small bowl and set aside.
2. Blend all the prawn spread ingredients in a blender until a smooth spreadable paste. You're after a similar consistency to butter.
3. Preheat a sauté pan or deep frying pan of vegetable oil until boiling hot. Ensure the oil is hot and bubbling (check by sticking chopsticks in – if bubbles form it's hot enough). If it's not hot enough it'll make the toast greasy and heavy.
4. Spread the prawn mixture on the bread and brush beaten egg on top.

5. Pour sesame seeds and spread a flat surface out on a plate. Dip the bread on the seeds to ensure the toast is covered; if there are some bald patches, dip again to cover with more seeds.

6. Carefully place bread in the oil, seed-side down, and use chopsticks to push the bread to submerge in the oil for even cooking. Or, you can freeze before frying to batch-make and preserve for another time. Place parchment paper in between slices to separate and ensure they are covered. You can fry from frozen, but allow slightly more time, 4–6 minutes, to ensure it's cooked all the way through and can keep for up to a month.

7. Cook until golden brown for 2–3 minutes. Keep an eye on the frying because prawns cook really quickly.

8. Cut into triangles and serve with salad and a variety of sauces. My favourites are sweet and sour, Thai sweet chilli or salad cream.

9. If you have leftover oil don't waste it or pour it down the sink. Let the oil cool, line a fine-mesh sieve with a cheesecloth over a container and strain the oil. You'll notice debris at the bottom of the oil, discard that and keep the extracted oil in a cool, dark place for reuse. There's no rules on how many times you can reuse oil, but it breaks down the more you use it and will still have hints of flavours of what it's previously cooked, so keep that in mind.

II

Competition Time

They say there is a soulmate out there for everyone. When you meet the love of your life it's sort of a lightbulb moment, you just *know*. I never thought I'd meet mine on my 18th birthday at a trash, alternative nightclub in Cardiff. A three-storey live-music venue, I was packed in a basement room full of sweaty bodies dancing to The Smiths and chanting indie bangers while drinking one-pound bottles of VK Blue.

I'm finally old enough to legally buy my own alcohol instead of using friends' IDs and sneakily asking my brothers to buy me beer for house parties. Exams are coming to a close and it's the last summer before we all go our separate ways, so we have to make sure it counts. Gelsei is dating Matt, who she met on Myspace, and that's where I met Matt's best friend, Tom. He's a year older than me and lives in the next village over. He has mousy-brown floppy hair, face plastered with adorable freckles and a goofy grin. I'm not exactly sure what my 'type' is, considering that I've only ever had one serious boyfriend before, but Tom brings me a fake plastic rose from a lady selling them in the street as a joke and I drunkenly kiss him back. Soon, we fall madly in love and become best friends. He makes me laugh like no one else I've ever met and being with him is like being in a warm bath. We double-date all throughout the summer before we're thrust into a long-distance relationship as we go to university. I stay local in Cardiff and Tom goes to Wrexham, three hours north near the Wales–England border. Just as we're starting our budding romance, the extra distance pulls us apart and tests our love for each other, but we're determined to make it work and call each other and Skype every night.

My parents drop me off to start my new life in the city. I don't take much with me except for new bedding, a red, white and blue laundry bag full of clothes and a dozen of Mum's premade dumplings in silver aluminium containers, enough to last me for the month. I've come to Cardiff at the University of Glamorgan to study journalism so that one day I can be an editor of a glossy fashion magazine, interviewing interesting people and creating the spreads I once had plastered all over my walls. Mum and Dad inspect my student room and the bathroom. We stand awkwardly for a moment.

'Wah, £87 a week for this shoebox? So expensive, lah. What a waste of money. You should've just lived at home. Only down the road,' Dad complains.

'Oh, be quiet. It's nice. Hope you settle in okay. Give

us a call if you need anything, we'll see you this week-end,' Mum says.

We wave each other off, then they drive away. I'm only half an hour away. Far enough to enjoy independence but still on a tight leash to be at my parents' beck and call for helping out on weekends. The majority of the takeaway responsibilities now fall on my shoulders, in-cluding keeping tabs on important bills, taxes and being on standby for any translation duties, as my brothers are about to fly the nest for good. Jacky is 21 and finishing his Master's in Cardiff; soon, he'll be off to Imperial College in London to study for his PhD. And Keen has scored his dream job designing video games for a com-pany in Manchester at 22. The Hui siblings are going their separate ways and it terrifies me not to have my brothers to fall back on in case anything were to happen.

My university is located on a main road in the city centre, next to the prison. It's a brand-new state-of-the-art building especially for those studying in creative and cultural industries, a modern glass building that juts out from the Victorian and Edwardian city skyline. My student halls are directly opposite the campus. Ideal for rolling into lectures five minutes before they start. My flat is on the 19th floor, with an open-plan kitchen, living room and five en-suite bedrooms. I had originally missed the deadline to apply for student accommodation because I'd been working late at the takeaway and my scattered, unorganised brain forgot. They were full up, but due to last-minute drop-outs I managed to squeeze into a spare room with third-year journalism students.

I walk into the kitchen to claim my shelf in the fridge and find my new roommates, Emily, Seren and Nia, decorating the shared living-room space with pink balloons, pink glittery banners and metallic pink streamers. They're getting ready to host pre-drinks for Nia's 21st pink-themed birthday. I run away and hide in my room. I'm sure they're nice enough people, but in the end we never really click. We mainly keep ourselves to ourselves because, in my mind, I feel there is too big an age gap. We are at different stages in life, like two passing ships. I am an outsider infiltrating on their turf and I don't want to intrude.

On my first night away from home I'm lying on my single bed looking up at the white ceiling in my room. I finally have my own space, privacy and no snoring mother beside me. It feels weird to have the freedom and independence I've craved for so long but, now that I have it, I'm not sure I want it. University is such a ruthless introduction to adulthood and it feels so finite. A chance to pave a way for myself; picking a career, deciding the person I want to be and finding friends I want to surround myself with, all while juggling rent, bills, and studying. Trying to forge a new life for myself for a better future can mean the past can quietly bleed in.

I can hear Nia having an afterparty in her room and she's brought back a massive crowd of randoms from their night out next door through the paper-thin walls; Seren on the other side is blasting bad dance music to drown out the noises. I miss home. I miss the takeaway. I stay up all night crying, as my anxieties eat away the insides of my brain. I'm starved of sleep by the time morning rolls around for my first full day of introductions, meeting lecturers and fellow classmates. I'm in a class of 30 students who are roughly around the same age as me, and the majority are Welsh and white. I'm so nervous that I can't summon the courage to speak to anyone. I try to blend into the background and stay silent throughout the day. I walk home to my halls thinking that I've made a huge mistake; maybe I should've stuck to what I know at the takeaway.

Luckily, the majority of my friends from school are still close by, studying the same art foundation diploma course in Treforest that Keen did. Tommy, Jamie, Claire and Gelsei coax me out for freshers' week and welcome me into university life to make me feel less alone. We go to an 80s nightclub in town, drink and dance our troubles away, celebrating my first night of independence on a Monday evening. The next morning, I feel like I've been hit by a car. I awake to a screeching alarm clock on my phone and four bodies sleeping in foetal positions strewn across my blue-carpeted floor. I tiptoe over them to the bathroom to splash my face with water to wash away last night's hazy drunken antics and catch a glimpse of myself in the mirror. *I look awful.* No time to brush my hair, I grab whatever clean item of clothing lying on the floor I can find and run to my second course induction.

My classmates are waiting in the foyer outside the lecture hall, already in their circle of friends. The morning sun pours in warmly through the high wall of windows, its rays blinding me and searing my aching head. Cliques are already forming and I'm struggling to make friends; on the outside looking in again. It feels like school's repeating itself, as I stand around awkwardly on my own like a lemon. My heart picks up speed and my head throbs, unsure if this is a panic attack from me overthinking that I'm going to be Billy No-Mates for the next three years or if I'm just suffering from last night's effects and worried that others can smell the booze radiating off me like cartoon squiggly lines. I spot two girls on their own in my eye line who are about the same height as me: a brunette freckled girl wearing a floral dress and a curly ginger-haired girl sporting a cosy grey jumper with leggings. They're already in mid-conversation and my mind goes into overdrive, thinking that I'm being rude for going to intrude, but I summon whatever liquid courage I have left inside of me, coax myself out of my hermithood and approach them.

'Hiya! Are you both in this class? I'm Angela, what's your name?' I ask, my voice quivering.

'Alright, I'm Hannah!' the ginger girl says, with a thick Welsh accent.

'Hiya, I'm Therese. Ah yeah, I recognise you from yesterday! Wait, you have a Welsh accent? Where are you from?' the other girl says, surprised.

'Ahah, yeah. I was born in Wales. I'm from the Valleys.'

I laugh nervously, shuffling my feet and not keeping eye contact. I can feel myself getting flushed and my confidence is disintegrating from the loaded ambiguous question. I know it is a simple, genuine question and they want to get to know me better, but I feel a pang of tiny annoyance every time someone asks where I'm from. The cumulative effect of these interactions adds up to a significant burden. My internal organs collapse into a rich mulch that coats my bowels and throat, my face falling, giving a gormless impression and perhaps also a bit on fire. I can see the cogs turning in their heads and the confused looks on their faces. How can a person like me, a descendant of Asian immigrants with Asian features, be from Wales? So, after what seems like the longest pause from my initial introduction, I blurt out and laugh, 'My parents are from Hong Kong and China, we own a Chinese takeaway and we sell egg fried rice for a living.'

'Oh, that's so cool!' they both echo. 'What was it like? How long have you owned the place for?'

'I'd love to visit some time,' Hannah says with a grin. 'I'm from Brynna and I grew up on a farm.'

I'm so conditioned into being confronted by questions that ask where I'm from geographically that I often pre-empt it without prompting because I'm defensive and uncertain of the real purpose behind this question. I know their questions are meant to be caring and not probing, but still, I joke so they can't make fun of me. The Chinese takeaway kid. It sort of becomes my

271

identity and makes me look at myself as the Chinese girl and nothing else, because that's what I think everyone else is thinking too. I'm so used to fighting off micro-aggressions and years of customers addressing me as a foreigner that I don't quite know what to do when I'm met with admiration and curiosity from these two girls. The three of us sit together for every lecture. I like them because the colour of my skin isn't a contentious issue, and they don't laugh at our main source of income or see it as less worthy. They accept me for who I am, rather than what I look like or sound like. They care about both takeaway Angela, *and* just Angela. Therese invites me to her house party this Saturday, but I'm working and tell them I'll try my best to make it when my shift finishes, even though I know this is another empty promise I can't keep.

We have a new counter assistant, Lowri, to help out every day of the week. She's a bubbly, young single mother who always has her blonde hair slicked back into a low ponytail. I start to relinquish a lot of responsibilities to her and take her under my wing, teaching her to memorise the takeaway dish numbers from the menu, how to log fridge temperature recordings for the hygiene inspectors and how to use the till. She's a natural. My parents adore her because she's hardworking and they manage to get by despite the language barrier, and I'm so grateful to have an extra set of hands I can rely on. Since I started university, I've started working part-time on weekends, but business in the shop has been slow and on a steady decrease. As I sit on the counter with Lowri, frantically trying to write a media-law essay that is due on Monday, tonight feels scarily quiet. We've been open for two hours and only a handful of customers have walked through the door. It might've been a drizzly and blustery autumn, but it's more than bad weather keeping the customers away. It's obvious we're losing customers.

Over the past two decades, we've been relatively lucky. Blessed with a great location and a loyal customer base that chooses to eat with us, our business hasn't done too badly. Our biggest issue, however, is that more Chinese takeaways are opening up nearby and the competition is on, which only makes Dad moodier. He moans but refuses to change or do anything about it. Chinese people don't hide their ambition to make money, they thrive on it, and the concept of money is so ingrained in our culture, it's not just a simple affection for it, it's an obsession. Lives revolve around how much you earn and how much you can spend. Money not only defines your social standing, but it's also your identity. When other Chinese families see an opportunity for good business to try to muscle in on our turf it becomes a game of cat and mouse. They lower their prices, we lower our prices. We introduce free prawn crackers, they introduce free cans of cokes. They cater to weddings, we don't bother. Usually, Chinese takeaways are kept to one per village to avoid direct competition, but it's inevitable that there's overlap. Rather than helping each other out or offering support, it's common for Chinese people to stick to what they know and focus on themselves.

'At this rate, we're going to go out of business,' Mum sighs, staring at the security-camera footage on the small TV from the kitchen, waiting patiently for customers.

'Well, if it ain't broke, don't fix it. We'll be fine, people will come,' Dad insists while sitting on a stool next to her, reading the sports section of a Chinese newspaper.

'Well, we have to do *something*. We're just pouring money down the drain trying to keep the lights on,' Mum argues.

This triggers another explosive argument. Dad takes it as a personal attack on how he's running things and how they aren't working. Mum has always been the business-savvy one and she thinks of creative ideas to help boost business, to try to set ourselves apart from the new competing businesses nearby. She's come up with new menu items, meal deals, changed prices due to inflation of supplies, taken items off that aren't as popular, and introduced a new loyalty-card scheme to attract more customers and ensure they'll keep coming back. For every £20 spent, customers get an inky Lucky Star stamp – our own takeaway seal specially engraved and personalised in Hong Kong. Collect three and customers can get a bag of prawn crackers for free. Collect five and they'll get ten pounds off.

'Haiya, too annoying,' Dad complains. Every time Mum tries something new, he shoots her down or finds something to protest about. He's risk-averse (surprising, considering he's always taking a chance at casinos) and doesn't want to wrap his head around the stamp scheme. But a month into the new vouchers and there's a spike in customers. Mum's idea and strategy for improving business is working and we haven't been this busy in months. Old and new customers flood in to make the most of the offer and try out new dishes. But with only two of them in the kitchen, me part-time, Lowri on the front and Dewi on weekend deliveries, we're now struggling to keep up with the influx of hungry people with limited staff.

The paper spike reaches the top with ticket orders. We're determined to make it work; to push and fight for survival. But my body aches in ways I didn't know could ache and my brain is running on 5 per cent battery. After my shift, when the takeaway has closed, Mum drops me off late at night along with another supply of dumplings in silver containers and an extra helping of leftover roast duck from the shop, in case I get hungry. I glance at my mobile: 11:45pm. My hair is slicked with chip grease and I reek of curry sauce fumes, no time for a shower. If I head straight downstairs to Therese's party I can still make it for a drink or two. Mum's inspecting my room, complaining how messy I am with little piles of clothes everywhere, and eyeing up my posters and pictures of friends on the wall. She notices the picture of me with Tom.

'Who's this?' she asks, and points.

'No one,' I reply, and nervously look at my feet because I'm a terrible liar.

'Is this your boyfriend?!' she shrieks, and pulls the photo off the wall to scan his face properly. 'How long have you been going out with him?'

'A year,' I mumble, still looking at my feet, refusing to make eye contact.

'A YEAR! You've had a boyfriend for a year without telling me!' she shouts, and lets the photo drop to the floor. She gathers her things, stomps down the stairs and slams the door shut behind her without saying goodbye.

She doesn't speak to me for the rest of the week, which is the longest I've ever gone without talking to her. This is exactly how I imagined her finding out about my boyfriend and this is precisely why I don't want my parents involved in my love life. Mum has the tendency to overreact and jump to conclusions before I've even had a chance to explain myself.

I don't go out to the party. I stay awake all night worrying I won't hear my alarm in the morning and I keep mentally going over and over what I should've done or said differently to Mum. I think about all the times I stayed at my cousins' houses in neighbouring villages, roughly half an hour's drive away from our takeaway, when I was young. My cousins, brothers and I would help out at my aunties and uncles' takeaways in the summer holidays when we weren't in Hong Kong. We'd mess about playing video games, spending all our pocket money on pick 'n' mix in the corner shops, and eating gravy and chips for breakfast. I cried and cried every single night because I was homesick. The ugly type of crying where your snot and tears merge into one and a whining that sounds like a high-pitched cat wailing. I missed Mum and I missed her smell. It felt weird and alien, sleeping in a bed that wasn't mine and in the same room with my Auntie Sarah and Uncle George. I used to follow Mum around everywhere, like I was her little chick. It got so bad once that my Auntie Sarah had to call my mother to tell her I was being unbearable and annoying everyone around me.

'Come take her home, she keeps calling for you and I'm fed up with her crying,' Auntie Sarah said.

'It's okay, mui, I'm here. We'll see each other soon in a couple of weeks,' Mum reassured me. Her calming voice always puts me at ease. I used to be inseparable from her and couldn't bear to be apart from her. Now, I feel a million miles apart from her and like I hardly know her. How did we come to this?

I Skype Tom on Sunday night and he can tell something is on my mind, but I feel like I can't share with him what's wrong or tell him what's bothering me because I feel like he wouldn't understand. Loneliness engulfs me. The next day, on my way to campus, I push myself to walk through bracingly cold air, repeating phrases in my head until they melt into limericks, a feeling of vastness consuming me for the rest of the week. Classes are a blur and none of what my lecturers are teaching us is registering in my head; all I can think about is Mum.

When the weekend rolls around, I get the bus home to go back to the takeaway to help out. The horror of the South Wales bus network is on full display as drivers decide to not turn up and routes are cancelled. What should've been a speedy half-hour journey took twice as long, winding through the peaks and troughs of the Valleys. When I finally arrive, I quietly let myself in through the front door and past the counter. I find Mum lying horizontal in the living room, having dozed off while watching her TVB dramas in the background on a low volume. She looks so peaceful when she sleeps.

'I'm sorry, Mum,' I whisper, and hug her. I embrace her so tightly that she's cocooned and can't escape.

Mum wakes and smiles. 'I'm not angry, I'm disappointed. I just wished you'd told me sooner,' she says softly, and hugs me back. I can still sense that something is off between us, but I'm glad we're talking again.

'I didn't know how to, and I was afraid of how you'd react. You always told me to go out with a nice Chinese boy. Always matchmaking and forcing your friends' friends' sons on me who I have no interest in,' I say.

'I only want what's best for you, and I want you to be happy. So, tell me more about him. Where's he from? How old is he? Is he in university?' she asks, and sits up, so she can talk to me properly.

We talk about Tom at great length. Where he grew up, what he's like and where he goes to university. It feels good. I haven't talked to Mum like this in forever and I've really missed her. As I grow older and we start to butt heads less, I realise I was expending a tremendous amount of energy trying, often subconsciously, to be a different person around my parents. Previously, living at home, being colleagues and spending every waking moment together, was one of the biggest blockers in my life. I was being inauthentic, and I pretended that I was okay with it when I wasn't. Now I want to break free of the old, debilitating pattern of putting on a different face, because that no longer serves the people in my life or me. I don't want to spend the rest of my life hiding certain parts of myself from the people I love, unable to be my cheerful, loving, authentic self. My authentic self is who I naturally am when I'm not trying. It's a profoundly fulfilling state of being, which I want to spend as much of my life in as possible. I want to be myself around my parents, enjoy my time spent with them, and love them with open arms. I would truly be living the best life. In order to do that though, I have to ruthlessly eradicate the blame, shame and guilt associated with my parents. As I have learned, these unresolved emotional wounds stand in the way of all my friendships and relationships, especially with my parents. Most importantly, I have to embrace old wounds that will inevitably come up. These are life-long challenges. I have to start somewhere, and it starts now.

It's a massive weight off my shoulders to be able to tell Mum about the boy I'm falling madly in love with, knowing that I can let my parents know what's going on in my life and I don't have to lie anymore. I tell Mum that I'm serious about Tom. I feel free and happy, finally being able to combine my two worlds together rather than separating them. I always had the notion that something bad was going to happen if they ever collided but, in fact, it couldn't have been further from that. Everything is fine and our lives are better for it. In that moment, I wish I'd opened up sooner to allow others to understand, rather than hiding my inner thoughts and feelings, being in constant fear of people's judgement.

'I wanted you to go out with a Chinese boy so I could communicate and understand,' Mum says. 'But I'd love to meet him.'

When reading week rolls around during the autumn semester, Tom comes back home and I invite him over to dinner for a family meal to meet my parents. He's the first boy I've ever brought back home to meet my parents and I'm terrified and a ball of nerves. I can tell Tom is bricking it too.

Ferrero Rocher or After Eights? Tom texts late the night before we're due to meet, in a fit of panic, worrying about which would make the better impression.

'Definitely Ferrero Rocher. They're known as "gold sand" in Chinese and Mum will appreciate the link to wealth and prosperity. She's bound to love you after these,' I reply.

Tom scores serious brownie points with the delectable chocolate candy. In Chinese culture, the act of giving is more important than the gift itself and gift-giving plays a vital role in maintaining a good relationship.

In return, Mum showers him with food and questions. She's making Cantonese-style cheung fun, a steamed, rolled rice noodle with a translucent wrapper that tightly adheres to the outlines of its fillings like cling film. Rice noodle rolls are all about the texture: soft and slippery, chewy with a little bit of bounce. They're so slick that they practically slide down throats, hugging the gullet on their way down.

It's a late Saturday afternoon, a moment of calm before the shop's due to open, and Dad is upstairs catching a quick nap before service. Tom and I sit on the sidelines in the kitchen on yellow plastic stools, observing Mum doing what she does best. We watch her work quickly, pouring batter and carefully releasing rice rolls using a cheesecloth in a special gigantic industrial-sized steamer, which reminds me of a silver robot hissing as it releases excess steam. A dinner and a show all in one. The intoxicating aroma of rice fills the room. Tom is keen to impress and asks if he can help out and, to my amazement, Mum actually relinquishes some kitchen responsibilities to him. Normally, she's very protective and likes things done a certain way – which is why I never dared overstep and tread into her territory – but she lets him help with chopping ingredients for the fillings. Seeing them cook together, slicing char siu, duck, plump king prawns and spring onions with a giant meat cleaver, soothes me. I never thought I'd see the day when my boyfriend would be in the takeaway. I didn't think Mum would be so open and accepting.

When the time comes to eat, I'm taken aback by what an adventurous eater Tom is; he eats whatever Mum puts in front of him without any qualms. He clearly knows the way to a Chinese mother's heart is through the rapturous enjoyment of her cooking. Despite never having eaten cheung fun before, and not being accustomed to this texture, he polishes off his plate, and requests seconds. Mum is notorious for cooking way too much food and for getting extremely upset when there's some left on the table, so there's no such thing as going overboard in this household, especially when it comes to showing appreciation for the food.

Prior to coming over and meeting my family, I taught Tom how to say 'delicious' and 'I'm full' in Cantonese, the two most important phrases in our language. He sagaciously uses them at the right moment as Mum is about to spoon his fifth serving of rice noodle rolls into his bowl. She's so impressed and amused that she lets him off the hook. (To this day, he still uses the same tactic at our family dinners and it still works like a charm.) Mum compliments him for 'eating well' and having a 'big appetite'. A good sign. My shoulders start to relax and I breathe a sigh of relief, knowing that they're getting along like a house on fire despite Mum's broken, jumbled English. They manage to communicate through smiles, expressive nods, hand gestures and pointing. As expected, she ends up making far too much, a mountain of cheung fun, white cylindrical tubes stacked on top of each other like a waiter coming around with a hot-towel tower. She claims she made extra to hand out to friends and family but, in reality, I think she would've kept feeding us until we exploded.

Tom sits behind the counter to keep me company while I serve customers. Soon, we are already making more plans to meet again in the future. We arrange for both parents to meet and this is the big one. We settle on meeting over dim sum at our usual haunt in Happy Gathering.

Tom's parents, Pippa and Glyn, are Welsh through and through, and this is their first time having dim sum. Prior to now, they've only ever had Chinese takeaway food, and I can tell by their faces that they are apprehensive about what is going to happen. The loud clamour and shouting between round tables in the banquet hall must be terrifying for them. I'm babbling nervously, making polite small talk, talking them through the process and facilitating between both parents, translating for everyone.

I'm worried because Tom's parents are not as adventurous when it comes to eating as I've trained Tom to be. Glyn and Pippa know what they like and stick to it, they have a predisposition towards not liking things before they've tried it, unless you give them a dish without telling them what it is first. Tom and I exchange nervous glances at each other as bite-sized dishes come out one by one in bamboo steamers, stacking higher and higher like a mountain summit in the centre of our lazy Susan. Mum, being Mum, takes over. She explains what each dish is and fills everyone's bowls with food. It's her way of expressing that she cares and a gesture that everyone's family now. They bite into fluffy cloud-like steamed buns, oozing with gooey char siu meat inside. They try to swallow silky cheung fun whole and chew on gummy, sticky har gao. Texturally, this is all new to them, there are things on the table that bear no resemblance to anything in Western cuisine and I'm worried that they'll go hungry and won't enjoy it. Plus, I know they will be too polite to say anything bad if they don't like it.

My family turn to these delicacies that inspire a sense of comfort and nostalgia in us, but induce shock – and, in some cases, rejection – from others. Texture that physically and philosophically challenges you. It forces you to figure out why you may (or may not) like it as a texture. It confronts deep-seated, subconscious ideas about what defines deliciousness. Dim sum demands – literally – that you take your time with it, to bask in it and to savour it. But if nothing else, it's just fun to eat. Yum cha is about slurping, biting down hard, crunching through and getting messy.

I wonder if Tom's parents feel the same joy when eating this food, but it doesn't matter whether they like it or not because both parents are chatting away, getting to know each other. Everything is going smoothly, without a hitch. I fall back into my chair, look at the empty plates and baskets in front of us and smile. While tradition retains its iron grip over East Asian families, like mine, family dynamics are no longer as black and white in the face of modernity. For years I have been on a treadmill of validation and vanity, trying to pick and choose which lane serves me best. As I slow down, basking in this moment, everything seems to click into place. Why pick, why not both?

Experimental Cheung Fun (Rice Rolls)

Without fail, I will always order cheung fun at a dim sum spread or get a polystyrene tray of cheung fun doused in hoisin sauce and peanut butter to go in the streets of Hong Kong. There's something about the chubby and squishy texture that makes me so happy. It's something that is unique to East and Southeast Asian palates, the sensation of using your molars to really chew and chew, as the rice noodle roll slips, squeaks and sticks in your mouth. I crave this constantly. There's no need for specialised equipment to make rice noodle rolls, this dish can easily be made using home equipment. Any large plate that can withstand heat or baking pans that can fit inside a wok work well. The secret to getting silky, smooth cheung fun is to steam a thin layer of batter on a greased plate or tray for several minutes. Mum used to let me play around with different ingredients and we'd mix and match like a kid choosing pick 'n' mix sweets (only less sweet, more savoury). I wouldn't say this is a difficult recipe to make per se, instead it's about trying to spread the batter evenly and thinly enough, as well as getting the rolling or folding technique down. Practice makes perfect, and be prepared to sacrifice a few, like you would do with spring rolls. There's always going to be a couple of ugly initial ones but have fun playing around and experimenting with the different filling combinations.

Serves: 4 | **Prep time:** 15–20 mins |
Cook time: 2–5 mins

Ingredients
For the cheung fun batter:
300g rice flour
32g wheat starch (about two heaped tbsp)
32g potato starch
32g corn starch
2 tbsp vegetable oil
1 litre cold tap water
250ml ice-cold water
Pinch of salt

For the fillings (optional):
Duck, sliced
Char siu, sliced
Chicken, sliced
King prawns, deshelled and deveined
Dried shrimp
Shiitake mushrooms, sliced
1 spring onion, sliced on a diagonal for garnish

For the dipping sauce:
½ onion, diced
3 tbsp vegetable oil
1 tbsp sugar
1 tbsp dark soy
1 tbsp oyster sauce

Chilli oil, optional

Method:

1. First, work on the dipping sauce to set aside for later. Cut and dice onion, submerge in oil and slowly cook for 15–20 minutes on a low flame until the onions turn golden brown. Sieve and discard onion (or save the crisp onion for another dish), so that you're left with fragrant onion oil. Add sugar, soy sauce and oyster sauce in a pan, cook on a low heat until sugar has dissolved. Add the onion oil, give everything a mix to combine everything together. Set aside.

2. For the batter, weigh out all the ingredients. Dry-mix the flour together and add the oil. Slowly incorporate the water with the flour a bit at a time to mix into a smooth paste. Keep mixing and slowly add a bit of water until everything is combined and there are no lumps. It's important to give the batter a good stir each time before using it, because flour, water and oil can separate and the flour can sink to the bottom. You'll know it's the right consistency when the batter coats the back of the ladle.

3. Set up your steaming equipment and set the flame to medium or high. Ensure the water underneath is at a high rolling simmer.

4. Liberally brush vegetable oil on the plate or baking tray to prevent sticking. Or, optionally, you can lay down a wet cheesecloth underneath to help with the sticking. It's a matter of preference and finding what works best for you. Add a ladleful of the batter to the tray and quickly swirl around. Tilt the pan so that it covers the entire base and reaches the edges evenly. You don't want a lopsided cheung fun. This is the time to add your desired filling of choice. Line up the fillings in a single line, but don't overdo it with the fillings, otherwise you can't roll it up.

5. Cover and steam for 2 minutes. You'll know it's done when the batter turns a solid white colour and bubbles up slightly.

6. While the cheung fun is steaming: fill up your sink with cold water or have a big bowl of cold water nearby. Place the plate or tray on top of the cold water to help the cheung fun cool down straight after steaming. This helps the rice rolls come off cleanly and easily.

7. After it cools down, liberally oil a dough scraper or rubber spatula to prevent sticking. Gently push to roll it up or fold up from one end. Aim for either cylindrical or folded rectangle shapes.

8. Garnish with spring onion and serve with dipping sauce.

12

Going Through Changes

'Matthew Hill,' the chancellor says into the microphone.

Everyone in the room claps.

'Sarah Hughes,' he calls.

Everyone in the room claps again.

'Angela . . . Hoo-wee,' the chancellor announces.

I can't believe it. One of my biggest achievements to date and the ceremonial head of my university butchers my name to the entire auditorium filled with graduates, lecturers, staff and proud parents. I visibly roll my eyes, which is probably captured on the livestream that's being broadcasted on the jumbo screen outside the venue. I've had people constantly mispronounce my surname my entire life and I know this is unintentional, he probably doesn't mean anything by it, but still, I can't help but feel irked by it. I let it slide because nothing can dampen this day. I can't believe that I've finally graduated. I wobble to the podium in my heels, cap and robe to shake hands with the chancellor, collect my cylinder blank piece of paper that's supposed to be my graduation certificate and pose for a photo. I can see Therese, Hannah, the rest of my housemates, classmates and my family in the crowd all clapping and cheering me on. I walk back to my seat, nearly tripping over in my too-high heels, to listen to more names being called out, further speeches, and generally enjoy the remainder of the ceremony.

It's scary to be graduating, leaving behind familiarity, the people and the city I've gotten to know and fall in love with over the past three years. I also feel triumphant, relieved and pleased. I've done it and finally joined the graduation club with my brothers. To be able to share this moment with my family, including Keen and Jacky who have travelled back to see me graduate, means so much. Mum and Dad are not good at expressing positive emotions, often using negative language to educate us. This means they'll never say 'I'm proud of you' to my face directly, which makes me crave for my parents' accept-ance even more; the more critical they were, the harder I had worked. I can't expect my parents to congratulate me now when they have no track record of doing so. For them, it's a matter of familiarity and for them to say the 'P word' feels as unnatural as them tucking me into bed or reading me and my brothers a bedtime story. I know me graduating university is a moment of pride for them, though, and they'll show it through their actions, like taking a million photos of me in scorching July sweating in my robes. 'Ooh, one more in front of the fountain!' or 'Another photo by your campus'. Later, these will be framed and hung on the staircase of our other home, the one my parents had eventually purchased with their hard-earned takeaway money. After graduation they take us all out for dinner at Happy Gathering.

Therese and Hannah score full-time graduate jobs in marketing and PR. A few classmates take a gap year to travel straight out of university and others take jobs in unrelated fields. I'm the only one on my course who isn't quite ready to enter the world of work or become a fully functional young adult yet. I'm 21 and unsure what I really want out of life. After graduating I'm left with a 'now what?' feeling, balancing the chase for self-actualisation via a fulfilling career, alongside my traditionally Asian family values that are more about my parents' self-sacrifices and intergenerational obligations.

I feel I have more to learn and I've managed to secure a last-minute scholarship to study a Master's degree in journalism at Cardiff University this coming September. The scholarship helps fund half my tuition fees, which is useful as there's no way I could have funded it myself. My parents help fund the other half and it helps them out too as I can continue to stay close by in case of any takeaway emergency. My parents want me to move back in with them to save money, but I'm adamant that I need to rent a place in the city. I've had a taste of freedom and independence, so for me to move back home above the takeaway would feel like being catapulted back into my old life. Tom has also graduated and is living back home with his parents. He's working part-time at a college, as well as working two temporary jobs as a dishwasher at an Italian restaurant and a sales assistant, a hardware store in Cardiff. This is the first time in three years we are in the same city together but we barely see each other because he's working so much and I'm preparing for my Master's course schedule. It looks so demanding that it feels like a full-time job.

I choose to live in a four-bedroom rented house in the student area of Cathays with my friends Jamie, Elis and Rhydian, who I've known for years at school. Living with three guys involves a lot of mess and mouldy, dirty plates, but the building is also worse for wear. We have a dodgy extension (you can tell because there's a massive crack right down the middle of our house from the outside) and the kitchen and the bathroom downstairs have a constant slug and woodlice infestation, which the landlord does nothing to resolve, only suggesting we buy salt and pour it by the doorways to prevent them from coming in. It is most definitely unfit for human habitation, but we live there anyway because it's the only thing we can afford; we treat the place more like a hotel. My parents won't let me hear the end of it because I'm not living with girls and they're wary that something is going to happen to me but, after much convincing and my promise that I'll come back every Saturday evening to help out and earn my keep, they let me be. At some point, I need to start living for myself and stop living in my parents' shadow at the takeaway.

I have the biggest room, facing a street-corner inter-section, two huge windows letting light in. Despite the stained cream carpets and mouldy walls, no matter how disgusting, I need a place to escape the weight of life. I am grateful to have my own space so Tom can come over to crash after his shifts and we can at least spend some time together. We are having a hard time readjusting to togetherness, but when he comes crawling in exhausted from work, curls up into a ball beneath the duvet and falls asleep beside me, it's such a wholesome emotion that fills me with joy, seeing a person so dear to me en-tirely calm. Seeing how peaceful he looks sleeping, and waking up beside him, makes me realise just how much I love him, and I end up falling in love with him all over again.

My new home for my Master's feels formal and seri-ous. It's a Grade II listed neoclassical building complete with a grand Roman column entrance and perfectly clipped grass surrounding it, a world away from the sleek, modern creative hub I was in before. It's intim-idating and serious, but it feels like the next level up. We share this site with the architecture students who occupy the top floor, while journalism students are lo-cated in the basement of the building. My alarm doesn't go off in the morning and I'm late for the first day of student orientation. Tom is still sleeping in my bed and he looks so serene and snug that I wish I could stay there all morning with him. I kiss him on his forehead and dash out the door.

The wind is gusting and clouds are rolling across the sky. I can feel the blood pounding behind my ears and rushing to my face as I run to class. I regret wearing a jacket because I'm going to be a sweaty mess. I get lost trying to find the room I'm supposed to be in, run-walking through a tunnel of long, shiny hallways where all the rooms look the same. When I finally arrive, over half an hour late and out of breath, my classmates are already sitting on grey chairs next to computers at their wooden desks on different clusters of islands. I sheep-ishly join the desk closest to the door without trying to cause too much of a disturbance.

One by one, everyone has to step up to the podium to introduce themselves, say what our hobbies and interests are and our favourite magazines. Ranging from motor-ing to sports and politics, it's an interesting and eclectic mix of people. Our lecturers and course leaders, Julia and Tony, are going through the syllabus for the rest of the year. They're like mother and father to us 24 class-mates and we will spend almost every waking moment together celebrating the highs and lows of postgraduate life throughout the year, getting through stressful press days, late nights designing magazine layouts and frantic last-minute calls trying to secure interviews or follow up on quotes together. I love the thrill of it all, to be with like-minded people who adore journalism and print magazines as much as I do, if not more. I feel blessed to be learning and studying next to a bunch of these crafty operators who are not only my friends but potential future colleagues and contacts in the industry. It teaches me the importance of making connections and to never burn bridges. I'm networking before I even know it's networking.

The first week of introductions are done and dusted, and I'm back at the takeaway for the weekend to help out on the counter. I can't believe how dead it is. It's so quiet that they don't even really need me back to work. With the benefit of distance, I can see that the times are changing. People want to eat more healthily and the competition has grown fiercer as more and more Chinese takeaways move into the area, stealing business away from us. Inflation rates for buying produce have skyrocketed and, while we still have Lowri, there's a shortage of staff wanting to help out because we don't pay as much as the other takeaways and Dad drives everyone away with his temper. Despite it all, though, my parents have used their hard-earned money to put me through university, pay mortgage repayments on the other home, pay staff and their overhead expenses at the shop. Fighting for survival is tough.

'Do you accept cards?' a customer asks while opening the door.

'No, but there is a cash point next door at the Co-op,' I say. I get excited that there is finally a customer, and I pop up like a meerkat from behind the counter and point left to the direction of the supermarket on the same street.

'No card? Buncha mad 'eds. Worr are yew on about?'

The customer closes the door, walks off and doesn't return.

I slump back down in my stool. This is happening too many times. I try to convince my parents to be set up for card payments over and over again, but they refuse because they don't understand. They think it's too difficult and they won't understand without me here. Not being able to digitise and go cashless means our takeaway is suffering. Card is king and money is tight. It feels pointless trying to keep up with what our competitors are doing when we are seriously lagging behind other shops. Mum puts me in charge of the digital marketing side of things to bring the business online because the competition has also done so. I set up a Facebook business page and create a website so that customers can see the menu online and we can get feedback. But customers still aren't able to order directly online (it was still done via in-person or on the phone) and we are still a fiercely cash-only business. After a frustrating weekend, Dad drops me back to my house, along with more of Mum's weekly food care packages, neatly labelled and dated.

I'm up late, making a start on my feature writing and video assignment before the deadline on Monday. No matter how many times it happens, I never learn to do things in good time and always rush my assignments just before crunch time, tricking myself into thinking I work better under pressure. Not long after I arrive back and have fired up my laptop, Mum calls. I assume I must've left something at the takeaway.

'Hey, mui, how's things going?' Mum asks.

'I'm good, busy. Deadline tomorrow. What's up? Can't talk for long,' I answer, with the phone wedged between my ear and shoulder. I'm half listening and half typing on my laptop at my desk.

'I forgot to tell you to read this letter. I'm not quite sure what it says, but I think it's from the doctors. I need you to come to the hospital with me next weekend to help translate. I have to go in for something called an M . . . I . . . R?' Mum says, her voice changing from her normal chirpy self to serious.

'Do you mean MRI scan? Is everything okay?' I ask, and stop what I'm doing, giving her my full attention.

'Yeah, I think so. I've been feeling more tired than usual and I have to sit down more. Sometimes, I have pins and needles or it goes numb on the left side of my body and legs. It's just a scan to find out what's wrong with me,' she explains.

How long has she been suffering from this without telling me? I start to worry and automatically assume the worst. The week goes by painfully slow until I am finally sitting in a dated waiting room with her. The plastic blue bench seats are uncomfortable and the silver boxy TV in the corner is showing *Homes Under the Hammer*. The presenters are interviewing a young couple who regret their decision of paying too much for a dilapidated property at auction. I try to focus, but my mind is elsewhere. Hospitals and doctors creep me out and I have always associated them with sickness and death. Now, here I am sitting with my potentially very sick mother. Nurses scuttle up and down the hallway with clipboards, an old man sitting opposite us with one leg in a cast spreads out, and there's a lady in a wheelchair who looks so ill I think she should be fast-tracked to see the doctor first.

'We've been waiting for ages. When is it our turn?' Mum asks, looking up from her Chinese gossip magazine she's brought from home.

'Jin Hui!' a young female calls out, as if she was listening, from beyond the double metal doors that read: 'No unauthorised access beyond this point'.

The nurse leads us to a room with blue curtains on either side. I help Mum answer and fill out the questionnaire about her health and medical history. I translate what the nurse is saying, explaining to Mum what is going to happen and what they are looking for when they're performing the scan. I ask her to sign a consent form to confirm. The nurse takes some of Mum's blood samples to send off to test, and afterwards we follow the nurse and a doctor, weaving through a series of confusing hallways, blinded by the halogen square lights in the polystyrene ceiling tiles. The buffed floors are so shiny that I can see my own reflection in them. Soon we are led into three cubicles where Mum has to change into a white hospital gown with a blue diamond print all over it. I help fasten the two ties at the back of her neck and waist and go to wait in the corner of the room. The nurse who is going to operate the machine tells Mum to lie on the motorised bed and instructs her to lie completely still, as she moves inside the open-ended cylinder feet first. The procedure is over within the hour and the radiologist tells us that they will send a report to the doctor, who will discuss the results with me over the phone in the next week or so.

We eat family meal at the takeaway later than usual when the shop opens because neither of us really have an appetite and we're late coming back from the hospital. I'm feeling drained from worrying about the takeaway business and Mum's unknown cause of deteriorating health, and stressed from the piling amount of university work I need to do.

'Sorry, mui, not very good dishes tonight. I'm too tired, so I only made congee in the rice cooker. We're trying to save money, too,' Mum says.

'Don't apologise! I love congee,' I protest.

I feel guilty knowing that my parents are making such sacrifices. Honestly, I don't mind what we eat. Mum could have served me instant ramen or a bowl of plain boiled rice and I would've been happy with whatever was put in front of me because she always puts care, thought and love into everything she makes. As we eat, Mum tells me one of her remarkable stories of overcoming adversity growing up poor and hungry in a country-wide famine. How as a child, she ate rotting, blackened sweet potatoes with thinned-out watery congee. She would eat the same thing every day for weeks on end because there was nothing else and all the crops on her family farm had been destroyed in the harshest of winters and pillaging. Sweet potatoes were often used by those who didn't have enough money to buy proper food but had to fill up their stomach, and she learned a multitude of ways to bulk up foods to make things last longer. As much as I love sweet potato congee, it's a reminder of a difficult time when food was difficult to come by and, as I look into the steaming bowl in front of me, I realise how privileged and blessed I am, knowing that I'll never go hungry like she did. To this day, it makes me proud to be her daughter.

I inhale a couple of spoonfuls of congee. I love the simplicity of it and the soft, lumpy texture that soothes each taste bud. The sweet potatoes give it a hint of natural sweetness that requires no extra seasonings and a contrasting texture that makes the congee filling and nutritious, a soothing hug from the inside out. The chunky, bright-orange hues floating in the bowl of rice porridge remind me of mini-sunrises peeking through, and that sunnier, happier days are there somewhere in the sea of gruel. Things might seem bad now, but good times will eventually come.

Congee has a powerful hold on me. It's a dish that's always been there for me in sickness and health, in part because nostalgia makes everything taste better and also because at home we cook this occasionally to cleanse or detox our bodies after a lot of good meals or when we are feeling unwell.

Mum and I are quiet when Dad walks in the kitchen. Whenever he enters the room there is always an awkward undertone to everything, a feeling of unease and uncertainty of what's going to happen. He peers into our bowls with a look of disdain and disgust.

'Congee, how boring. *I'm* not going to eat that. I'll just whip up shredded crispy beef for myself,' Dad says. He turns around to face the wok station and flicks the switch for the extractor fans to whizz into action. Firing up the wok, a blue-orange flame shoots up.

'You have such a bad diet! No wonder you have gout all the time. Don't come crying to me when your foot swells again,' Mum shouts, speaking to him like a baby, but he either doesn't hear or ignores her.

'Order! One chips, small chicken curry and barbecue spare ribs,' Lowri says, walking into the kitchen and placing the ticket on the nail.

'Mui, my legs are killing me. I need to lie down in the living room. Would you cover me while I rest?' Mum says.

I nod and get up without hesitation. I leave my lonely bowl of congee to go crusty on the table while I tend to the one customer who has come in. I add another basket of chips into the vegetable oil, which sizzles on contact, the heat from the oil driving off the moisture and forming tiny steam bubbles, crackling and hissing in the amber pool of searing-hot oil beneath me.

For the next few weeks while we wait for Mum's results I barely sleep, in some fugue state, neither living nor dead. Every moment my eyes are open, I'm either reading about the ethics of journalism and media law and what is deemed as public interest, practising my Teeline shorthand, or thinking about Mum in a hospital gown and what is going to happen to her. I'm feeling more worried as the days go by with no results; most likely I've had too much time to think about it. I've always pictured her as being strong as an ox (she was born in the Year of the Ox, after all), how she is invincible and nothing can harm her. Suddenly, she's not as fit and healthy any more. When I look at my mother, all five feet of her, lying horizontal on the sofa, barely able to stand, I see a mix of things – the naysaying qualities of a matriarch with the mindset of a bulldozer and a small, broken woman who got dealt a bad hand in life, but smiles and pushes through.

I had left my number as the emergency contact for the hospital so they could contact me directly with the results and I could relay the information back to Mum. Suddenly, my phone vibrates and flashes. The screen shows: NO CALLER ID.

This is it. Deep breaths. The doctor says that we need to come in for a face-to-face consultation next week so they can discuss the results and what is going to happen next. This only makes things worse and sends me into a panicked downward spiral. I wish they had just told me there and then on the phone what was wrong, because now I have to go through another excruciatingly long week worrying myself sick until we're back in the doctor's room again. When the appointment finally arrives, the doctor explains that Mum has calcium deposits in the peripheral arteries of her legs, most likely caused by her long days and nights at the takeaway. Her prolonged standing and the subsequent calcium build-up is the reason for the symptoms she'd been experiencing: numbness, tingling sensation, pain, spasm and sometimes an acceleration of the onset of fatigue in the muscles of her legs. The doctor suggests surgery to remove some of the calcium to fix the issue and Mum instantly freaks out.

'No surgery! No surgery! No surgery!' Mum shouts.

'I'll give you a week or so to think it over. I'll get the nurse to send you a letter with all the details and we can potentially book in another appointment for treatment,' the doctor says.

Mum nudges me to ask the doctor for crutches from the hospital because she's in constant pain and needs the crutches to help support her. On our way out, Mum is giving her new silver crutches a test-drive in the car park, slowly shuffling on the gravel and getting used to using them. I'm hovering close by in case she falls. We're both silent on the drive home from the hospital, still absorbing and letting the news sink in. I can't believe the takeaway is actually making her ill. I knew that it was back-breaking hard work, but not quite so literally. I keep turning around from the passenger seat to look at the two silver crutches balanced on the back seat. *Will she be on crutches for the rest of her life?* I think to myself.

As we roll to a stop at a set of traffic lights, I try to convince Mum to change her mind about the surgery.

'Mum, please reconsider. I just want you to get better,' I say.

'No way. I believe in traditional Chinese medicine and no Western doctor is going to cut me open. They treat the symptoms, but not the root of the problem. I'll never be the same again,' she protests, without looking at me, her eyes focused on the road.

'Mum, this is serious. If left untreated it could get worse,' I insist.

'Mm, okay, lah. Be quiet now, I'm trying to concentrate on driving,' she says, shushing and shutting me down. She knows I will not let this go. I only want what's best for her, but Mum won't listen. For as long as I can remember she's always believed in the healing power of traditional Chinese medicine and rarely in science. It's not so much a belief itself, but more something that's been ingrained into her from an early age. She's as stubborn as ever and I know she's already made up her mind to fly back to China to see a specialist there.

Even though Mum is ill, she refuses to take time off work as we can't afford it. For most restaurant and takeaway workers, any time spent away from working is a missed opportunity to make more money. Mum knows that we need her to keep the lights on, to bring food to the table and to keep the cogs in motion. Without her, we'd be nothing. I plead for her to rest, but she refuses to listen and is still manning the deep-fat fryer with her crutches hooked around her arms. Dad still doesn't see the severity of it.

'Stop exaggerating. You're fine,' Dad remarks.

'I'm on crutches! I can't walk! How serious does it have to get? Do you think I want to be like this?' Mum snaps.

Dad doesn't like what Mum says and he gets loud with her. Then she gets louder, and they start arguing in the middle of service again. The volume creeps to the front, which garners a worried look from Lowri, who pokes her head around from the counter to peer in. I shake my head at her like some secret language that says, 'I'm not calling for you and everything's under control.'

'You have issues! I've been so accommodating to you, and you don't even care,' Mum continues.

She huffs and throws down the chip basket to one side, splattering flecks of hot oil and loose chips everywhere. She grabs her crutches and hobbles off to the living room to walk away from this argument, to cool off and rest for a bit.

'Stop it, both of you!' I say sternly, as if I'm scolding two children. I automatically pick up where Mum left off, shaking off excess oil from the basket and bagging up the steaming-hot chips. 'Dad, can't you be a little more considerate?'

'The woman pushes my buttons!' he says.

'Be nicer to her!' I reply, raising my voice to tell him off.

He doesn't say anything and carries on cooking, flicking the wok up and down, but I'm surprised he's actually listened to me for once instead of always having the last word. Tonight has been an eerily quiet Saturday night. We barely make enough to cover our costs. The lights are turned off and the closed sign flipped. I help Lowri with the sweeping and from the window I can see it's a calm and starry night. The blackness envelops everything.

'Here, wong dai lui,' Dad says, and hands me £30 in cash. I know there is barely anything left in the till and I try to decline. I can't accept his money knowing full well how badly the business is struggling and that they are paying out of their own pocket for me to stay in university.

'Nonsense. You worked hard tonight and earned it. I won't take no for an answer. Take it.' Dad pushes the notes into my left hand and closes it. I almost flinch from the skin contact. I've never really hugged or had any real affection towards my Dad. His callused hands over my own small, soft hand feels alien. He chuckles and winks at me. 'Don't worry about it. I've got more money.'

I don't want to argue back because I know I'd never win with him, so I accept the money and thank him. I also know that the reason Dad is in such a good mood and didn't completely lose it earlier is because he won big at the casino the night before. Regardless, whether he won or lost, it always makes my blood boil. We all dislike how his gambling is spiralling out of control and he knows it. I just hate how his winnings dictate our life and how we are always at odds with each other; it's fifty-fifty on what mood he'll be in, and I hate those chances.

'My lift's here! Goodnight, Ange, Jin and Gary! See you tomorrow!' Lowri says, waving and letting herself out the door.

'Oh, uh. Bye, Lowri!' I wave and lock the door after her. I pause for a moment to take in the perfect midnight velvet sky once again, gazing up at the sea of stars so brilliant that they dazzle. I'm amazed by the brightness, the street's even reflecting on it. I look for constellations and find Orion's Belt, which my brothers taught me to spot as three stars in a line when we were younger. The stars' pretty twinkle from a distance calms me and I see a shooting star blitz across. I wish that Mum will get better and Dad will quit gambling, and I hope that things will get easier soon. My head follows the trail until I can't see it any more.

Sweet Potato Congee

Congee's origin is one born out of poverty and necessity. This dish doesn't actually contain that much rice because the liquid really helps stretch out the meal to make you feel more full. Congee wasn't created because people wanted another texture of rice; the dish naturally has broken grains and was eaten by poor farmers in hard times who couldn't afford even the most basic grains. It was used to fill stomachs; rice porridge is what civilisations were built on. During the Cultural Revolution, sweet potatoes were one of the few crops that were available and sustained thousands of people through the Great Chinese Famine, and they were used to bulk up dishes. It's a nod to Mum's rough childhood, a reminder that no matter what life throws at us, as long as we have each other we'll make it through. Congee is peasant famine food, it's what you eat in times of need, and it can cure all. It's healing food when you're sick, whether you're young or old. This particular recipe is a blank canvas where you can add any topping for more sustenance.

Serves: 4 | **Prep time:** 5–10 mins | **Cook time:** 80–90 mins, plus soaking rice overnight

Ingredients:
200g (1 cup) white rice, soaked overnight
1 tbsp salt
2 slices of ginger, peeled

1.3 litres of water or chicken stock
3 tbsp dried scallops, soaked for 1 hour and shredded (optional, but adding dried scallops adds
   more depth and umami)
2 sweet potatoes, peeled and chopped into chunks

Toppings and suggestions (optional):
All ingredients can be found in a Chinese supermarket (the world's your oyster as there are no rules
when it comes to congee toppings – I've even tried
blitzed up Scampi Fries and Monster Munch dust)

A pinch of white pepper
A drizzle of soy sauce
A small bunch of coriander, diced
Deep-fried garlic flakes
Deep-fried onion bits
1 spring onion, diced
Handful of pork floss
½ salted egg or century egg
Handful of mui choi (pickled Chinese cabbage), diced
Handful of salted peanuts
1 tin fried gluten

Method:
1. You don't have to soak the rice overnight, but by
soaking the rice it helps break down the grains and
cooks it faster. If you don't have time, feel free to skip
the soaking part. Wash and rinse rice until clear.

2. To the washed, soaked rice, add salt, ginger, water (or stock) and the optional dried scallops all together in a pot or rice cooker. If using a rice cooker, set to congee setting and it should be done in an hour's time. For the pot, turn to high heat. Stir everything together and keep occasionally stirring to prevent sticking to the bottom of the pot. Cook with lid off for about 20 minutes until the rice starts to break down.

3. Once the rice starts to thicken, add the sweet potatoes, then cover with a lid and cook for a further hour.

4. Check on consistency. It depends on preference, but some people prefer a thicker, creamier texture while others prefer a loose, runnier texture. Add more water to adjust and thin it out depending on preference. Serve in a bowl, season with white pepper and a dash of soy sauce on top and add optional toppings.

13

Final Order

I open Microsoft Word and type up a poster in Chinese on my laptop advertising the takeaway.

'No, no, no. Let's make it £160,000 or nearest offer,' Mum says, pointing at the screen, as if it's a touchscreen. 'Don't want to go too low, right?'

'You sure? No going back now?' I question.

She nods and I hit print. We put the takeaway on the market and advertise within our circles, putting up posters in the shop window and at the wholesalers in town. Mum has emotionally and physically checked out; riddled with chronic pain and burn-out. The years of exhaustion and toll have caught up with her; while everyone else around her is having a good time, her schedule is off balance from the rest of the world. She has already made up her mind and will spend half the year in Guangdong, near her ancestral village, for her traditional Chinese medicine treatment. She'll be splitting her time between there and back in Wales to help out at the shop while still recovering on crutches.

Mum rejected surgery, even against everyone's wishes, showing me it's okay to do what's right for you and leave situations which, for one reason or another, no longer serve you.

'I can't do this any more. I'm tired, so very tired,' Mum says.

'Fine! Go to China to see your doctor and I can carry on with the shop without you. I can do it on my own. I don't need you! Come hell or high water, I'm not selling. You can put posters up, but I'm going down with this ship!' Dad screams in her face, his face turning a bright beetroot shade.

'Fine with me!' Mum huffs back, while angrily chopping onions, taking her frustration out on the chopping board.

Every time they talk about the future of the shop it always ends in the same painful dialogue and heated volatile conversation that's doomed from the start. Perhaps time and distance apart will be a good thing for them and they need their own space. Mum is 58 and Dad is 64. They're both getting old and frail, no longer young and active like they once were. Dad also has a catalogue of health problems. He's riddled with gout and has problems with high blood pressure and tuberculosis due to his bad diet and lack of self-care. He keeps forgetting to take his medication, despite our concerns and worries. Though they're both ageing, they're at different stages in life. Mum: acceptance. Dad: anger.

We barely speak to Mum while she's in her doctor's

care in China. This is mainly because she and technology are not the best of friends, but is also thanks to China's firewall blocking many of the social networking apps, so communication is limited. She pings me an update on WeChat (China's most popular messaging and calling app) every once in a while telling me she's okay. She sends pictures of herself covered in needles mid-acupuncture session and dark-red angry circles on her back post-cupping therapy to draw out the toxins from her body. Dad decides to man the shop on his own, with Lowri out front on the counter and Dewi on deliveries. My brothers and I come back occasionally on the odd weekends to help out. We plough on like tired marathon runners, limping towards the finishing line. Dad's interest and quality of cooking is also going downhill. He cuts corners, burns things and lets the food's quality slide. Customers notice and complain. He, too, is tired and doesn't have the stamina, heart and passion he once had. Mentally, we all agree it is time to close the book on the takeaway chapter, but Dad refuses to do so, even though it's already on the market.

I'm 22 and have officially flown the nest across the Severn Bridge. I feel free, grateful and happy to be able to do what I want working as a journalist in London without my parents' watchful eye, but I also feel guilty because I feel like my parents are my responsibility and I have abandoned them. I'm the last Hui to carry on the takeaway legacy and I've turned my back on it. I'm a city worker now and I have to get used to a morning diet of emails, black coffee, deadlines and existential despair, instead of standing on my feet eight hours a day deep-frying chicken balls and answering phone calls. My parents continue to nag me though, trying to convince me to move back to be physically closer in case anything happens.

'Haiya, you're all so far away now. Why couldn't you all get a job closer to home like your cousins?' Mum leaves a voice note on WeChat. 'Come back soon to help your father when you can.'

Despite being thousands of miles away on the other side of the world and seven hours ahead, Mum is still worried about the shop and her husband running things alone. They might have argued constantly, but she still cares. Later, another notification pings on my phone. A picture of an out-of-focus blurry letter pops up.

'What does this say?' Dad asks too closely on the microphone on the family WhatsApp.

I leave him unread. Since moving, I have been enumerating my father's flaws and shutting out Mum's pleas and requests. Out of sight, out of mind. Sometimes I don't have the headspace to deal with their drama; I will eventually get back to them at a later date. I feel selfish, but I deserve to be selfish for once; to think and focus on myself. A young working professional getting her foot in the door and starting on my career ladder, all I want is to live my new life in peace. I find it excruciating for me to spend time with my parents, as I'm notionally filled with angst. Any form of communication is painful and I dread and avoid phone calls, messages or any time they ask me for help. My brothers and I fall into a bad routine of passing the buck.

'I'm busy, can you help them renew their car insurance, Keen?' I message in our siblings Whatsapp group chat.

'Jacky, it's always me and Angie that ends up doing things. It's your turn,' Keen replies.

'Can't. Deadline tomorrow. Stacked,' Jacky texts back.

'Fine, fine, fine. I'll do it,' I moan.

We go back and forth, talking about whose turn it is to help our parents do such menial tasks on top of our full-time jobs. We complain and resent it a bit, of course we all do, because it feels like we have all been forced to grow up quickly in order to help out when our parents don't understand something. Translating letters, being the interpreter, filling out staff taxes, looking over utility bills and logging daily food-safety checklists from afar, like an umbilical cord attached to our parents that refuses to be severed. It's a hard club to be a part of at times but, although we moan, we'll always find time to help and begrudgingly be happy to be a part of it. We learn to embrace our roles because it is our way of giving back to our parents, for all that they have done for us. I'm happy to sacrifice my time and energy to an immigrant parent who has sacrificed so much for us to be British. Even as a teen or young adult, translating legal and financial issues is intense as one becomes fully aware of the fragility of our family's situation. They've taken care of us all these years, now it's time for us to take care of them.

The selling process is slow and sluggish. We have a few potential buyers who are interested and people come around to view the shop. Some even make offers but, when it comes to moving on to the next step of the process, Dad backs off and gets cold feet. He can't make up his mind. To sell or not to sell? As the months go on, sales dwindle from week to week and business naturally slows, cash becomes tighter, and we barely break even. The thing that we've spent so many hours building and loving just isn't working out. We have to admit to ourselves that none of us are happy with the takeaway and it isn't going to get any better, but Dad just can't admit defeat because it feels like acceptance, and that acceptance is what he needs to escape.

After two long years of being on the market and living in limbo, we finally find a suitable buyer through a friend of a friend. It's a relief to see Dad finally be able to pull the parachute cord; it has been too long and we're beginning to crash into the trees. A young Chinese family from Swansea buys the takeaway – they have been working and living in Chinese restaurants, just like my parents had been when they first came to the country 30 years ago. They have two young daughters and need their own place for their growing family. They remind me of us in a lot of ways. Fresh-faced, ambitious and with a sense of hope and excitement about the future. We have a date set for selling: 31 August 2018. Coincidentally, it has been exactly 30 years this month since my parents opened up shop. The timing of it all . . .

Mum calls. 'When are you coming back from London? It's our last week before selling. Last chance before it's too late.'

'We're coming back Friday straight after work. Tom will be seeing and staying with his family, but he'll pop over for family meal,' I say on the phone, cradling the phone between my head and shoulder as I type in work.

Tom and I get the Megabus back to Wales to say goodbye. We have been living together in north London, at last. For years, it felt like we were never in sync or in the same location. We have spent most of our eight-year relationship long-distancing, but everything finally fits together like a jigsaw piece. However, neither Jacky nor Keen can make it home to see off the shop one last time. Jacky has just relocated to New York permanently for work and Keen has quit his job in Manchester to travel and work and currently lives in South Korea; all of us spread so far on different continents. They're gutted and tell us to take lots of photos to send to them.

I put my headphones up high to drown out the noise of other passengers and gaze out the window, admiring my city. I can see the sun gradually dropping out of sight, leaving behind its peaceful pastel summer rays. We crawl at a snail's pace, stopping and starting in traffic, made even worse being the August bank holiday and everyone getting out of the capital. Seeing grand tourist attractions in the distance and crossing over Tower Bridge as we drive under its twinkling lights, it fills me with the same excitement as a kid in a sweet shop. London is my home now, the majority of my friends from Wales have moved here too and I love this hectic, eclectic city. I feel more at home in the city in London than I have ever felt in all my years in the countryside in Wales. I don't feel singled out for my race either, because London is home to one of the most ethnically diverse populations in the world, which makes people more accepting and less reliant on media depictions of other races and nationalities. I can just be me. But whenever I return to Wales, there is an inexplicable hiraeth* pull on me; a yearning for a home of my past.

By the time we arrive back in Beddau it's late and the streets are pitch black. I crash in the same bed I grew up in and crawl under Jacky's old Manchester United football bed sheets. Our shared lilac room, next to Mum. My favourite band posters have all been taken down ready for the move, leaving behind flecks of chipped paint and Blu-Tack marks on the walls – it feels strangely empty. I sleep through the night like a baby, even through Mum's incessant, floor-shaking snoring. The next day, I awake to an empty bed next to me; Mum is already up, pottering about. I put on Mum's well-worn work clothes: joggers covered in crusty old batter and

---

* Hiraeth – a Welsh word that has no direct English translation, meaning homesickness tinged with grief and sadness

an oversized white Kangol T-shirt with multicoloured flecks of sauces and see-through oil stains seeping in. We're the same size and I didn't bring anything suitable to wear or that I didn't want to destroy.

'Hey, mui, you hungry?' she calls from the kitchen, sauntering from one corner to the other while clinging on to her crutches. 'I can make you Spam and egg macaroni soup? Something quick and easy, okay? Or would you like something else?'

I walk towards her, down the narrow white hallway, and try to rub the sleep from my eyes. I look up at the white kitchen wall clock wrapped in a plastic bag to protect against grease. It's 12:30 pm. I really slept in, huh?

'You know I'm always hungry. I'm easy for whatever,' I say with a grin. I had forgotten that living at home means being bombarded with food from the instant I wake up. I miss my mother's food and she makes up for my absence from the fruits of her labour with plentiful nutritious food. Tom drops by from his parents' house in the next village over to see me and my parents early, knowing full-well by now to bring a bag of oranges as a gift. Mum and Dad are always so delighted to see him. There is something to be said about Asian parents and unreasonably high expectations. They love Tom, though, because he is kind and hardworking (but mainly because he brings them oranges).

Tom takes photos of the three of us standing outside the shop before we're due to open for the very last time. Mum smiles for a bit, her cute, freckled, round cheeks complementing her short, red-dyed bob, then suddenly her usual sprightly self seems to evaporate into thin air. I look to my right and I can see Dad's eyes welling up. A tough, stern balding man – who normally doesn't say much, except to shout – but at this moment in time no words are needed to convey how he and we all feel. He looks down at his feet, breathes a heavy sigh and stands there in silence. I've never seen them like this before, they look so broken, so defeated. At that moment, not one of us utters a word as we reminisce silently and stare up at the shop sign that reads:

LUCKY STAR
Chinese & English Hot Meals to Take Away

Absorbing the realisation of it, the weight of it all and reflecting on the years, there is some directionless shuffling. Should we put on our aprons for tonight's shift? Grab our knives to start prepping? Stay and talk it through and hug it out? Instead, we carry on standing there, at a loss for words, taking it all in. I'm numb. Nothing I can do or say can change the situation. Part of me isn't ready to let go; part of me wants to shout, 'Good riddance!' and never look back. Looking around our rural street lined with rows of quaint terraced homes and surrounded by rugged, lush, green mountains, I finally see the beauty of it. I'm going to really miss this place.

'We had some good times, right?' I say to no one in particular.

Mum is holding back tears. Dad looks to the ground and pats me on the back.

'Well, since Tom's here I'll get started on my ribs,' he says with a chuckle, trying to lighten the mood, walking back into the shop rubbing his hands together.

The three of us put on our striped aprons and get to work while Tom stands awkwardly on the sidelines observing. I make a start on tackling some of the prep work and get a tray of eggs from the pantry to start whisking them for old time's sake. Mum's busy battering chicken balls. She's wearing her signature yellow Marigolds and gently lowers the chicken into the blistering oil below. Meanwhile, Dad gets to work on his ribs. He has already prepared the ribs the day before, chopping all the ingredients and hacking the ribs into bite-sized pieces with his trusty cleaver, bashing through the bone on the round wooden chopping board. He's put on a blue vinyl glove to make the process cleaner. His fingers fix into a claw shape, mixing in a clockwise motion, combining the flavours and ensuring the ribs are covered in the dark-brown viscous sauce. You can somehow taste the emotion in his food, channelled through his hands. He takes the ribs out of the gigantic fridge and we all duck out the way. I'm not going to miss that fridge. Dad scoops everything into a pot to simmer and steep on the hob for hours, stirring occasionally. He keeps a watchful eye to see it slowly thicken and break down, the flavours getting to know each other with every minute. He lets the pot of ribs be as he moves on to other prep work, chopping char siu slices for tonight's service. Mysterious bubbles form and pop like a swamp coming to life. The intoxicating fragrance fills the kitchen, tempered with aromatics, spices and condiments. Whenever Dad makes this dish he does it with such pizazz and showmanship. This is his signature dish and he wants everyone to know it. The ribs bring out the best in him. I can see his excitement, happiness and craft come to life in this dish. I love seeing his giddy anticipation as it all comes together and, using a spoon to blow on it to cool down, he tastes his work. Dad's truly a great chef when he puts his mind to it.

'It's a time-consuming process and there are too many sauces to name. It's too hard for you to learn,' Dad remarks, swatting me away like a fly.

'But I've got loads of time and I want to make this dish in London,' I say, peering on the side, looking down at the bubbling pot. Ever nosy when food is around.

'Next time, lah,' Dad says, stirring the pot with the steam reaching higher with every rotation. He is always so secretive and resistant to giving me his recipes and I'm never sure why he is so adamant to hold on to the secret, as if I'm some spy trying to learn his tricks and steal what is his property. I can understand wanting to keep a recipe or tradition feeling like it's something really special by keeping it a secret, but it's always 'next time' with him, with both of them. Soon, it might be too late, and I don't want my parents to pass away without ever sharing their trade secrets. Plus, what good is a tradition if you don't pass it on to your children? I don't want to be deprived of something that could have always reminded me of them and I don't want to be left with a little bitterness in its place. I'll try and persuade him next time. We huddle around the silver kitchen island worktop for the last family meal. What a feast. My parents really did go all out. Dad's famous ribs; gai lan choi with oyster sauce; steamed sea bass with ginger and spring onion; braised dried oysters and black sea moss; salt pepper fried squid; and steamed razor clams with garlic vermicelli. All served with a rice cooker filled with boiled rice ready to go, and a pork rib watercress soup as a digestif.

'Wow!' Tom and I say in unison, shocked and taken aback by how many dishes there are in front of us. 'Are you sure you cooked for four people? This could easily feed an army.'

'Don't want you to go hungry,' Mum says, as she fusses setting the table with bowls and chopsticks. She prods my ribs. 'London's making you skinny. You need to eat more.'

'Well, don't just gawp. Sik fan!' Dad chuckles, and ushers us to take our stools to eat. Mum spoons ribs into each of our bowls and keeps filling them up with more food, sneaking in a razor clam here and there.

'We can do it ourselves, Mum!' I comment, rolling my eyes. 'You gotta eat, too.'

Tom takes a bite of Dad's ribs and it instantly becomes one of his favourites. He says that we should've put the ribs on the menu, and that if we'd sold them we would've made a killing. We never did. Some things are best reserved. We gave every part of ourselves to the takeaway and we deserved at least one thing for ourselves. The ribs were strictly off-menu and they were off-menu for a reason. I take that first bite of glossy, sticky and succulent rib and I'm home again.

On our last night of trading, customers are saddened to hear we are selling. Word gets out about our closing and more people come to enjoy their final order to show their support. Some even give us cards and gifts. We're truly touched.

'Your barbecue sauce was the best! It's not going to be the same without Gary and Jin,' a male customer chuckles, handing Lowri a crisp ten-pound note.

'Do you know what's going to replace you now?' a neighbour in our street asks while ordering a half-and-half tray of chicken curry with fried rice and chips. 'I hope it's another Chinese.'

'But where will I get my rice and curry from now?' boiled rice granny says as she slides over coins on the counter. 'What happened? How come you're selling?'

'Oh, haha. Thank you for all your custom over the years. My parents are retiring,' I say, taking her money.

'Congratulations to them! I hope they have a happy retirement. I'm going to miss them,' she replies.

We're peppered with questions. It's a relief but exhausting to finally get everything out in the open and off our chests. It feels like a lie telling people that my parents are retiring. Technically, they are retiring, but those who aren't on the inside know little of our situation or the real reason why we're selling. We're grateful for their custom over the years and I wonder if us being here all this time has affected not just local economies but the fabric of communities.

After my last shift, I wave across the counter to Dewi, who's handing in his insulated delivery bag. I lock the door to prevent any more customers from coming in and turn the lights half-off to signal closing time. I'm met with a strange mixture of longing and nostalgia from our longest-serving employee.

'Thanks so much, Dewi, and thanks for sticking by us for so long. Best of luck for the future and I wish you and your sons the best,' I say with a smile.

Dewi and Lowri take over the counter, stacking coins, putting notes into neat piles and unravelling crumbled order tickets. They're counting tonight's earnings to check if they match. They hover by the till waiting to be paid and we say our goodbyes.

'Thank you for everything, Lowri, and thank you for working right up to the end. We couldn't have done it without you.' I hug her.

'Aww, it's been my pleasure. An honour to work for your family. I'm going to miss them and you,' Lowri beams. 'Keep in touch.'

'In a blink of an eye and just like that, it's been years.' Dewi grins and waves. 'Tell your parents thank you and happy retirement. Hope to see you around.'

I wave to them for the last time as they leave and

while I'm sweeping the floors, it hits me. I have spent 26 years in the same place, 30 for my parents. I remember the times running up and down the hallway being a nuisance, blocking Cecilia's way, the birthday parties in the waiting room with friends and cousins, cramped family meals over the coffee table that took up most of the living room and everything in between. I know all the grooves of Lucky Star's white artexed walls, where each cracked brown floor tile is located, the stained light switches from the grease build-up and the leaky pot filler above the wok station as well as I know my own body. All of it will be gone by the end of the week and I have to head back to London tonight for work tomorrow.

We're passing the baton on to the next generation and all we're left with are memories and scars, but sometimes great things and determination come from terrible scars. Whether it's the deep-fried oil splatter on my left eyelid narrowly missing my eye or the cut on my right pinkie finger from a drastic cleaver accident, scars tell stories. Scars are proof of hard work, scars are our badges of honour and scars are a sign of a life well lived. An eventful, traumatic childhood filled with highs and lows, but the takeaway itself leaves the biggest scar on my heart. My parents have put their lives into this for 30 years. It's not easy to leave it all behind.

As I get ready to board the late-night Megabus back to London, I hug my parents tightly, for what feels like the first time in ages, and I don't want to let go.

'Mm okay, lah, okay, lah. Wong dai lui. You can let go

now,' Dad chuckles, clearly feeling awkward from our bodies touching, and he pats me on the back.

I'm 26 and he still calls me princess. I laugh at the silliness of it all.

'Safe trip, mui. We'll see you soon and visit you in London. I mean, we have a lot of time on our hands now!' Mum waves, with a crutch still attached to her arm.

I step onto the bus with Tom and wave my parents off through the window. As we begin to pull away and Cardiff's skyline begins to blur behind me, I start to cry. The tears flow out of my eyes like a waterfall refusing to stop. I am profoundly sad over the loss of our beloved takeaway. I cry because life will forever be altered and bittersweet. I cry because there are no words to adequately express how I am feeling, but these aren't tears of sadness, these are tears of joy. I have learned one of the most important lessons in my life today: my family is my biggest strength and weakness. They were the very thing that was holding me back as a child. Keeping me safe and healthy, but also making me awkward, shy and not very outgoing, because I couldn't gain a lot without being able to risk a lot. But, without the shackles of the takeaway holding us back, we are all free. No longer chained to the unsociable hours, evenings and weekends are ours again. No overheads to think about, no staff to worry about and no dealing with drunk customers ever again. I'm overwhelmed with gratitude for the independence, and in many ways that is a gift in itself. As

I get older, I find that financial security isn't everything. In our rat race to assimilate, provide and survive, we've missed out on a lot of things that we couldn't do when we had the shop. We missed out on quality time and family trips away, which was the gruelling price we paid. Now, we have to find what's necessary for our happiness.

The absence of the takeaway leaves an awkward space in me, like a corner of a room you can't find a good use for, a dead space grasping for its own utility that serves no purpose any more. I feel my body rearrange itself, like a Rubik's cube, figuring out how to reconfigure and reshuffle myself. Takeaway life and post-takeaway life. What now? Who am I without the shop? What person will I be? But empty, unused space means opportunity. I want to forge my own path as a woman through my mother's example. A millennial woman who can only take inspiration from someone as headstrong, independent and self-sufficient as her. Someone who is never limited by circumstances. By all means, my mother was a poor migrant woman with three children (four including Dad, maybe five including the shop as well) but she had ambition, dignity and perseverance. As complex as our relationship is, I still love Dad too, and I look up to him. His humour, unwavering loyalty and pride light my way. I'm trying to mend the past hurts; maybe one day they'll have little power to cause me pain in any lasting way and Dad will take accountability and grow. While I don't regret not taking over the takeaway, I wish I'd given my parents more credit when I was growing up, rather than just being so painfully embarrassed by them and angry at my life all the time. They broke their backs and busted their balls in order to not only put food on the table but to make sure we did better than them. They weren't just takeaway cooks, they were so much more than that. They were savvy business owners, teachers and providers.

The takeaway has watched me grow up, whipping vital life skills into me, shaping me into adulthood, and has seen me take my first steps out into the real world. I've spent more than a quarter of a century in the takeaway. All of us are still so unsure of what is to come. My parents now face no clear path or direction on what to do next in life because the takeaway was their whole existence. The takeaway had been something so concrete and central in our lives. The nostalgia is experienced in real-time. It requires every ounce of who I am, squeezes every last drop, wrings me out, hangs me out to dry and asks for more. Shutting the doors is a massive blow to me personally. I still can't get over it. None of us can. Life has changed irrevocably and it's something I don't think we'll ever get over.

I'm trying simultaneously to numb the grief I feel for losing something so dear and to burrow into that grief, so that I can stand behind it and serve at the counter one last time. My parents turn the sign over, turn the lights off, we give our keys to the new owner and we call it a day.

Dad's Off-Menu Ribs

I've always liked to think that food is how my parents express their love to us. We didn't have big heart-to-hearts or have family day trips, but watching Dad painstakingly braise pork ribs until they fell off the bone for our enjoyment and satisfaction was all I needed to see. This sweet, sour, spicy and umami pork ribs recipe is my father's secret off-the-menu dish. We typically served a skinnier deep-fried barbecue version of ribs on the takeaway menu for customers, but we reserved the fattier, succulent, bite-sized version for our family meal. I loved watching him huddle over the hob, checking the temperature and occasionally stirring to prevent burning. Going from one corner to the other, rummaging around the kitchen and scouring fridge shelves looking for the right sauces, splaying out almost every condiment we had on the silver worktop island. No matter how many times I make it, it's never as good as his version. Be patient with this one, as time is the most important factor for tender meat.

Serves: 4 | **Prep time:** 5–10 mins |
Cook time: 90 mins

Ingredients:
2 spring onions, sliced into 2cm strips
1 thumb ginger

2 tbsp sweet chilli sauce

2 tbsp light soy sauce

4 tbsp Chinkiang black rice vinegar (if you can't find use malt vinegar)

2 tbsp Shaoxing wine

1 tbsp oyster sauce

1 tbsp ketchup

1 tsp chilli powder

4 tbsp granulated sugar

1 kg pork ribs (Dad usually goes to the butchers' section within the Asian supermarkets, as their cuts are fattier and meatier)

Method:

1. Chop spring onions and ginger.

2. Mix all ingredients together and ensure the sauce is rubbed into the pork. Marinate for at least three hours or overnight in the fridge for best results.

3. Add everything in a heavy-bottomed pan. Cook on low heat for an hour and a half. Stir occasionally to prevent the bottom from burning. Keep going until the liquid has thickened to a sauce or adjust the sauce by adding a splash of water if needed.

4. Serve with boiled rice and choi.

Further Reading / Siu yeh

I want to highlight and pay my dues to those before me. I know my story isn't unique; thousands of Chinese takeaways were born after different waves of migration occurred and me and my family were one of the latecomers. Our grandparents and parents came here before we did, started families and set up shop in a similar, if not more hostile, environment. I have been learning just how resilient mine and many other immigrant parents were in this chapter of life. From China's communist revolution to the Cultural Revolution and the Sino-Hong Kong handover – I am just beginning to understand the depths of my parents' goal in life to move across the world for a better life for their children.

I want to acknowledge that segregation, that feeling of loneliness and not knowing your footing in the world in an alien place. With age you start to find your sense of belonging and realise that others out there, in different towns and villages, have their own local takeaways and

335

ANGELA HUI

that there is a common thread running through each and every one of us takeaway babies.

However, that doesn't mean all of our anecdotes, emotions and stories are the same; we may have had upbringings that run parallel, but each takeaway story is uniquely ours and should be celebrated. I want this book to be a talking point and to start the bigger conversations. Here's to all the immigrant parents who never victimised themselves in the process and are still working through their trauma while choosing to view life with wonderment. I am honoured to carry on this generational knowledge and resilience. I want to use this section for recommendations on other books by East and Southeast Asians that tell their own stories in their own way revolving around food, identity and race.

Ann Hui – *Chop Suey Nation*
Anna Lo – *The Place I Call Home*
Cathy Park Hong – *Minor Feelings*
Celestial Peach – *Lost in Translation: An A–Z of Chinese Food* (online)
Charles Yu – *Interior Chinatown*
Claire Kohda – *Woman, Eating*
Elaine Hsieh Chou – *Disorientation*
Erika Lee – *The Making of Asian America: A History*
Helena Lee (ed.) – *East Side Voices*
J.A.G. Roberts – *China to Chinatown: Chinese Food in the West*
Jenny Zhang – *Sour Heart*

Julie Ma – *Happy Families*
Karen Cheung – *The Impossible City*
Lillian li – *Number One Chinese Restaurant*
Ly Tran – *House of Sticks*
Mary Jean Chan – *Flèche*
Michelle Zauner – *Crying in H Mart*
Min Jin Lee – *Pachinko* and *Free Food for Millionaires*
Nichole Chung – *All You Can Ever Know*
Nina Mingya Powles – *Tiny Moons: A Year of Eating in Shanghai* and *Small Bodies of Water*
Ocean Vuong – *On Earth We Are Briefly Gorgeous*
PP Wong – *The Life of a Banana*
Qian Julie Wang – *Beautiful Country*
Romalyn Ante – *Antiemetic for Homesickness*
Rowan Hisayo Buchanan – *Harmless like You* and *Starling Days*
Sharlene Teo – *Ponti*
Sue Cheung – *Chinglish*
Tash Aw – *Strangers on a Pier*

Acknowledgements

I find writing acknowledgements weird because in my mind they are reserved for award ceremonies when you've actually won something. *Takeaway* has been a huge collaborative effort and it wouldn't exist without the input of many, many people, some of whom have not been thanked enough. There have been countless hours put in and sacrifices made not just from my end, but from others involved working behind the scenes for this book to happen and to produce the very thing you are holding in your hands. To be able to pull that off and to pull it off during a pandemic, well, that in itself feels like an Oscar-worthy moment to me. Thank you Pomodoro technique for kicking me up the arse to write this book. I will live and die by you, you genius tomato clock.

Ah ma, thank you for teaching me from all the right to the wrong, for teaching me how to not just enjoy food, but to cherish, love and appreciate it. You've guided me to be the fully realised version of myself, both as a creative and as a person. I am eternally indebted to you and your sacrifices. If I can ever be half the woman you are, then I'll die happy.

Ba ba, I know we have a complex, complicated relationship. I'm still processing, working through the past hurts and trauma. I hope one day, before it's too late, we can be closer and get to know each other better. I'll always be your wong dai lui.

My big brothers, Keen and Jacky. The best colleagues I've ever had. Thank you for your guidance and protection. You've taught me so much in life and I'm so grateful for the close bond we share, despite being on different continents and different time zones.

Tom, my rock and love of my life. I'm sorry for abandoning you for the past two years trying to write this and all the lonely nights you've had to endure while I tapped away until the early hours of the morning. Thank you for your kindness, patience and unconditional love. I'd be lost without you.

My book editors Ru Merritt and Shyam Kumar, thank you for plucking me out of the digital realm. I'm impressed you somehow managed to turn this incoherent blob of nothingness into something that's actually palatable for readers. Everyone at Orion and Trapeze, who helped edit, typeset and launch this story, thank you for believing in me, letting me tell my story and for taking a chance on me. My wonderful agent Nicola Chang at David Higham, I'm so grateful to you for holding my hand through the entire process and guiding me. Thank you all for just getting it, without me having to explain myself a hundred times over.

Georgie Leung, thank you for the beautiful illustrations that have brought some of the closest and most personal recipes to life. I'm so proud of how far you've come and I love watching you go from strength to strength. You're such a talented powerhouse, an inspiration, and I admire you so much.

My in-laws: Glyn, Pippa, Hannah, Hugh, Carys and Jenny. Thank you for your endless love and support.

To the extended Hui clan and cousins. Thank you for the sleepovers, cheese and potato pies, late-night video game sessions, gravy and chip breakfasts and the lut pei lut gwut games. Growing up in a similar Welsh Valleys Chinese takeaway environment wasn't always easy, but I'm so grateful that we share this bond together. I wouldn't have had it any other way.

Ayi, Beyond, Sammy, Sean, Kinki and Winnie. I miss you dearly and can't wait to be reunited in Hong Kong soon. Bring on the 30-degree sweaty hot pots again.

Fun auntie, Uncle, Ray, Jess, Amy, Shirley, Selina, Mila, Mason, Harper, Yaingy, Natalie and Gary. Thank you for being like family through thick and thin. I'm lucky to have you in my life.

My Beddau buddies. I cannot believe you're still by my side after all these years. Lauren Ilyas, Tommy Davies and Jamie Davies, you bring so much colour, joy and silliness into my life. I hope that we'll be friends until we're old. Time for that tombstone tattoo to commemorate?

Betsan Jones and Ross Clarke. Thank you for being two of the first readers of the early drafts of this book. I'm eternally grateful for your advice and your patience. Diolch yn fawr legends.

Stay weird and rad: Zack Piercey, Elinor Brinselly, Danny Jak Midwinter and Lizzie Morgan.

Love you gals endlessly and I appreciate you all so much. Cassy Bhairo, Diane Dao, Emilia Ullmann, Attalia Yaacov-Hai, Therese Wynn Davies and Hannah Perry.

The himbo appreciation society: Jenny Lau, Tiff Chang, Cherry Tang and Emily Chung. Thank you for keeping me sane with your hilarious, vulgar real talk and advice. I'm lucky and glad to have you in my life.

Nerds: David Jay Paw, Jessy BB Wang, Simran Hans, Jonathan Nunn, Feroz Gajia, Sirichai Kularbwong, Adam Coghlan, James Hansen, Anna Sulan Masing, Emma Hughes, Nick Bramham, Rebecca May Johnson, Shekha Vyas, Chris Prowler, Ana Gonçalves, Zijun Meng, Mandy Yin and Guan Chua. Thank you for sharing your bottomless pit of wisdom, entertainment and support. You really have taught me how to eat and I've learned so much since knowing you all. Your food nerdiness astounds me and it knows no bounds. I count down the days until our next food crawl.

Corridor crew: Alex Sims, Katie McCabe, Kate Lloyd, Izzy Aron, Samantha Willis and Jess Philips. Thank you for being some of the biggest cheerleaders and best agony aunts, offering an ear to listen to my panicked moaning throughout the entire writing process.

Zing Tsjeng and Phoebe Hurst. Thank you for taking a chance on me and believing in my writing early on in my career. I am in debt to your guidance and kindness. Without you, I wouldn't be the writer I am today.

Besea.n gals and pals. Amy Phung, Viv Yau, Karlie Wu, Charley Wong, Isabelle Pan, Mai-Anh Peterson, Amy Lau, Mike Tsang, G-Ma, Anna Chan, Shu Lin, Mildred Cheng and Suyin Hayes. Thank you for all the work you do in advocating, educating and providing a beacon of light and hope in these troubled times. For all the ESEA brothers, sisters, allies and all the takeaway kids out there. Know that you're not alone, relish it, be proud and enjoy your access to all the free chips, spring rolls and chicken balls while you can, because it's not going to last forever.

Our long-serving staff and everyone who's ever helped out or worked at the takeaway. I'm not even sure if you'll ever read this book, but thank you for your acceptance, hard work, generosity, understanding and years of service. You've impacted me and my family's lives in more ways than you think.

Most importantly, thank you to our loyal customers over the last 30 years. Without you, we would be nothing. You kept a roof over our heads and made us a part of the community. Cymru am byth.

About the Author

Angela Hui is an award-winning journalist, editor and author. Her work has been published in BBC, *Guardian*, *Financial Times*, *HuffPost*, *Independent*, *Lonely Planet*, *Refinery29*, *Vice*, and more.

Currently, she is freelance and was the former editor at REKKI, a free app transforming the way chefs order ingredients, and former food and drink writer at *Time Out*.